KU-063-822

Documents in Contemporary History

General editor
Kevin Jefferys
Faculty of Arts and Education, University of Plymouth

Espionage, security and intelligence
in Britain, 1945–1970

MANCHESTER
UNIVERSITY PRESS

Documents in Contemporary History is a series designed for sixth-formers and undergraduates in higher education. It aims to provide both an overview of specialist research on topics in post-1939 British history, and a wide-ranging selection of primary source material.

Already published in the series

Stuart Ball *The Conservative Party, 1940–1992*

John Baylis *Anglo-American relations since 1939*

Alan Booth *British economic development since 1945*

Stephen Brooke *Reform and reconstruction after the war, 1945–1951*

Steven Fielding *The Labour Party: 'socialism' and society since 1951*

Sean Greenwood *Britain and European integration since the Second World War*

Kevin Jefferys *War and reform: British politics during the Second World War*

Scott Lucas *Britain and Suez: the lion's last roar*

Ritchie Ovendale *British defence policy since 1945*

Harold L. Smith *Britain in the Second World War: a social history*

Chris Wrigley *British trade unions, 1945–1995*

Forthcoming

Rodney Lowe *Britain's postwar welfare state*

Ralph Negrine *Television and the press since 1945*

Documents in Contemporary History

Espionage, security and intelligence in Britain 1945–1970

Edited by
Richard J. Aldrich

Senior Lecturer in Politics, University of Nottingham

Manchester University Press
Manchester and New York
Distributed exclusively in the USA by St. Martin's Press

The right of Richard J. Aldrich to be identified as the author of this
work has been asserted by him in accordance with the Copyright,
Designs and Patents Act 1988.

Published by Manchester University Press
Oxford Road, Manchester M13 9NR, UK
and Room 400, 175 Fifth Avenue, New York, NY 10010, USA

Distributed exclusively in the USA by
St. Martin's Press, Inc., 175 Fifth Avenue, New York, NY 10010, USA

Distributed exclusively in Canada by
UBC Press, University of British Columbia, 6344 Memorial Road,
Vancouver, BC, Canada V6T 1Z2

British Library Cataloguing-in-Publication Data
A catalogue record for this book is available from the British Library

Library of Congress Cataloging-in-Publication Data applied for

ISBN   0 7190 4955 5   *hardback*
       0 7190 4956 3   *paperback*

First published 1998

05 04 03 02 01 00 99 98   10 9 8 7 6 5 4 3 2 1

Printed in Great Britain by
Bell & Bain Ltd, Glasgow

For Libby
(each volume to be mauled savagely)

Contents

Contents

Acknowledgements

Many individuals and institutions have offered kind assistance during the preparation of this book. Part of the research was made possible by a Fulbright Fellowship at Georgetown University and also by grants from the Economic and Social Research Council and from the University of Nottingham. The documentation has been gathered over a long period of time and many individuals have offered advice and encouragement down the years. I would particularly like to thank Matthew Aid, Christopher Andrew, Pat Andrews, Michael Coleman, Gervase Cowell, Anthony Gorst, Ted Harrison, Michael Herman, Michael Hopkins, Sheila Kerr, Julian Lewis, Scott Lucas, Kate Morris, David Painter, Tilman Remme, Wesley K. Wark and John W. Young. I have enjoyed happy co-operation with a cognate project on the command and control of British nuclear weapons conducted by Len Scott and Stephen Twigge at the University of Wales at Aberystwyth.

Many archivists, librarians and records officers have been more than helpful, but none more than those behind the long counters of the Public Record Office. The Waldegrave Initiative on Open Government, and all who have worked to implement it, have been important in facilitating this volume. Transcripts from Crown-copyright records in the Public Record Office, the India Office Library and Records, and elsewhere are reproduced by permission of the Controller of Her Majesty's Stationery Office. Permission to quote from the papers of Lord Avon was given by Lady Avon. Permission to quote from the diaries of Barbara Castle was given by David Higham Associates. Material from the memoirs of C. M. Woodhouse is reproduced by permission of Curtis Brown Ltd, London. The cartoon on the cover is reproduced by kind permission of *Spectator* magazine.

It is friends and family who are perhaps most conscious of the time and effort involved in the preparation of such a study. Even after the

Acknowledgements

screen has been switched off, the arcane acronyms of this subject continue to spill out into everyday life. Above all, I should like to thank my wife Libby, for tolerance, unfailing support and endless assistance.

The School of Politics
University of Nottingham
Nottingham NG7 2RD

Chronology of events

1942

October The Holden Agreement on naval signals intelligence is concluded between Britain and the United States.

1943

April The BRUSA signals intelligence agreement is concluded between Britain and the United States.

1945

April Franklin D. Roosevelt dies and Harry S. Truman becomes President.

May V-E Day: Berlin placed under US, Soviet, British and French occupation.

July Clement Attlee becomes Prime Minister.

October The Communists are the largest party after the first French post-war elections.

September Igor Gouzenkou, a cipher clerk working for Soviet military intelligence, defects in Canada.

September Truman authorises negotiations for continuation of large-scale signals intelligence exchange with Allies.

September Decision to create the Joint Intelligence Bureau.

November Chiefs of Staff resolve to continue large-scale exchange of signals intelligence with Allies.

December The Secret Intelligence Service is reorganised.

1946

January Chiefs of Staff confirm merger of remnants of the Special Operations Executive with the Secret Intelligence Service.

February	Arrest of a major spy-ring in Canada revealed by the Gouzenkou defection in September 1945.
April	Decision to form the Foreign Office Russia Committee.
May	Alan Nunn May, British atomic scientist, is jailed for spying for the Soviets.
July	Irgun (Jewish terrorist group) bomb the King David Hotel in Palestine.
August	The McMahon Act becomes law in the United States and Allied co-operation on atomic intelligence becomes difficult.
December	British and American zones merge in Germany.

1947

July	American National Security Act and the creation of the CIA.
September	Formation of the Cominform by the Soviet Union.
December	Work on VENONA decrypts reveals a Soviet agent inside Australian government.

1948

January	Plans for the Information Research Department receive Cabinet approval.
February	Remit of the Joint Intelligence Committee is revised and expanded.
April	Christian Democrats win the elections in Italy after considerable covert funding from the CIA.
June	RAF electronic intelligence gathering programme around the Soviet Union is intensified.
June	Emergency declared in Malaya against 'Communist terrorists'.
June	Berlin is blockaded.
September	Staff Conference held by the British military on the conduct of the Cold War.
October	The UKUSA signals intelligence agreement is concluded.
November	RAF–USAF joint agreement on target intelligence completed.
November	Russia Committee discusses special operations against the Eastern Bloc, beginning with Albania.

1949

January	Chinese Communists capture Beijing.
January	Establishment of Comecon.
February	Permanent Under-Secretary's Committee created.
March	MI5 officers visit Australia and help to create the Australian Security Intelligence Organisation.
July	The atomic scientist, Klaus Fuchs, is placed under surveillance.
August	The first Soviet atomic bomb is exploded.
September	The Joint Scientific/Technical Intelligence Committees system abandoned in favour of a Director of Scientific Intelligence.

1950

January	Burns–Templer agreement on the sharing of UK–US military information.
February	The atomic scientist, Klaus Fuchs, is sentenced to ten years imprisonment.
February	Senator Joe McCarthy claims that there are over 200 pro-Communists in the State Department.
March	British defector policy is finally agreed and set out in JIC (49) 107 (Final).
June	Korean War begins.
July	London Controlling Section revived and renamed the Directorate of Forward Plans.
July	Soviet 'bugging' device detected in the British Embassy in Moscow.
September	The atomic scientist, Bruno Pontecorvo, defects to the Soviet Union.

1951

April	The Rosenbergs are sentenced to death for espionage.
March	The diplomat, Donald Maclean, is placed under surveillance.
May	Guy Burgess and Donald Maclean escape to the Soviet Union. Kim Philby falls under suspicion.
May	Anglo-Iranian Oil Company nationalised by Iranian Prime Minister Mossadeq.
October	Attlee approves positive vetting.
October	Winston Churchill returns as Prime Minister.

1952

January	The Foreign Office attempts to secure a reduction in the scope and scale of American covert action against the Soviets.
January	Soviet 'bugging' device detected in the American Embassy in Moscow using British equipment.
May	Australian Secret Intelligence Service established with British assistance.
November	Dwight D. Eisenhower wins the American elections.
November	American National Security Agency created.

1953

March	The death of Stalin.
March	An RAF Lincoln bomber is shot down over the inner German border, killing all seven crew.
May	An RAF Canberra establishes a new world altitude record of 63,000 ft.
June	The Rosenbergs are executed.
June	Demonstrations in East Berlin are put down by the Red Army.
July	Beria, the head of the Soviet MVD, is arrested.
August	UK–US sponsored coup topples Mossadeq in Iran.
December	Beria, the head of the Soviet MVD, is executed.

1954

February	A UK–US telephone tap tunnel into East Berlin, Operation Gold, inaugurated.
March	Chiefs of Staff consider Brundrett Report on the future of scientific intelligence and the Davies Report on the future of atomic intelligence.
April	A Soviet MVD officer, Vladimir Petrov, defects in Australia with information about further Soviet agents in Whitehall.
April	Operations against Albania cease, following show trials in Tirana.
June	Government Communications Headquarters and the US National Security Agency discuss the creation of a Centralised Comint Communications Centre in Britain.
June	CIA topples radical President Arbenz of Guatemala.
August	The American Communist Party is outlawed.

1955

February	Baghdad Pact signed.
April	Anthony Eden becomes Prime Minister.
May	End of the Western occupation of Germany. Germany joins NATO.
May	General Templer's report on colonial security is completed.
June	The revision of the American McMahon Act.
September	Information from the Petrov defection appears in the British press.
October	Government White Paper on Burgess and Maclean published.
October	President Diem emerges as ruler of South Vietnam.

1956

February	Khrushchev's 'secret session' speech attacking Stalinism.
April	Berlin telephone tap tunnel, Operation Gold, uncovered by the Soviets.
April	American U-2 aircraft arrive at RAF Lakenheath in Suffolk.
April	Commander Crabb incident during the visit of Khrushchev and Bulgarin to Britain.
May	Permission for U-2 flights from Britain withdrawn and the first operations are moved to Germany.
May	High level UK–US discussions on Operation Straggle in Syria.
June	'Poznan Rising' of Polish workers put down by the Polish army.
October	Operation Musketeer – the Suez invasion.
November	A photo-reconnaissance Canberra is destroyed by Syrian fighters over Lebanon.
November	The Soviet Union invades Hungary and installs Kadar as leader.

1957

January	Harold Macmillan becomes Prime Minister.
January	Army Intelligence Corps reorganised.
March	Macmillan renews permission for U-2 flights (Aquatone) from Britain.
August	First stage of the Distant Early Warning system begins

	operation in North America.
August	Test of first Soviet intercontinental ballistic missile announced.
October	Launch of the Soviet space satellite, *Sputnik*.

1958

March	Khrushchev becomes Soviet Prime Minister.
March	Macmillan approves British participation in special operations to aid rebels against President Sukarno of Indonesia.
May	Operations against Sukarno end unsuccessfully.
May	British pilots begin to participate in the U-2 programme.
May	Nuclear test controls agreed.
June	Imre Nagy, Hungarian reformist leader, is hanged.
July	The American Atomic Energy Act restores aspects of Allied atomic co-operation, including atomic intelligence.
July	American marines arrive in Lebanon to support President Chamoun and British paratroops arrive in Jordan to support King Hussein.
October	Moratorium on atomic tests.

1959

January	Castro takes control in Cuba.
January	Britain agrees in principle to participate in the Ballistic Missile Early Warning System (BMEWS).
December	Eisenhower, Macmillan and de Gaulle invite Khrushchev to a summit in Paris in 1960.

1960

May	Gary Powers's U-2 spy-plane is shot down over the Urals. Eisenhower denies, then admits, that the United States was engaged in espionage. Khrushchev arrives in Paris and cancels the East–West summit.
July	End of the Malayan Emergency.
August	Gary Powers imprisoned.
August	Colonel Penkovsky offers to spy for the West.
August	Two American National Security Agency personnel, Martin and Mitchell, defect to the Soviets.
August	Eisenhower authorises the American satellite reconnaissance programme.

| September | Macmillan and Kennedy discuss the loss of reconnaissance aircraft. A new UK–US agreement on spy-flights from British bases is completed. |
| November | John F. Kennedy wins US presidential elections. |

1961

January	Two Soviet agents, Harry Houghton and Gordon Lonsdale, are arrested in Britain.
January	Khrushchev speech announces a programme of 'wars of national liberation'.
February	Ex-premier Lumumba murdered in the Congo.
March	Controversy over Templer proposals for new intelligence arrangements on guided missiles.
April	Bay of Pigs invasion, sponsored by the CIA.
August	Construction of the Berlin Wall begins.
September	UN Secretary-General Hammarskjold killed in an air crash over the Congo.
September	Sir Robert Thompson's advisory mission to the Diem government arrives in South Vietnam.

1962

February	US Military Assistance Command established in Vietnam.
October	Colonel Penkovsky arrested in Moscow.
October	An American U-2 aircraft photographs launch-sites for nuclear missiles in Cuba. At the end of October a U-2 is shot down over Cuba and Khrushchev agrees to remove the missiles.

1963

March	Anatoli Golitsyn, defector and evangelist of massive Soviet penetration, begins an extended visit to Britain under the aegis of MI5.
June	John Profumo resigns as Secretary of State for War.
August	Test Ban treaty agreed by Unites States, Soviet Union and Britain.
September	President Sukarno of Indonesia launches 'Confrontasi', the sporadic border war with Malaysia.
November	President Diem of South Vietnam and his brother Nhu are toppled in a coup and executed.

November	Kennedy is assassinated and Lyndon B. Johnson becomes President.

1964

January	BMEWS station at Fylingdales declared fully operational.
September	CIA predicts first Chinese atomic bomb.
October	Harold Wilson becomes Prime Minister.
October	China explodes its first atomic bomb.
October	Khrushchev is overthrown and is replaced by Brezhnev and Kosygin.

1965

April	China launches the 'Cultural Revolution'.
July	Creation of Defence Intelligence Staff.
August	Wilson Cabinet consider the introduction of a thirty-year rule on document release.
September	Failed bid to overthrow President Sukarno of Indonesia and subsequent elimination of many Indonesian Communists.

1966

February	Soviet writers, Andrei Sinyavsky and Yuli Daniel, are imprisoned, and the KGB campaign against dissidents intensifies.
March	General Suharto takes power in Indonesia and the Communist Party is outlawed.
March	A special organisation within the Ministry of Defence's Defence Operations Centre is created to collate intelligence on the IRA.
August	George Wigg reports on security in the Foreign Office, Government Communications Headquarters and the Ministry of Defence.
October	George Blake escapes from Wormwood Scrubbs prison.

1967

January	Britain, the Soviet Union and the United States sign a treaty banning nuclear weapons from space.
March	Svetlana, Stalin's daughter, defects to the West.
April	'The Colonels' seize power in Greece and repression follows.

June	USS *Liberty*, an American signals intelligence dedicated vessel, is attacked by Israel and thirty-two crew are killed.

1968

January	Geoffrey Prime, an RAF signals intelligence specialist, offers his services to the Soviets.
January	North Korea seizes the USS *Pueblo*, an American signals intelligence dedicated vessel.
January	The Tet Offensive in Vietnam.
January	Britain's accelerated withdrawal East of Suez is announced with a target date of December 1971 and it is proposed to reduce the Secret Vote by 10 per cent.
February	Kim Philby's memoirs are published.
May	Student unrest in Paris.
August	Invasion of Czechoslovakia.
November	Richard Nixon wins the American presidential elections.

1969

April	American EC-121 spy-plane shot down by North Korea.
July	Nixon announces the Guam Doctrine and 'vietnamisation'.
August	Sino-Soviet border clashes.
September	Geoffrey Prime transfers to Government Communications Headquarters and spies for the Soviets until his arrest in 1982.
November	SALT talks begin in Helsinki.

1970

May	Work begins on a large American National Security Agency signals intelligence collection station at Menwith Hill, Harrogate.
June	Edward Heath becomes Prime Minister.
December	Participation of British pilots in the U-2 programme ceases.
December	MI5 begins efforts to recruit Oleg Lyalin, a KGB officer in London. His eventual revelations lead to the expulsion of 105 Soviets 'diplomats' from London in 1971.

List of abbreviations

ACAS(I)	Assistant Chief of the Air Staff (Intelligence)
ASIO	Australian Security Intelligence Organisation
BMEWS	Ballistic Missile Early Warning System
BRUSA	British–United States signals intelligence agreement 1943
'C'	Chief of the British Secret Intelligence Service (MI6)
CAS	Chief of the Air Staff
CIA	Central Intelligence Agency (American)
CNS	Chief of the Naval Staff
Comint	Communications intelligence
Comsec	Communications security
COS	Chiefs of Staff (British)
Cosmic	A high level of NATO security clearance
DFP	Directorate of Forward Plans
DIS	Defence Intelligence Staff
DSI	Directorate of Scientific Intelligence
Elint	Electronic intelligence
GCHQ	Government Communications Headquarters
GRU	Soviet military intelligence
ID CCG	Intelligence Division of Control Commission, Germany
IRA	Irish Republican Army
IRD	Information Research Department of the Foreign Office
JCC	Joint Concealment Centre
JCS	Joint Chiefs of Staff (American)
JIB	Joint Intelligence Bureau
JIC	Joint Intelligence Committee
JS/TIC	Joint Scientific/Technical Intelligence Committees
KGB	Soviet intelligence and security service
LCESA	London Communications-Electronics Security Agency
LSIB	London Signals Intelligence Board
LSIC	London Signals Intelligence Committee

List of abbreviations

MI5	Security Service (British)
MI6	Secret Intelligence Service (SIS) (British)
MGB/MVD	Precursors of the KGB
MoD	Ministry of Defence
NATO	North Atlantic Treaty Organisation
NSA	National Security Agency (American)
OSS	Office of Strategic Services (American)
PUSC	Permanent Under-Secretary's Committee
PUSD	Permanent Under-Secretary's Department
PV	Positive vetting
PWE	Political Warfare Executive
RAF	Royal Air Force
SAS	Special Air Service
SHAPE	Supreme Headquarters Allied Powers Europe
SIFE	Security Intelligence Far East (joint MI5/SIS)
SIME	Security Intelligence Middle East (joint MI5/SIS)
Sigint	Signals intelligence
SIS	Secret Intelligence Service (MI6)
SLD	Services Liaison Department
SOE	Special Operations Executive
SSU	Strategic Services Unit (American, post-war became OSS)
STIB	Scientific and Technical Intelligence Bureau of ID CCG
TCS	SIS Technical Co-ordinating Section (scientific intelligence)
TRIC	Technical Radio Intercept Committee
TUC	Trades Union Congress
Ultra	British classification for signals intelligence
USA	United States Army
USAF	United States Air Force
USN	United States Navy
UKUSA	UK–USA signals intelligence agreements 1948
VISTRE	Visual Inter-Service Training and Research Establishment

Additional abbreviations used in references

AIR	Air Ministry records
CAB	Cabinet records
CO	Colonial Office records
DDRS	Declassified Document Reference System

List of abbreviations

DEFE	Ministry of Defence records
FO	Foreign Office records
FRUS	*Foreign Relations of the United States*
HW	GCHQ records
IOLR	India Office Library and Records, Blackfriars, London
LAB	Ministry of Labour records
PREM	Prime Minister's Office records
PRO	Public Record Office, Kew Gardens, Surrey
RG	Record Group (US National Archives)
USNA	United States National Archives, Washington DC
W O	War Office records

Introduction

The growth and importance of modern secret service

If the nineteenth century is primarily defined by the 'Industrial Revolution', then the twentieth century could be characterised by the 'Information Revolution'. Both these revolutions had a profound impact upon the conduct of international affairs by states and upon their general security. This impact was most clearly observable in the conduct of war. New technologies lent armed forces enhanced mobility and manoeuvrability, opening up the hitherto unknown possibility of devastating surprise attack on a strategic scale – the threat of the 'knockout blow'. By the Second World War the majority of strategic initiatives by both the Axis and the Allies sought to achieve this form of devastating surprise attack. Pearl Harbor, the attack on the Soviet Union, D-Day and the Ardennes offensive of 1944 constitute major examples of this. States responded to the threat of surprise attack in a number of ways, one of which was seeking new warning mechanisms in the form of enhanced intelligence. Intelligence, faced with the new challenges presented by modern warfare, also sought to exploit technological developments, turning to aerial reconnaissance and machine cryptanalysis, and thereby securing remarkable achievements.[1]

The steady rise in the importance of intelligence staffs therefore moved hand in hand with the increasing mobility of forces provided by rail, then road and air. But modern secret services were also ambiguous: they were seen by defenders as a possible antidote to the new problems of strategic surprise, and by aggressors as providing techniques to multiply the effectiveness of surprise through such means as strategic deception. During the early Cold War there were many factors that ensured the steady growth of intelligence services, but it was, above all, the fear of strategic surprise – the 'nuclear Pearl

Harbor' as some in Whitehall called it – that ensured the continued development of modern British intelligence services after 1945.[2]

The importance of the intelligence services in British post-war policy-making is confirmed by their relative size and centrality in the Whitehall machine. The open literature of the post-war period can be misleading on the matter of the relative scale of their operations, and official publications are notably unhelpful. A cursory glance at a copy of the British *Diplomatic List* for 1960 reveals the names and detailed employment of approximately 10,000 staff in the Foreign Office and in diplomatic missions around the world. Unsurprisingly, this *Diplomatic List* contains only a modest reference to the British post-war signals intelligence organisation, the Government Communications Headquarters (GCHQ), which was subordinate to the Foreign Office. From this, few would suspect that the overall British signals intelligence effort at this time employed about 11,500 staff, more people than the Foreign Office itself.[3]

If strategic-technical and military-industrial developments help to explain the growth of intelligence services within British government in the twentieth century, then it is ideological developments that explain, in almost equal measure, the rise of other aspects of modern British secret service. Fenian terrorism, followed by exaggerated fear of German espionage, had laid down the basis of a British internal security service before the First World War. But it was ideological subversion, most clearly characterised by the Bolshevik revolution, with what appeared to be a globally orchestrated pattern of conspiracy, that dominated the British understanding of subversion in the twentieth century. In that respect, the work of MI5 (the Security Service) after 1945 represented nothing very new, merely a return to its familiar inter-war focus on communists, radicals and 'agitators'.[4]

But what *was* new after 1945 was the British determination to join the Communists at their own game, trying out the techniques of peacetime subversion and 'black' propaganda for themselves for the first time. This was buoyed up by the perceived recent success of these techniques in wartime against the Axis. Although these post-war initiatives were first conceived of in an anti-Communist context, they proved to be more effective against other types of British opponents. Again, inspection of the *Diplomatic List* for 1960 would not reveal that the Information Research Department (IRD), Britain's main post-war 'black' and 'grey' propaganda organisation, funded on the Secret Vote, was the largest and fastest-expanding department of the post-war Foreign Office.[5]

Expansion cannot be achieved without budgets and resources. In the post-war period, for the most part a time of perennial government stringency, the levels of spending upon secret service activities are reliable indicators of priorities chosen at the centre of British government. Spending, as Sir Leo Pliatzky once observed, is akin to choosing, and so this provides us with a relatively objective and quantifiable measure of their perceived importance. Whatever one's interpretation of the nature and significance of secret service within British government, there is no escaping the fact that during this period, secret government was big government.[6]

A different, but equally significant, indication of the importance accorded to secret service in post-war Britain was offered by the developing core executive machinery for policy-making in the area of national security. Unlike France, where secret service has always remained a less than respectable activity, consigned to the fringes of government, in post-war Britain it was at the very centre. The mechanisms for its control and management were also those designed for the high-level supervision of British national security policy as a whole. This is most clearly demonstrated within the Foreign Office, where, in the 1950s, the new Permanent Under-Secretary's Department (PUSD) became synonymous with 'special activities' and the Secret Intelligence Service (SIS or MI6). Indeed, in the 1960s, the new SIS headquarters, an office block south of the Thames on Westminster Bridge Road, were officially described as accommodation for the PUSD. The proliferation of Cabinet committees, dealing with intelligence, security, counter-subversion and propaganda, managed by the Cabinet Secretary, is further confirmation of this.

Accordingly, no historical analysis of British national security policy between 1945 and 1970, indeed even British government as a whole, could be complete without an extended consideration of the work and influence of the secret services in a broad range of areas. But the documentary record does not inform historical understanding for reasons of mere antiquarian interest. In this field particularly, history is frequently pressed into service to inform current debate on present and future aspects of secret service.

This is true in both the official and public arenas. As Christopher Hill has pointedly observed, academics and foreign policy practitioners constitute 'two worlds'. The latter regard the rarefied theoretical literature on international relations, produced by the former, as a spectacular waste of time, and they do not read it. That is not to assert that policy-makers are completely without recourse to theory. The foreign policy style of practical incrementalism has long been informed by an apparatus that might be broadly described as one of contemporary historical analogy. Landmark events in the preceding half-century, often personally experienced, point the way to an unspoken coda of received wisdom, which is deployed mostly unconsciously, but sometimes, at moments of crisis, quite stridently. During the Falklands War, the fraught discussions in Whitehall and Westminster were peppered with references to Munich and Suez, but allusion to the 'advanced literature' on theories of crisis management were nowhere to be found.[7]

History is also critical in informing current public debate and never more so than now. In the 1990s Britain embraced a new era of increasing openness and accountability of the secret services on a statutory basis. But the details of current activities are identified as 'sensitive' and, quite properly, remain closed. Those who wish to discuss policy in this area in the public arena, be they officials or non-officials, are inevitably forced to deploy hypothetical examples, or to rummage through recent history in search of examples to illustrate their contentions.

The latter approach is an established one and has an intellectually respectable pedigree, albeit there are pit-falls. The writings of Carl von Clausewitz are perhaps the most impressive example of the employment of contemporary history to 'stand in' for reality, when testing strategic nostrums. But recent practice is probably closer to that of Soviet Army strategists during the Cold War who, anxious to avoid discussing sensitive current issues, conducted their discussions over developing strategic ideas in professional journals through analogous debates on aspects of the Great Patriotic War. If the contemporary history of British secret service continues to be used in this way, and there is every indication that it will, then the importance of a sound historical understanding based upon reliable data, rather than hearsay, becomes paramount.

The study of secret service

British secret service has long been a matter of intense public interest, and its historical, political and legal perspectives have attracted extended press coverage throughout the twentieth century. In contrast, the establishment of this field as a subject for serious academic study is relatively recent. The study of its legal aspects attained a high profile in universities relatively early, invigorated by the publication of David G. T. Williams's notable study, *Not in the Public Interest*, in 1965.[8] Academics in the field of international relations and diplomatic history were slower off the mark. Current studies of British foreign policy written by political scientists in the first three post-war decades, often produced under the auspices of major think-tanks and institutes that were close to Whitehall, mostly avoided the subject.[9] Contemporary history fared no better, and the Joint Intelligence Committee (JIC), Britain's highest intelligence authority, devoted no small amount of time to the issue of how matters such as 'Ultra' intelligence and deception could be kept out of official histories. In the event they chose to indoctrinate official historians, who then became part of the process of deliberate obfuscation.[10]

But in the 1970s the release of the archives for the period to 1945, revelations concerning the 'Ultra' secret and finally the publication of the first volume of the official history of British intelligence, combined to transform our understanding of the Second World War. Then in 1982 two historians, Christopher Andrew and David Dilks, in a landmark volume, urged international historians to pay more attention to intelligence in international history generally, defining this as the 'missing dimension'. This was followed in 1986 by the launch of an inter-disciplinary academic journal devoted to this subject, *Intelligence and National Security*, which has become required reading. By the end of the 1980s, there had been an explosion of academic interest in this subject and a considerable body of scholarly literature had begun to emerge.[11]

It is perhaps too early to attempt to offer a developed historiographical schema of writings on British secret service. However, a number of categories are already evident. The most obvious is probably orientation towards the issue of the costs and benefits of secret service work. Early examples of critical studies are the work of Bloch and Fitzgerald on intelligence, and Richard Norton-Taylor's study of positive vetting, while those emphasising the value of secret service have been most strongly represented by official historians, more often than not themselves former practitioners.[12] But this distinction is not polarised and the majority of writers in the 1980s and 1990s have defined themselves as doubters rather than dissenters, broadly favourable to the existence of secret services, but critical of their management. Current policy-prescriptive writings could also be categorised in this way.[13]

A more useful approach to the dissection of the literature is the division between institutionalist and contextualist writings. The early national literatures on secret service in most countries have been dominated at the outset by an institutionalist approach, setting out to offer a basic description of hitherto little known services and their 'organisational cultures'. Early work often took the form of sensational and ill-researched accounts that earned themselves the generic title of the 'airport bookstall' school of history. But the quality of institutionalist studies improved dramatically in the 1980s, and the strength of such work is the light they throw upon culture, tradecraft and the inner world of intelligence, all of which is capable of standing alone as a significant subject in its own right.[14]

Nevertheless, the institutionalist approach is always vulnerable to the charge of separateness and self-absorption. Moreover, the anxiety of the British authorities before 1990 to suppress every detail of postwar secret service undoubtedly exacerbated this, with writers sometimes reacting with an equal determination to catalogue every available fact. Robin Winks has offered the most articulate criticism of this approach, insisting that intelligence studies tended to ignore the 'So What?' question, that is, failing to demonstrate the impact of secret service upon the wider fabric of policy-making, and the history of the period in general. Winks advanced a powerful argument for the contextualist approach.[15] Although his charge was a valid one, it is not difficult to see why the contextual history of intelligence was thin on the ground. The explanation of the detailed impact of intelligence upon a major historical event is a task of labyrinthine complexity. It is no accident that the most formidable examples of a contextualist approach to the study of British intelligence remain the official histories of intelligence in the Second World War (bearing the sub-title *Its Influence upon Strategy and Operations*). These magisterial volumes were the work of a team of historians. Nevertheless, sophisticated contextualist work on secret service has emerged in the 1990s.[16]

The growing body of reliable literature has facilitated the academic teaching of this subject, and by 1990 the study of intelligence, subversion and domestic security constituted a major growth area in universities and colleges. It also drew strength from the separate but related field of propaganda and communication studies, which had its own distinguished path of development. Secret service is now ubiquitous on degree courses in history, politics and international relations at the BA and MA level. In the English-speaking world there are now over 200 such courses at universities which include Cambridge, Edinburgh, Harvard, Oxford, Toronto, Yale, the Australian National University and the LSE. Specialist MA programmes focusing on secret service have existed in Britain since the 1980s, and the teaching of this subject as an integral part of undergraduate courses in international relations, politics and modern history had become widespread by the early 1990s. But 1997 marked an exciting new development with the launch of a mainstream three-year BSc Econ degree in International Politics and Intelligence Studies in the Department of International Politics at the University of Wales, Aberystwyth. Although British academics have never hesitated to tackle resistant subjects, there is a clear relationship between the quantity of reliable information opened to public inspection by the authorities, and the development of the academic study of secret service. The legislative changes of the 1990s seem to point to the continued expansion of this subject.[17]

The British secret service archives

A noted intelligence historian once defined the status of British secret service archives as a 'Never-Never Land'. Prior to 1981, British departments of state were warned that secret intelligence materials were 'never released' to the Public Record Office (PRO). Subsequent to the Wilson Committee White Paper on public records in 1981, this guidance was changed and departments were thereafter instructed that 'the word never should never be used'. The Wilson Committee considered that in the fullness of time all such records would eventually find their way into the public domain.[18] But for those outside Whitehall, this intriguing double negative seemed to signal little material change and secret service archives remained 'a far-off place' that no independent historian was ever likely to visit.[19] By contrast, the experience of intelligence historians working in the United States is continually identified as being very different.[20]

The 1990s have seen a number of important changes in the management of secret service archives on both sides of the Atlantic. These changes have been instrumental in facilitating this volume of documents. In Britain, the Waldegrave Initiative on Open Government has resulted in the release of substantial amounts of intelligence material, mostly for the period before 1945. Only limited post-war materials were released, but there have been some positive responses to the specific requests of historians for closed material. Meanwhile, in the United States there have also been notable changes. Surprising materials continue to be released into the American National Archives, but the operation of the Freedom of Information Act has become erratic, and promises of declassification made by the Clinton administration have sometimes been broken.[21]

The Waldegrave Initiative on Open Government, announced in July 1993, claimed to revise the conventions governing the release of sensitive documents. Opinion is divided as to whether this is a significant development which has materially changed our understanding of aspects of Britain's recent past or, alternatively, a mere publicity opportunity for government which involved major claims accompanied by only marginal change. On the one hand, government press releases maintain that there has been nothing short of a major revolution, with the default setting of Whitehall now upon releasing, rather than withholding, information. This has been accompanied by some startling changes, not least MI5 openly advertising for recruits in the pages of the *Guardian* in May 1997.[22] On the other hand, there is a significant school of opinion that views this as nothing more than a transition from the 'stonewalling' approach of the Thatcher era to a more sophisticated form of active 'information control' for the 1990s. Moreover, this latter school maintains that change was not undertaken willingly, but instead was prompted by a reluctant recognition that mechanisms such as the European Court would make some change inevitable.[23]

Openness, or secrecy, relating to secret service issues has been at the centre of the Waldegrave Initiative. This is partly because a high proportion of the PRO documents closed for more than the normal thirty years have been retained precisely because they relate to secret service. It is also because William Waldegrave deliberately chose to make 'revelations' in the area of secret service history, and also current secret service practice, a flagship element in the presentation of Open Government to the media.[24] The government correctly presumed that revelations about even the most antiquated aspects of secret service would guarantee headlines such as 'MI5 thrills historians by opening up its files'.[25]

8

Unsurprisingly, it is upon the period *prior* to 1945 that the Waldegrave Initiative has had the most impact. Materials from this period represent the majority of hitherto closed files retrospectively released into the PRO. They include Churchill's 'Ultra' decrypts, specially selected for him from the work of Bletchley Park against Axis and neutral communications traffic, and amounting to several thousand files. The Special Operations Executive (SOE), Britain's wartime sabotage organisation, constitutes another important release and its files will eventually number over 10,000. The level of public interest in the Second World War has ensured quick exploitation by journalists and popular historians as well as academics.[26]

The Waldegrave Initiative has had two types of impact in the area of secret service history. The first, and most radical, is upon subjects that are specialist and technical and, accordingly, were hitherto almost completely closed. Only with the gradual opening of the detailed files of Bletchley Park, its outstations and collaborators, have we seen the development of a substantial body of non-official 'Ultra' history. The extent to which this new work has already begun to challenge official history on fundamental issues, such as the 'shortening' of the duration of Second World War by 'Ultra', underlines the importance of this new work.[27] The second pattern concerns its impact upon broader subjects that were already partly open. SOE is a good example of this. Well-documented and authoritative non-official studies of SOE have been appearing in profusion since the mid-1970s. New and intriguing aspects of this organisation can now be investigated, but there has been no recent shift in our overall understanding of SOE.[28]

There has been continuity as well as change. For example, the use of the 'oblique approach' is alive and well. In the 1980s crafty historians worked through military and diplomatic files to get at copies of supposedly 'closed' SOE documentation. In the 1990s historians are working through these and newly released SOE files to open up the history of its still-closed British sister service, the SIS, during the Second World War. New debates have been ignited and old arguments re-examined. The credibility of the picture of a bankrupt SIS, offered by Kim Philby in his controversial KGB-sponsored memoir *My Silent War*, has been at the centre of this. Some former practitioners have long condemned this as an unreliable product of Soviet propaganda, while non-official historians have come to the conclusion that the new material reveals a picture of wartime SIS that was, if anything, worse than Philby's caricature.[29]

The flood of Second World War secret service files opened to public inspection under the Waldegrave Initiative has had a further, rather unexpected, effect. Some historians are clearly attracted to the challenge of an awkward and inaccessible subject. Accordingly, as many more records are released for the Second World War, there are some historians who will be discomforted by this, and who will transfer their attentions to more recent, still classified, events. Doubtless this was not the intention of the Waldegrave Initiative.

The record of Waldegrave is patchy on secret service and it is not easy to cast up a satisfactory overall judgement. This is partly because Whitehall departments have continued their time-honoured tradition of interpreting the same guidelines differently. Some are more generous than others and have placed post-war materials of a genuinely new type into the PRO. The arrival of records from the Ministry of Defence's (MoD) Directorate of Scientific Intelligence (DSI) during the early Cold War was nothing short of a major breakthrough. The same can be said of the release of the files of the British Military Mission or 'BRIXMIS' in East Germany, which engaged in massive legal and semi-legal surveillance of Eastern Bloc military activities. All this has permitted the detailed study of some 'front line' intelligence operations of the Cold War.

The impact of the Waldegrave Initiative remains unclear. Those who wish to minimise its importance point to the fact that much of the material discussed might have been expected about now, at the fifty-year point, even under the previous regime. Ambiguity even extends to the more surprising release of some post-war intelligence materials such as 'VENONA'.[30] 'VENONA' is the codename for the KGB communications traffic decrypted by both GCHQ and the Americans in the 1940s, leading to the initial exposure of members of the 'Cambridge Comintern': Kim Philby, Guy Burgess, Donald Maclean, Anthony Blunt and John Cairncross. This is not material that historians would have remotely expected to see before the advent of Waldegrave. Yet sceptics would argue that this release has not been motivated by a new British spirit of openness, but instead by pressure from GCHQ's American partners, the National Security Agency (NSA). A large selection of the American 'VENONA' material has been put on the NSA's Website in a way that would have been difficult to ignore. Perhaps the Internet will act as an agent of 'globalisation' in the area of declassification policy.[31]

There are important differences in the way in which the British and the Americans have managed the release of secret service archives. Most obviously, Britain's programme is running about a decade behind that of the United States. While Britain is still processing the archives of the wartime SOE and of Churchill's wartime 'Ultra' materials, releasing them at approximately the fifty-year point, the Americans released much of their equivalent material at the forty-year point. For example, the Americans have released almost all their wartime records for the Office of Strategic Services (OSS) – their main agent-based secret service – to 1947.[32] As a direct result of this, in the 1980s American historians were able to locate retired OSS veterans and conduct interviews that could be compared with the written record. A rich and sophisticated literature on the history of OSS is now emerging from the synthesis of oral testimony and written records. By comparison, as equivalent British records become available in the mid-1990s, there are few survivors still available to talk about the policy-level. The full meaning of these arcane documents will not necessarily be self-evident to future historians.[33]

In Britain a squeamish distinction is still made by the authorities between secret service activities conducted during war and those during peacetime, and thus only limited post-war British secret service material has been opened to public inspection. In contrast the Central Intelligence Agency (CIA) has recently deposited hundreds of files relating to its changing internal organisation prior to 1953. American National Intelligence Estimates on the Soviet Union are available up to 1989, while the equivalent British JIC reports are available only up to 1953. Accordingly, historians working on post-war American subjects have been able to integrate the intelligence dimension into their wider work, encouraging a more contextual approach. In Britain the debate on intelligence records has focused narrowly upon the release of 'secret service' records held by SIS, MI5 and GCHQ, while in the United States greater recognition has been given to the importance of Army, Navy and Air Force intelligence activities. Prior to 1953, in both Britain and the United States, service intelligence personnel outnumbered those in the 'secret services'. American service intelligence records have now been released for the period up to 1955.[34] The United States has also taken more care to preserve regional or 'theatre command' intelligence records.[35] Some fine studies of American policy in Europe and the Far East have drawn extensively upon them.[36]

A profusion of British materials has reportedly long been available in the American archives, but their exact extent has never been clear. Two important distinctions can be drawn. The first is simply chronological: for the period up to 1945 a vast quantity of British intelligence records of many different types abounds, much of it not yet available in the PRO. British historians have been continually irritated that there are materials generated by Bletchley Park which are not available in Britain but which have been released into the American archives. Bradley F. Smith, in a path-breaking study of Anglo-American co-operation in the field of signals intelligence to 1947, has illustrated just how much British material is available in Washington DC.[37] The archive of the American OSS contains not just isolated documents, but often entire files of British material.[38]

But for the post-war period, which constitutes the central concern of this book, the story is rather different. Archivists in the United States often refer to an agreement between the State Department and the British government with guidelines detailing the categories of material that London requests be withdrawn from American files. Nevertheless, there are inconsistencies, and about 10 per cent of post-war British JIC reports are extant in Washington.[39] In the papers of American organisations like the US European Command, a substantial proportion of the papers of the British Intelligence Division, Control Commission Germany (ID CCG) are to be found for the 1940s and 1950s. It is disturbing that a reasonable history of this important British organisation could be written in Washington but not in London, where the main records have been destroyed.[40]

Finally we should consider the field of memoirs. During the 1980s the literary efforts of retired British secret service officers were greeted with concerted official hostility. This approach might be contrasted with the American system by which retired intelligence officers are required to submit their memoirs for clearance, a process which usually results in sections of the memoirs being sanitised. It is not only historians who have benefited from memoirs that have appeared under this regime. Arguably, the widely quoted memoirs of the late William Colby have done much to encourage a sympathetic view of the place of the CIA in American post-war history.[41]

There is now a strong case for Britain to look again at a similar system of official clearance for memoirs. The most forceful argument for this is derived not from the past American experience, but from future developments in the former Soviet Union. In the early 1990s numerous retired KGB officers, some of them quite senior, sat down and began to write their memoirs. Their numbers are increasing and, as a result, we will soon have a substantial picture of British intelligence in the post-war period, albeit from a dubious source. It will be dubious not only because some of these officers are bitter, unreconstructed Communists with an axe to grind, but also because retired KGB officers naturally wish to present the achievements of their own service in the best possible light. There is a growing danger that the history of British intelligence will be written by its enemies. In 1993 there were unconfirmed reports that the British government had made representations to the Russians asking them to keep certain aspects of their archives relating to Britain closed. However successful this approach was, it will not address the problem of KGB memoirs. There have been welcome signs of a more balanced British approach to secret service memoirs, with the unopposed publication of the memoirs of Desmond Bristow, *A Game of Moles*.[42]

There are lessons to be learned from recent developments in the release of British secret service records. The sternest lesson is that their sheer volume presents significant problems. During the period 1945–89 the Western intelligence community enjoyed steady growth and so the quantities of old intelligence records awaiting declassification will increase for the foreseeable future. At the same time these types of records are awkward, expensive and time-consuming for officials to process for release. In the 1990s the main barrier to further and faster release of secret service material is not secrecy but resources. In order to deal with these sorts of problems a government requires not only a carefully considered Open Government policy, but also the commitment of adequate resources and the effective management of those resources through a clear dialogue with historians. Historians, given a picture of what governments hold in their archives, will readily articulate their priorities.

There is also a need for a climate of greater trust between historians and departments of state. This will develop only slowly, for secret service historians who took a critical line on official policy in the 1980s have largely concluded that they were right about excessive secrecy. This is clear from the nature of some of the documents finally released in Britain in 1993. These included records that had been closed for two centuries – for example the documents relating to secret postal interception for the period 1742–92.[43] It is hardly surprising that historians initially greeted the announcement of the

Waldegrave Initiative in 1992 with scepticism, but this attitude has softened with the release of many thousands of new files.[44]

Organisation and selection

Central to the growth of the academic study of British secret service has been the recognition that, with careful research, a surprising range of reliable primary source materials can be identified. Clear documentation is of the first importance when attempting to offer accurate description and interpretation in a field dogged by sensationalist accounts and unreliable memoirs. This book exploits new primary source material gathered from two main sources. Firstly, some documentation has been released as a result of the Waldegrave Initiative on Open Government. This includes files that were declassified in specific response to requests by the present editor. Secondly, a great deal of documentation has been gathered in the United States which is not yet available in British archives. Diaries and private papers have also been surveyed, but they have been somewhat disappointing: compared to their predecessors during the Second World War, post-war practitioners seem to have been less imbued with a need to record 'History'. There has been less emphasis on published materials in this volume, for these are more widely available to the reader. The material reproduced in this book is scattered and time-consuming to locate and consult, and therefore one of the principal objectives is to bring some of it together in a coherent and readily accessible format.

Although it is important to analyse the development of the British intelligence and security services as institutions in themselves, nevertheless, as their name implies, the primary purpose of these organisations was to provide a 'service' to the wider policy-making community in Whitehall and Westminster. Accordingly, there is something to be said for the superiority of the contextual approach, demonstrating the way in which secret service impacted upon the 'big themes' of this period: nuclear weapons policy, decolonisation and Britain's relations with her main partners – the United States, Europe and the Commonwealth. However, the quantity of documentation required to sustain a contextual approach to these sorts of issues would have been far beyond what can be accommodated within this volume. Therefore, a range of approaches has been used to select the documents reproduced here.

This book attempts to offer a sound documentation of the post-war development, activities and significance of the British secret service. But no collective term happily embraces the remit of the book. Although 'secret service' captures some of its flavour, the network of intelligence, security and counter-subversion activities examined here, together with their associated assessments and management staff, is rather wider than the term implies. Definitions are rendered particularly problematic by the seamless overlap between the work of MI5 and SIS on the one hand, and 'information and cultural activities' on the other. Some important tasks that lay within the province of the CIA in the United States during this period, were conducted in Britain by 'straight' Foreign Office departments.

The selected timespan runs from the end of the Second World War through to 1970. The volume terminates in 1970 for three reasons: it marks the end of Harold Wilson's second administration; it marks the implementation of Britain's withdrawal East of Suez, announced in 1968, with its consequent abandonment of a global military role; and it also marks the last decade for which substantial documentation is currently available in Britain and the United States. The massive expulsion of Soviet 'diplomats' from London, decided upon in the early months of 1971, is also a landmark in secret service history. Although material abounds on British secret service for the period after 1970, its texture is very different and it would not sit comfortably alongside the documents selected here.

The organisation of this volume reflects a presumption that the links between different parts of the British intelligence and security apparatus are sometimes quite tenuous. Accordingly, instead of attempting a chronological survey tracing the development of a coherent British secret service community over time, a functional approach has been taken which emphasises the roles and responsibilities of different services and departments. These boundaries are problematic and some of the more interesting documents do not belong in any obvious single category.

Notes

1 R. K. Betts, 'Analysis, War and Decision: Why Intelligence Failures are Inevitable', *World Politics*, 31, 1 (1978) 961–88. See also

M. I. Handel, 'Intelligence and the Problem of Strategic Surprise', *Journal of Strategic Studies*, 7, 3 (1984) 229–82; 'Clausewitz in the Age of Technology', *Journal of Strategic Studies*, 9, 3 (1986) 51–92.

2   Minute by the Director of Intelligence, Air Ministry, September 1945, AIR 20/3420, PRO.

3   A. Bullock, *Ernest Bevin: Foreign Secretary* (New York: Norton, 1983), p. 101n.; Paymaster General, George Wigg, to Prime Minister, Harold Wilson, enclosing 'The Organisation of Security in the Diplomatic Service and Government Communications Headquarters', 17 August 1966, PREM 13/1203, PRO.

4   C. M. Andrew, *Secret Service: The Making of the British Intelligence Community* (London: Heinemann, 1985); B. Porter, *Plots and Paranoia: A History of Political Espionage in Britain, 1790–1988* (London: Routledge, 1989); R. Thurlow, *The Secret State: British Internal Security in the Twentieth Century* (London: Blackwell, 1994).

5   L. Smith, 'Covert British Propaganda: The Information Research Department, 1944–1977', *Millennium*, 9, 1 (1980) 676–83.

6   L. Pliatzky, *Getting and Spending: Public Expenditure, Employment and Inflation* (London: Blackwell, 1984). Exactly how much was spent remains elusive. Until the 1990s, aside from the Secret Vote, significant expenditure on secret service activities was hidden in the budgets of other departments.

7   C. Hill and P. Beshoft (eds), *Two Worlds of International Relations: Academics, Practitioners and the Trade in Ideas* (London: Routledge, 1994); A. M. Haig, *Caveat: Realism, Reagan and Foreign Policy* (London: Weidenfeld and Nicholson, 1984). A perceptive commentary on analogous reasoning by policy-makers is offered in Dan Reiter, 'Learning, Realism and Alliances: The Weight of the Shadow of the Past', *World Politics*, 46, 2 (1994) 490–526.

8   D. G. T. Williams, *Not in the Public Interest* (London: Hutchinson, 1965).

9   J. Frankel, *British Foreign Policy, 1945–73* (London: Oxford University Press, 1975); W. Wallace, *Foreign Policy-making* (London: RIIA, 1972).

10   JIC (47) 81st mtg. (1), Confidential Annex, 'Use of Special Intelligence by Official Historians', 21 November 1947, CAB 159/2, PRO.

11 F. W. Winterbotham, *The Ultra Secret* (London: Weidenfeld and Nicholson, 1974); F. H. Hinsley *et al.*, *British Intelligence in the Second World War: Its Influence on Strategy and Operations*, Vol. I (London: HMSO, 1979); C. M. Andrew and D. Dilks (eds), *The Missing Dimension: Governments and Intelligence Communities in the Twentieth Century* (London: Macmillan, 1986).

12 J. Bloch and P. Fitzgerald, *British Intelligence and Covert Action* (Dingle, Ireland: Brandon, 1983); M. Hollingsworth and R. Norton-Taylor, *Blacklist* (London: Heritage, 1988). The first official history of British secret service was M. R. D. Foot, *SOE in France* (London: HMSO, 1966).

13 For example, P. Gill, *Policing Politics: Security Intelligence and the Liberal Democratic State* (London: Frank Cass, 1994) is critical, while M. Herman, *Intelligence Power in Peace and War* (Cambridge: Cambridge University Press, 1996) is complementary.

14 A recent example of this approach is Tom Bower's biography of Sir Dick White, *The Perfect English Spy* (London: Heinemann, 1995).

15 J. L. Gaddis, 'Intelligence, Espionage and Cold War Origins', *Diplomatic History*, 13, 2 (1989) 191–213.

16 See for example W. S. Lucas, *Divided We Stand: Britain, the US and the Suez Crisis* (London: Hodder and Stoughton, 1992).

17 For a survey of the current literature see P. H. J. Davies, *The British Secret Services: A Bibliography* (Oxford: ABC Clio Press, 1996).

18 Wesley K. Wark, 'In Never-Never Land? The British Archives on Intelligence', *Historical Journal*, 35, 1 (1992) 195–203.

19 On the problems of British intelligence archives see also Andrew, *Secret Service*, pp. xv–xvii, and in 'Whitehall, Washington and the Intelligence Services', *International Affairs*, 53, 2 (1977) 390–404.

20 Typically John Costello identifies the National Archives in Washington as 'a model national institution', *Mask of Treachery: The First Documented Dossier on Blunt, MI5 and Soviet Subversion* (London: Collins, 1988), pp. 12–13.

21 Cmnd 2290, 'Open Government' (London: HMSO, 1993).

22 *Guardian*, Tuesday 20 May 1997.

23 P. Gill, 'Reasserting Control: Recent Changes in the Oversight of the UK Intelligence Community', *Intelligence and National Secu-*

rity, 11, 2 (1996) 313–31.

24 For example, in October 1993 William Waldegrave launched a booklet describing the work of the JIC in co-ordinating the activities of the secret services, *Central Intelligence Machinery* (London: HMSO, 1993) with a foreword by John Major.

25 For example, 'MI5 Thrills Historians by Opening up its Files', *Sunday Times*, 18 May 1997.

26 See David Stafford, *Churchill and Secret Service* (London: John Murray, 1997).

27 R. Bennett, *Behind the Battle: Intelligence in the War with Germany, 1939–1945* (London: Sinclair-Stevenson, 1994), pp. xx–xxi. A limited quantity of detailed Ultra material was released into the class DEFE 3 as early as the late 1970s, but a great deal has only just been released.

28 For an example of new work on SOE see M. Thomas, 'The Massingham Mission: SOE in French North Africa, 1941–1944', *Intelligence and National Security*, 11, 4 (1996) 696–721.

29 R. Cecil, 'Philby's Spurious War', *Intelligence and National Security*, 9, 4 (1994) 764–8; E. D. R. Harrison, 'More Thoughts on Kim Philby's *My Silent War*', *Intelligence and National Security*, 10, 3 (1995) 514–26; R. J. Aldrich, 'The British Secret Intelligence Service (MI6) and the Pacific War', *Modern Asian Studies*, 32, 1 (1998) 113–43.

30 'Release of Records of GCHQ: Signals Intelligence Relating to the Venona Project' (HW 15), 1 October 1996, PRO Press Pack.

31 This argument is based on conversations with officials in December 1996. The NSA's Website is available at http://www.nsa.gov:8080/docs/venona/venona.html

32 American signals intelligence records are located in RG 457, while OSS records are kept in RG 226, both at the United States National Archives (USNA) in Washington DC.

33 A fine example of a history of OSS which benefited from the combination of both primary record and oral testimony is R. Winks, *Cloak and Gown: Scholars in America's Secret War* (London: Collins Harvill, 1987).

34 Air Force Intelligence Records are presently held in the USNA in RG 341, while Naval Intelligence material is held at the same location in RG 38, and Army Intelligence in RG 319.

35 The files of Far Eastern Command are in RG 332, USNA.

36 M. Schaller, *Douglas MacArthur: The Far Eastern General* (New

York: Oxford University Press, 1989); L. Hunt, *The Secret Agenda: The United States Government, Nazi Scientists and Project Paperclip, 1944–1990* (New York: St Martin's, 1991); J. Gimbel, *Science, Technology and Reparations: Exploitation and Plunder in Post-war Germany* (Stanford: Stanford University Press, 1990).

37 B. F. Smith, *The Ultra-Magic Deals and the Most Secret Special Relationship* (Shrewsbury: Airlife Publishing, 1993).

38 An example of British material available *en bloc* is the reports of Security Intelligence Middle East (SIME); they are available in a collated form for 1945 at Folder 81, Box 19, Entry 120, RG 226, USNA.

39 See for example British JIC Report, 'Perimeter Review as at 9th December 1952', File 2-36282, Box 69, DI/HQ Series, RG 341, USNA. Perimeter reviews have not yet been released in the UK.

40 In 1993, under the auspices of the Waldegrave Initiative, the author requested declassification of records of this organisation. However, the MoD have established that almost all of these records were destroyed during a previous review. MoD Deputy Departmental Record Officer to author, 1 February 1994, D/CS (RM) 1/6/1/3.

41 W. Colby, *Honorable Men: My Life in the CIA* (New York: Simon Schuster, 1978).

42 There have been unconfirmed rumours of British approaches direct to Boris Yeltsin in an attempt to keep certain archives closed: David Connett, 'Tell-tale Spy the British want to keep in the Cold', *Independent*, 13 June 1993, p. 5. D. Bristow's autobiography, *A Game of Moles: The Deception of an MI6 Officer* (London: Little, Brown and Company, 1993), appeared with remarkably little fuss, perhaps because of its unsensational nature.

43 These records were released into the PRO at class HD 3/17 in 1993.

44 For further discussion of this subject see R. J. Aldrich, 'Never-Never Land and Wonderland? British and American Policy on Intelligence Archives', *Contemporary Record*, 8, 1 (1994) 132–50; and 'Did Waldegrave Work? The Impact of Open Government Upon British History', *Twentieth Century British History*, 9, 1 (1998) 111–26.

PART I

THE SECRET INTELLIGENCE ORGANISATIONS

In the twentieth century, the majority of British government departments developed some capacity to collect or analyse information that was considered to be secret, and which was therefore dignified with the term 'intelligence'. Accordingly, the range of subjects to be surveyed within this book is potentially very large. However, this section concerns itself specifically with the two main organisations whose primary purpose was to collect intelligence overseas by secret means. The first is SIS, often referred to as MI6, which conducted operations with human agents. The second is GCHQ, whose main work was to gather intelligence by technical means, through the intercepting and deciphering of signals. Although the term GCHQ was employed as early as 1942, this organisation was sometimes referred to by its pre-war title of Government Code and Cipher School or as Bletchley Park after 1945.

SIS did not perform particularly well during the Second World War. Starved of resources in the 1930s and handicapped by a 'clubland' recruitment system that had resulted in distinctly mediocre staff, it struggled to deal with the challenges presented by the speed of modern warfare. SIS was saved politically by the fact that it controlled 'Ultra', produced by the celebrated wartime Bletchley Park signals intelligence centre. Operationally too, intelligence from Bletchley Park gave SIS great advantages in conducting human operations against its Axis adversaries.

Although SIS was somewhat antiquated in its methods and organisational culture – its chief, Sir Stewart Menzies, was certainly an intelligence officer of the old school – nevertheless SIS began to re-organise for the Cold War early, certainly no later than the summer of 1944. It set up a complete new anti-Soviet section before the end of the war, probably at the prompting of the Chiefs of Staff, who, to the intense dismay of the Foreign Office, had begun to think about re-arming Germany against the Soviets in 1943. At the end of 1945, SIS underwent a full re-organisation which resulted in two main sections: 'Production', which handled the operational collection of intelligence and which was organised on a geographical or regional basis; and 'Requirements', which dealt with enquiries from, and distribution of intelligence to, the customers of SIS across Whitehall.

Although the post-war period brought an influx of more able, university-educated SIS officers, and a gradually improving organisational culture, SIS faced severe challenges. The police states of the Eastern Bloc and, after 1949, Communist China presented a stern test of operational skills. Recruiting agents and gathering intelligence in these countries became progressively more difficult as these regimes tightened their control. A high proportion of agents working in Communist countries were lost. This did not prevent SIS from attracting defectors and running operational agents of high value. The supreme achievement of SIS prior to 1970 was almost certainly the work of the GRU Colonel, Oleg Penkovsky, who had access to details of Soviet missile development and high-level strategic thinking. Controlled jointly with the CIA, Penkovsky provided useful intelligence for the Berlin crisis of 1961 and for the Cuban missile crisis, before being arrested by the KGB in 1962, tried and shot. Penkovsky provided abundant proof of the continuing high value of human agent operations, and of their unique ability to shed light upon intentions as well as capabilities, in an era when technical intelligence collection commanded larger and larger budgets.

After 1945 the British codebreaking organisation underwent considerable change. The Second World War had already transformed it from a small national organisation of specialist cryptographers working by hand, into a large international organisation working with machines and computers. Having enjoyed a spectacularly good war, GCHQ emerged to free itself from the control of SIS to become more a secret service in its own right, answerable directly to the Foreign Office. Thereafter, it secured increasing policy direction over the signals interception activities of the three armed services, including the vast new field of electronic intelligence or 'Elint'. Elint involved the interception of non-communication signals from radars and eventually telemetry signals from missile tests. This contrasted with the American system which, although enjoying greater resources, lacked centralisation and was beset by internecine struggles before 1960. In 1963 GCHQ secured detailed control over the activities of Army, Navy and RAF monitoring stations, administering them through the Composite Signals Organisation.

The rise of GCHQ was assisted by the post-war continuation of the 'English-speaking alliance' of British, Commonwealth and American signals intelligence organisations. In September 1945 President Truman had authorised American codebreakers to join negotiations to create a major Western post-war signals intelligence alliance. In November 1945 the British Chiefs of Staff had decided to seek '100 per cent' exchange with the Americans in this field. Patient negotiations resulted in the creation of the UKUSA agreements of 1948, the foundation stone of a remarkable signals intelligence alliance which continues to this day.

Partly because of the extraordinary size of its main alliance partner, the American NSA, GCHQ probably constituted Britain's most important intelligence organisation during the period 1945–70. Yet it remains one of the most secretive and least understood of British intelligence organisations. What is clear is that the main post-war targets presented GCHQ with problems. Most ciphers used for high-grade Soviet wireless traffic proved to be unbreakable, and so there was no equivalent to the wartime triumphs of 'Ultra' against Axis communications. There were limited but important exceptions, such as the successes of the VENONA programme (discussed below). But the British and the Americans were also troubled by security leaks, which undermined some of their better projects, including VENONA.

The volume of intelligence produced by GCHQ after 1945 was, nevertheless, fantastic. Intelligence was gained from tunnels built under Berlin and Vienna to allow the interception of Soviet landlines and telephones cables, from lower-level Soviet wireless traffic, and from the less secure communications of many other states. All this informed decisions in Whitehall on a daily basis. It is now quite clear that important targets for GCHQ included its European partners, such as the French and the Italians. The French were also intercepting British and American communications during this period. Some Third World states adopted the German Enigma machine encipherment system after 1945, believing that it provided a secure means of communication, until the 'Ultra' secret was revealed in 1974.

Although SIS and GCHQ are rightly perceived primarily as secret intelligence collectors, they also had important security functions. SIS was responsible for active counter-intelligence as well as intelligence outside British territory. Accordingly, in the Middle East and the Far East, some of its activities were merged with those of MI5. Equally, GCHQ not only collected signals intelligence, but, together with the London Communications-Electronics Security Agency (LCESA), worked to protect enciphered British communications from attack. In 1969 these latter organisations, which had not enjoyed a happy co-existence, were merged.

1

The Secret Intelligence Service (MI6)

1.1 **From World War to Cold War: SIS in 1943–44**

Sometime in 1943–44, SIS began to turn its attention from the Axis powers to the Soviet Union and set up a new anti-Soviet section. This was not an isolated development and needs to be seen against the background of a volatile debate developing in Whitehall at this time as to whether the Soviet Union should be considered benign or malignant for the purposes of post-war planning. The Chiefs of Staff forecast that the Soviet Union would be malignant. The Foreign Office insisted that whatever the future might hold, any anti-Soviet planning would probably leak out. They feared the impact of this on relations with the Soviets and the Americans. Both predictions proved correct. By the end of the war the head of the new SIS anti-Soviet section was Kim Philby, a long-term Soviet agent. His memoirs, reproduced below, are being re-evaluated by historians in the light of new evidence. They are now regarded as factually accurate, but at the same time strongly propagandistic because the facts he chooses to present are selective.

Long before the end of the war with Germany, senior officers in SIS began to turn their thoughts towards the next enemy. Between the wars, the greater part of the service's resources had been devoted to the penetration of the Soviet Union and to defence of Britain against what was generally known as 'Bolshevism', i.e., the Soviet Government and the world-wide Communist movement. When the defeat of the Axis was in sight, SIS thinking reverted to its old and congenial channels; and a modest start was made by setting up a small section, known as Section IX, to study past records of Soviet and Communist activity. An officer named Curries, approaching retiring age, was imported from MI5 to get the section going. He was hampered by deafness and ignorance of SIS procedure; and the exceptional secrecy imposed upon him hampered him in getting access to the papers relevant to his work. It was understood, however, that his appointment was a stop-gap one, and that, as soon as the reduction of work against Germany allowed, he would be replaced by a regular SIS officer ...

Kim Philby, *My Silent War* (London: MacGibbon and Kee, 1968), p. 68.

1.2 SIS and UK–US co-operation after 1945

After the war, SIS continued to supply many British intelligence reports to Washington through the remnants of the wartime American secret service, then known as the Strategic Services Unit (SSU). In 1947 the newly formed CIA became the main recipient of this material. It was then circulated around Washington on a restricted basis. In the late 1940s SIS negotiated a formal treaty with the CIA, as it had done with preceding American organisations.

1. Certain British Intelligence Service reports of special interest are currently received by us. In general, these reports deal with political problems of importance in Europe. Those of recent date have been of immediate interest in reporting on Germany and Austria; they discuss the political forces current in that area. Reports on that area as well as on others seem to me to be of considerable importance, not only because of their content but because of their source.

2. This material is received by us under special conditions and, up to the present time, no distribution has been made outside of this organisation. However, it would seem to me that you may wish to have, by some special arrangement, significant reports from this Service for highly restricted use.

3. If you should wish to receive this intelligence, I suggest that it be identified only by the source cryptonym WARWICK/COVENTRY, that you may wish to confine its use to yourself and your immediate staff, and that it not be sent to your regular files. These documents, usually presented in memorandum form, could be sent to you by special courier.

4. I would appreciate knowing whether this material is a matter of interest to you and, if it be, whether the arrangement suggested would be agreeable to you.

Head of SSU, Brigadier General John Magruder, to Assistant of Air Staff, US Air Force Intelligence, Major General Elwood R. Quesada, 7 December 1945, Secret, 'Special Reports from British Intelligence', Director of Intelligence USAF HQ files, File 1-200, Box 37, RG 341, USNA.

1.3 **SIS and its Whitehall customers, 1947**

The British secret services have often been portrayed as working in obscure isolation. In the post-war period this was rarely the case. Wartime pressures had forced organisations such as SIS to develop elaborate systems for liaising with its customers across Whitehall for receiving feedback on the value of its efforts and on changing requirements. The document below represents a routine meeting between SIS (here denoted as MI6) and the sub-sections of Military Intelligence, each with their specific responsibilities. It discusses the conventions for tasking SIS with enquiries, through 'Standing Questionnaires', which defined subjects of permanent interest, and 'MI6 Special Question' forms, which were used by customers for issues of more transient interest. The latter forms also had attached cancellation slips for use when a request had been met.

Present:	[name retained Section 3(4)]	M.I.6
	Capt. I.A. Lomax	M.I.2(b) [China]
	Major G.W. Davis	M.I.2(a) [South East Asia]
	Capt. A.C. Hare	M.I.3(a) [Middle East]
	Capt. J.T.C. Howard	M.I.3(b) [Eastern Europe]
	Capt. E.J. Frost	M.I.3(c) [Soviet Union]
	Capt. R.L. McGibbon	M.I.4(a) [Germany]
	Capt. P.N. Steptoe	M.I.4(c) [Spain/Italy]
	Capt. C.H. Gurney	M.I.10(a) [weapons tech.]
	Capt. R.A. Storey	M.I.10(b) [radar tech.]

1. Future M.I.6. Meetings.
With reference to the discussion which took place at Liaison Meeting

No. 21, it has now been decided that the M.I.6. Liaison Meetings will continue to be held every month as hitherto, and M.I.6. is accordingly arranging for room 218 to be made available at 15.00 hours on the first Thursday of each month during 1948.

It is felt that after the proposed cut in the establishment of the M.I. Directorate comes into effect, the frequency of personal liaison visits of M.I.6. officers to M.I. Sections may have to be curtailed to a certain extent so that the Monthly Liaison Meeting, providing as it does an opportunity for M.I. Sections to get together, will become increasingly useful.

It is proposed to ask sub-sections at three-monthly intervals to give their views at the meeting on the general value of CX material [SIS intelligence reports] received during the previous quarter. The first of these general reviews will appear on the agenda for the January meeting and sections are accordingly asked to be prepared to give their assessment of CX reports received during October, November and December 1947.

2. Phrasing of Special Questions.

The attention of sub-sections was again drawn to the necessity for careful phrasing when putting Special Questions to M.I.6. Where possible, a short background explanation should be given and the question related to it. Thus instead of asking point blank for, say, the whereabouts of the 5th Inf. Division, sections should preferably say something on the following lines:-

'It has been reported that the 5th Inf. Div. has left its old location at "Blacktown" and is now thought to be in the area of "Whiteberg", the move is thought to have taken place in early November. Conformation of this move is required together with the new location of the Div. H.Q.'

A similar procedure would apply for questions on organisation, equipment, personalities, etc.

It should always be borne in mind that the ultimate source to whom the question is put is unlikely to be in possession of the background knowledge which would guide him in obtaining the required information. It is appreciated that security of information held by the War Office is an important factor and it is NOT, therefore, suggested that sub-sections should include delicate information in such background.

3. Standing Questionnaires.

Although the Standing Questionnaires, which have been drawn up by individual sub-sections for M.I.6 are designed to cover the permanent over-all requirements of that sub-section, it may well be that changing conditions may require changing emphasis on various points of detail which they contain. Sub-sections are accordingly invited to look at their Standing Questionnaires from time to time and, if necessary, to revise them, or to supply Special Supplementary Briefs to cover any points which cannot be adequately dealt with by normal 'Special Question' system. This may apply particularly to those sub-sections which cover several countries, where the changing pattern of events may bring into prominence certain aspects of a country which may not hitherto have been sufficiently emphasised in the Standing Questionnaires.

4. In answer to a question by M.I.3b the terms 'Casual' 'Occasional' and 'Reliable' were explained by M.I.6. representative.

'Casual' is applied to a source of a transient nature, i.e. one who appears by chance, gives a piece of information, consciously or unconsciously, and then passes on his way. Reports of this nature can rarely be referred back to source.

'Occasional' is applied to a source, similar to the 'Casual' one, but who crops up from time to time. While such a source is not normally 'steered' by M.I.6., a follow-up of his information is sometimes possible on request.

'Reliable' is reserved for someone of known integrity (normally a British officer or official) who, while not being a regular M.I.6. 'steered' source, is able to pass on a piece of information which has come his way.

Thus, information from sources described in these three categories does not necessarily emanate from the same sources, but where two or more reports are received from the same 'Occasional' or 'Reliable' source, this will be pointed out by M.I.6. in their note ...

M.I.6/203/1353, 'Minutes of M.I.6 Liaison Meeting No. 22 Held at the War Office Room 218, at 1500 Hrs, 4 Dec 1947', Top Secret, WO 208/4749, PRO.

1.4 **SIS agent drops, c.1950**

The scale and purpose of SIS operations in the Soviet Union
itself during this period remain unclear, but are reviewed in
this rare SIS memoir. CIA accounts also mention three groups
each of six agents dropped into the Ukraine by SIS in early
1951. Both British and American operations of this type,
whether launched into the Soviet Union or Communist
China, sustained high losses. Insertion was achieved from airfields in the Mediterranean. These 'special duties' flights
seemed to have gone undetected by Soviet air defences, but
problems began once agents were on the ground.

Most of the intelligence coming out of the Soviet Union via émigré
organisations was considered suspect for two basic reasons, and all
reports of émigré sources were labelled *Mauve*.

The first reason for suspicion was that the various organisations
were not primarily set up as intelligence-gathering units and were
both insecure and often penetrated by the KGB. Secondly, we found
that émigré officers who passed us this information could never re-
frain from gilding the lily.

So it was that Menzies obtained authority for SIS to train and drop
our own agents in to the Soviet Union and PROJECT 1, the first such
operation was set up ... The officer in charge was Colonel Harold
Gibson, an old hand in SIS who had been Station Commander in
Prague at the outbreak of war ...

At suitable phases of the moon, teams of two or three highly
trained agents were dropped into the Ukraine or Byelorussia. I knew
that PROJECTS II, III, and IV went ahead and after arrival the
dropped agents made radio contact with their base station in Western
Germany. However, several of the agents were captured, tried – some
in show trials – and then shot. Today I still wonder whether those
who did continue in radio contact did so under KGB control.

Anthony Cavendish, *Inside Intelligence: The Revelations of an MI6
Officer* (London: Harper Collins, 1997), pp. 50–1.

30

1.5 **The SIS station in Berlin in the 1950s**

Germany and Austria were the front line for British intelligence during the early Cold War, nowhere more so than Berlin. The key reason for this was money. In the 1950s some SIS agent networks had to be 'laid off' due to budget cuts. But in Germany, most costs were met by the German taxpayer until the end of the occupation in May 1955, an event which prompted the re-organisation of the SIS station in Berlin. The plethora of intelligence organisations working in Berlin, and the decline of the black market by 1950, meant that a surprising proportion of Berliners were working as agents for an intelligence organisation or even many at the same time. George Blake, an SIS officer whose memoirs describe the Berlin station, was also in that category. His identity as an agent for the Soviets was deduced from leads from a senior Polish intelligence officer who defected to the Americans in 1959.

Berlin station was the largest station SIS had in the world. The reasons for this were not hard to seek. The Western Sector of Berlin was a small island, an outpost of the Western world in Communist territory ... it was as easy to travel from West to East Berlin and back as from Hammersmith to Piccadilly. Although there were check-points on the main streets, people could cross freely in both directions. On the underground there was no check at all. All this made Berlin the ideal centre for intelligence activities ...

Apart from the operational facilities created by the special conditions obtaining in Berlin, the status of Great Britain, as one of the four occupying powers, offered financial and administrative advantages to SIS which did not exist elsewhere. In Berlin SIS was operating not under diplomatic cover, but under that of the Army or the Control Commission. Both organisations were large enough to provide an umbrella for any number of personnel the Berlin station might require without attracting attention. Financial considerations were equally important. The whole SIS establishment was paid for out of occupation costs, which were borne in their entirety by the German taxpayer. All this was fully exploited ...

Berlin station had a complement of about a hundred officers, secretaries and ancillaries. Each officer had his own car. Every day these fanned out in all directions from the Olympic Stadium, where the

31

British headquarters were situated, to take their occupants to clandestine meetings on street corners, near underground stations, in cafes, night-clubs or safe flats in the Western sectors of the city.

The station was divided into several sub-stations, each with its own particular sphere of activity. There was a section responsible for the collecting of political intelligence and the penetration of the Soviet headquarters in Karlshorst (a suburb of East Berlin). Another had the task of collecting information on the Soviet and East German Armed Forces. A third was exclusively concerned with the collection of scientific intelligence. Finally there was the section concerned with the planning and execution of technical operations of various kinds.

G. Blake, *No Other Choice* (London: Cape, 1990), pp. 166–8.

1.6 SIS and strategic trade, 1953

In the late 1940s Britain joined Western efforts to prevent 'strategic' materials reaching the Eastern Bloc. This amounted to approximately a hundred key items, from raw materials such as uranium, copper and industrial diamonds, to complex electronic components and other 'technology transfer' items. This was a controversial issue between the Western Allies, especially *vis-à-vis* Communist China because of the Korean War. In the early 1950s SIS formed a new section to address this problem, which was headed by Desmond Bristow. One of its tasks was to prevent British firms becoming blacklisted. The extract below, from Bristow's memoirs, describes his section's work using human agents. Other passages make clear that considerable information was also derived from intercepted commercial communications.

The office [SIS] and the CIA set up agents in jobs that would enable us to monitor sea traffic as closely as possible. Once goods arrived in the country, customs officers would carry out random investigations on the receiving companies.

I will use Chile as an example since it produced copper, which was in very high demand behind the Iron Curtain. In Chile both the consul and the commercial counsellor worked for us and had a network of agents who passed on information about shipping. These agents usually worked in the import and export department, or in the shipping telegraph station. When the consul or commercial counsellor heard about a particular ship, carrying copper, which had been leaving for Oslo and then received instructions to redirect to Gdansk, they would send me details, often very explicit, perhaps even including the captain's name. I would then inform the naval intelligence department. The navy would follow the passage of the copper carrying ship, and at a strategic point intercept it and redirect it to an English or a French port. The cargo would usually be confiscated and put on the market, and the receiving company in Oslo would be investigated and blacklisted. We worked very closely with the CIA in our endeavour to monitor developments of strategic trade.

D. Bristow, *A Game of Moles: The Deceptions of an MI6 Officer* (London: Little, Brown and Co., 1993), pp. 236–7.

1.7 **The death of Commander Crabb, 1956**

In April 1956 Commander Crabb died while undertaking an SIS-sponsored operation to investigate electronic equipment on the underside of a Soviet cruiser in Portsmouth harbour. His headless body was later recovered from the sea. The cruiser was carrying Khrushchev to a summit with the Prime Minister, Anthony Eden, in London and the resulting furore caused Eden no small embarrassment. It seems that Eden had been consulted beforehand and had expressly forbidden the operation, but his orders were disregarded. An angry Eden ordered an immediate enquiry. He also requested that the JIC undertake a full investigation into the range and balance of current intelligence objectives, as well as the procedure for their approval. This had implications for future UK–US operations (see document 7.5).

I. I wish you to carry out on my behalf an enquiry into the circumstances in which Commander Crabb undertook an intelligence operation against the Russian warship in Portsmouth harbour on April 19.
   Your enquiry should include the following points:-
   (a) what authority was given for the operation, and
   (b) why its failure was not reported to Ministers until May 4.
   My objective is to establish, by independent enquiry, what the

facts are and where responsibility lies. When the report of this enquiry is available, I will consider, with the responsible Ministers, what disciplinary action, if any, should be taken.

I have been asked by the Minister in charge of the Departments concerned to give whatever instructions are necessary to ensure that officers in their Departments give you all the assistance you may require in carrying out this enquiry.

Prime Minister, Anthony Eden, to Permanent Under-Secretary to the Treasury, Sir Edward Bridges, M.104.56, 9 May 1956, AP20/32/78, Avon Papers, Birmingham University Library.

I have now had an opportunity of studying the report by the Joint Intelligence Committee which was forwarded to me by Sir Edward Bridges, on certain questions arising out of the Crabb affair.

I approve the recommendations in this report relating to future procedure. I also approve the recommendations by Sir Edward Bridges that Mr Dean should, in his personal capacity, undertake an enquiry into the question of the balance between military intelligence on the one hand, and civil intelligence and political risks on the other.

I am sending a similar minute to the Foreign Secretary and to Sir Norman Brook [Cabinet Secretary].

Prime Minister, Anthony Eden, to Minister of Defence, Antony Head, 22 December 1956, AP20/21/228, Avon Papers, Birmingham University Library.

1.8 Colonel Penkovsky and the Cuban missile crisis, 1962

In August 1960 Colonel Oleg Penkovsky, an officer in the Soviet military intelligence (GRU), and with a range of high-level contacts in the Soviet command structure, offered his services to the West. Over the next two years he provided intelligence of extraordinary quality on Soviet war plans, missile programmes and intelligence activities. Most importantly he gave new insights into Soviet decision-making and into Khrushchev's intentions towards the West. This information played a part in American decision-making during the

Cuban missile crisis. However, each delivery of fresh intelligence exposed him to risk. During the summer of 1962 Penkovsky became increasingly aware of KGB surveillance, but he could not determine what had excited their suspicions. He delivered his last minox camera film of Soviet documents to a case officer on 27 August and was arrested in October. Following his interrogation he was tried and shot. The passage below is taken from the recently released text of Penkovsky's debriefings by a joint SIS–CIA team during his visit to London as part of a Soviet delegation. Sir Dick White, then the head of SIS, met him personally.

You should know what is going on in the leadership and how Khrushchev is promoting generals to win their loyalty. Among the leadership there exists a secret opposition, which remains secret because the majority are still Khrushchev's protégés and the others don't want to lose their jobs. But there could be a realignment of forces and a split as a result of the Berlin question. All of those aware of the economic and military points will say, 'it is too early to go to war. We've got to wait. What's the point of heating up the situation because of a Berlin which has existed for the last sixteen years?'

Meeting No. 23, London, 28 July 1961, paragraph 31, quoted in J. L. Schecter and P. S. Deriabin, *The Spy Who Saved the World: How a Soviet Colonel Changed the Course of the Cold War* (New York: Scribner, 1992), pp. 212–13.

2
Signals intelligence

2.1 GCHQ and wartime planning for peace, 1944

By September 1944 it was increasingly clear that the end of
the war against Germany was less than a year away (although
the war against Japan was then thought likely to drag on into
1946). Attention was already turning to the future shape of
British intelligence. In September 1944 three influential
GCHQ officers prepared a report for its Director, Sir Edward
Travis, entitled 'The General Problem of Intelligence and
Security in Peace'. This paper addressed some of the most
fundamental issues of national intelligence organisation and
called for a more centralised 'Foreign Intelligence Office'. In
an appendix they also attached a more specific note on the
future of GCHQ (part of which is reproduced below). It is
interesting for its frank self-criticism, and for its anxiety to
relegate the importance of the war against Japan in favour of
long-term post-war concerns. It reveals an anxiety to assert
control over related areas such as signals security, the signals
intelligence work of the three services and also the new field
of electronic intelligence. By 1946 GCHQ had escaped the
control of SIS to become more a separate service in its own
right, but it was 1969 before its ambitions to control all
aspects of signals work were achieved.

RECOMMENDATIONS
17. We would therefore suggest three immediate objectives:
    (i) the creation of the Foreign Intelligence Office, which will in-
clude Signals Intelligence and Signals Security as part of its sphere of
activity;
    (ii) the remoulding of G.C. & C.S. [GCHQ] in the framework of
the Foreign Intelligence Office as an organisation which will compel

the respect of the Services and take its proper place as the unchallenged headquarters of all Signals Intelligence;

(iii) the development of a first-class Signals Security organisation with an expert and professional understanding of communications and communications engineering.

18. We are strongly of the opinion that the pursuit of these objectives should take priority over the part played by G.C. & C.S. in Signals Intelligence for the Japanese war, for the following reasons and to the extent explained below.

19. Before the German war, G.C. & C.S. was little more than a cryptographic centre. There was no Intelligence Centre, or anything like it. There was little appreciation of the coming importance of engineering, and little conception of the coming need for the sort of planning and coordination provided for in our diagram [not reproduced]. Early recruiting produced a few leaders, who, with the few men of wide outlook on the permanent staff, have managed to collect a reasonably good supporting staff and make a passable show in this war. But the Japanese war, with its need for major organisation overseas, presents a far more complicated problem of planning and coordination. It is entirely different in every way from the German problem, and it is doubtful if even the best of the men who have been exploiting German signals could have any appreciable effect at this stage.

Very few men in G.C. & C.S. have shown ability in general planning and coordination. Indeed, it would be difficult to count as many as a dozen, although there are plenty of good men with the right temperament for specialised work. We recommend, therefore, that as soon as the German war is over, as many as possible of the few potential planners should be set to work in the direction of our three immediate objectives, instead of devoting more of their time to Japanese problems. We also recommend that a sufficient number of the best supporting staff on the German side should be retained to help them. However, it is also important that the planners shall not lose touch with developments of the Japanese problem, since there is perhaps more to learn from experience in this sphere than from the easier German sphere.

From Gordon Welchman, Harry Hinsley and Edward Crankshaw to Sir Edward Travis, 'A Note on the Future of G.C. & C.S. [GCHQ]', Top Secret, 17 September 1944, HW 3/169, PRO.

2.2 **UK–US co-operation on VENONA from 1947**

In 1945 the Americans informed the British about the efforts of American Army codebreakers to decipher Soviet diplomatic communications. Soviet cryptographic systems were of high quality, but weaknesses had been introduced by poor procedure, notably using the same cipher pads twice. This provided the Western cryptanalysts with a 'way in'. Limited headway had been made by the end of 1946 and in early 1947 a British cryptanalyst joined the American team based at Arlington Hall, Virginia, just outside Washington. At the end of 1947, breaks into Soviet secret service (MGB, later the KGB) traffic showed the presence of a Soviet agent inside Australian government (see document 10.3). This Commonwealth dimension prompted GCHQ to devote more effort to this programme which was given the codename VENONA. VENONA pointed to the presence of important Soviet spies, such as the atomic scientist Klaus Fuchs in 1950 and the diplomat Donald Maclean in 1951. Although VENONA was betrayed to the Soviets by an American defector in 1948, work continued on previously recorded Soviet radio traffic from the 1940s, and this provided clues about Soviet espionage as late as 1980. The document below is an intercepted message, addressed to General Pavel Fitin, Head of the Foreign Intelligence Directorate of the MGB, referring to their agent, the atomic scientist Klaus Fuchs. It underlines the very technical and painstaking nature of cryptanalytical work.

From: NEW YORK
To: MOSCOW
No.:   195   9th February 1944
Personal to VIKTOR[1]
In reply to No.302[2]

On 5th February a meeting took place between 'GUS'[3] and 'rest'.[4] Beforehand GUS' was given a detailed briefing by us. REST greeted him pleasantly but was rather cautious at first, [1 group unrecovered] the discussion GUS' satisfied himself that REST was aware of whom he was working with. R.[5] arrived in the COUNTRY[STRANA][6] in September as a member of the ISLAND[OSTOV][7] missions on ENORMOUS[ENORMOZ].[8] According to him the work on ENORMOUS in the COUNTRY is being carried out under the direct control of the COUNTRY's army represented by General SOMERVELL [SOMMERVILL][9] and STIMSON:[10] at the head of the group of ISLANDERS [OSTOVITYaNE][11] is a Labour member of Parliament, Ben SMITH.[12]

The whole operation amounts to the working out of the process for the separation of isotopes of ENORMOUS. The work is proceeding in two directions: the electron method developed by LAWRENCE [LAURENS][13]

[71 groups unrecoverable]

separation of isotopes by the combined method, using the diffusion method for preliminary and the electron method for final separation. The work

[46 groups unrecovered]

18th February, we shall report the results.

No.92 ANTON[14]

Intercepted MGB cable from New York to Moscow, 'Meeting Between "GUS" and "REST": Work on Enormous' (1944), VENONA – TOP SECRET, NSA Website, http://www.nsa.gov:8080/docs/venona/venona. html

1   Lt General P. M. Fitin.
2   Not available.
3   'Goose' Harry Gold.
4   Dr Emil Julius Klaus Fuchs.
5   Again, Dr Fuchs.
6   The United States.
7   Great Britain.
8   The US Atomic Energy Project/Uranium.
9   Lt General Brehan Burke Somervell, Commanding General Army Service Forces, War Department.
10   Henry Lewis Stimson, Secretary of War.
11   British.
12   Rt Hon. Ben Smith, Minister Resident in Washington for Supply from 1943.
13   Professor Ernest Orlando Lawrence.
14   Leonid Romanovich Kvasnikov.

2.3 The JIC and signal intelligence requirements, 1948

The JIC was the principal co-ordinating body for British intelligence in the immediate post-war period. One of its tasks was to review the overall hierarchy of requests made to

GCHQ for defence priorities on an annual basis. The JIC gave top priority to the four areas of Soviet activity related to strategic air attack and defence, including nuclear, biological and chemical weapons. Despite the high priority accorded to these subjects, little hard information on Soviet strategic weapons was forthcoming and the detonation of the Soviet atomic bomb in the autumn of 1949 took the UK by surprise. It should be noted that this list was prepared for 'defence purposes' only and does not appear to indicate the requirements of the Foreign Office. These requirements were then passed to the London Signals Intelligence Board (LSIB, or the 'Sigint board'), which reconciled what Whitehall wanted with what GCHQ thought operationally practicable.

We have examined our intelligence requirements for Defence purposes from Sigint sources in order to guide the Sigint board in allocating its resources.

2. We have consulted the Colonial Office and the Commonwealth Relations Office (India Department).

3. We have listed subjects of defence interest and have grouped them into five priority classes. They are attached at Annex. We realize however that technical factors will influence the final allocation of priorities.

4. Any further requirements that the department may pass to L.S.I.C. should in future be related to this list, by bearing an indication of priority.

5. We propose to review these requirements in a year's time.
Ministry of Defence S.W.1.
11th May 1948

ANNEX
PRIORITY LIST
(No attempt has been made to arrange subjects in order of importance within each priority class)

PRIORITY I
1. Development in the Soviet Union of atomic, biological and chemical methods of warfare (together with associated raw materials).

2. Development in the Soviet Union of scientific principles and inventions leading to new weapons, equipment or methods of warfare.

3. Strategic and tactical doctrines, state of training, armament and

aircraft of:-

(a) Soviet long-range bomber force.

(b) Soviet metropolitan fighter defence force (including P.V.O.) [ground-based anti-aircraft units].

4. Development in the Soviet Union of guided weapons.

PRIORITY II

5. Manpower, call-up and mobilisation of Soviet armed forces.

6. Strategical and tactical doctrines, state of construction and training and construction programme (especially new types) of:-

(a) Soviet submarines.

(b) Soviet air forces.

(c) Soviet airborne forces.

7. Strategic industries (e.g. armaments, aircraft, fuels, steel, chemicals, power) in the Soviet Union.

8. Strategic stock-piling in the Soviet Union.

9. Railways in the Soviet Union.

10. Soviet economic successes or reverses (such as the drought of 1946) likely to have an effect on foreign policy.

11. Organisation and activities of Soviet espionage and counter-espionage services.

12. Significant internal political developments in the Soviet Union (especially question of succession to Stalin).

13. Soviet reaction to associations (actual or proposed) between powers outside the Soviet sphere of influence.

14. Soviet intentions in Germany and Austria, including Soviet employment of German Service and other personnel.

15. Organisation of, and foreign assistance to, Greek rebels (including any international brigade activities).

PRIORITY III

16. Strategic and tactical doctrines, training and morale of Soviet armed forces (except as already detailed in I and II).

17. Organisation of Soviet armed forces, including high command and M.V.D. [Ministry of Internal Affairs] troops.

18. Unit and formation identifications, locations, and movements of Soviet armed forces, including M.V.D. troops.

19. Present and future warship construction (with details of performance and armament) in the Soviet Union.

20. Weapons and equipment in the Soviet army (technical details).

21. Airfields in the Soviet Union, and areas under Soviet influence.

22. Location, organisation and activities of defence research and development establishments in the Soviet Union.

23. Movements and activities of leading personalities concerned with scientific research and development in the Soviet bloc and Soviet occupied countries.

24. Scientific and technical education in the Soviet Union.

25. Movement of Soviet officials or service personnel to disturbed areas on the borders of the Soviet sphere of influence, such as Germany, Albania, India, Pakistan and the Far East.

26. Relations of India, Pakistan and neighbouring countries with foreign counties, particularly the Soviet Union, and with each other.

27. Soviet relations with Jews in Palestine (particularly extent of Soviet and satellite assistance of emigration).

28. Organisation and activities of national communist parties and communist-inspired movements (including Cominform).

29. Indications of establishments in foreign countries in peace of Soviet agencies designed to assist the Soviet Union in wars.

PRIORITY IV

30. Soviet assistance to satellite armed forces.

31. Developments of bases, harbours and strategic waterways in the Soviet Union and satellite countries.

32. Soviet administrative network with particular reference to its vulnerability in war.

33. Arctic developments by Soviet Union, particularly extension of meteorological research and aircraft patrols.

34. Relations of satellite counties with neighbours outside Soviet Union.

35. Arab nationalism and relations of Arab states with U.K. and U.S.A.

36. Attitude of Soviet Union, France, Italy and Arab states towards future of ex-Italian colonies, especially Libya.

37. Organisation and activities of satellite espionage and counter-espionage.

38. Soviet intentions in India, Pakistan and Moslem countries.

PRIORITY V

39. Unit identification of Yugoslav armed forces.

40. Static defence system in the Soviet Union and satellite countries

(other than P.V.O.).

41. Any marked increase of telecommunication facilities in frontier areas of the Soviet Union and satellite countries, notably Caucasus, Balkans, White Russia.

42. Contributions by the satellite countries to Soviet industrial potential.

43. Deliveries of grain by the Soviet Union to other countries.

44. Relations between satellite countries.

45. Soviet intentions in China and Korea.

46. Organisations and activities of Chinese penetrations of non-Chinese territories in the Far East, particularly their intelligence services.

47. Organisations and activities of:-

(a) Zionist movements including its intelligence services.

(b) Clandestine right wing French and Italian Movements.

(c) Right wing movements in the satellite countries.

JIC (48) 19 (0) (2nd Revised Draft), 'Sigint Intelligence Requirements – 1948' (draft report by the Joint Intelligence Committee), Limited Circulation – Top Secret, 11 May 1948, L/WS/1/1196, IOLR.

2.4 **The UKUSA Signals Intelligence Agreement, 1948**

Little documentation is available pertaining to the complex series of letters and memoranda of understanding that constitute the so-called UKUSA Signals Intelligence Agreement of 1948. However, the discussions below of one of its component parts – a draft letter of understanding between the Americans and Canadians – gives a clear indication of its overall texture. It also illustrates that: a) this was essentially an elaboration of its predecessor, the wartime BRUSA agreement of 1943, and b) that those negotiating UKUSA were reluctant to permit an information free-for-all amongst all its signatories. Each clause was carefully crafted and its complex nature meant that UKUSA took over a year to negotiate.

1. Reference is made to USCIB [US Communications Intelligence Board] 3/19, dated 17 May 1948, and to USCIB 3/11, dated 24 May 1948.

43

2. With the exception of paragraphs 5, 6a and 17, the Air Force Member of USCIB concurs with the amended version of the proposed letter from the Chairman CCRC [Canadian Communications Research Committee] to the Chairman USCIB.

3. In the interests of clarity of understanding with the Canadians, and to insure that the understanding with the Canadians is the same as with the British, it is considered that paragraph 5 should be amended to use substantially the same definition as is used in BRUSA ...

6. Paragraph 6a is not considered sufficiently restrictive. In effect, it provides for the complete exchange of information. Not only is it considered that the Canadians will reap all the benefits of complete exchange but wider dissemination of the information could jeopardise the security of the information. It is believed that the exchange should be related to mutually agreed COMINT activities or on a 'need to know' basis.

7. While there is no objection to the assumption that there will be liaison officers as stated in paragraph 17, it is believed that the assumption should be qualified in such a manner as to permit control of these activities of the liaison officers.

[ENCLOSURE 1]
TO
PROPOSED CANADIAN LETTER AS AMENDED
5. *Scope of these arrangements*
These arrangements will govern the relations of the above mentioned authorities in regard to Communication Intelligence which will be understood to comprise all processes involved in the collection, production and dissemination of information derived from the communications of countries other than the U.S.A., the British Empire, and the British Commonwealth of Nations. It is realised that collateral material is often required for technical purposes in the production, and the proposed arrangements for exchange of such material are dealt with separately in this letter.

6. *Extent of Exchange of Information Related to Communication Intelligence*
The two Communication Intelligence authorities will exchange the following information on the bases indicated:
a. Translation and gists will be exchanged:
(i) On the request of each authority to meet the requirements of the

COMINT centers for assistance in the efficient discharge of their mutually agreed-upon COMINT activities and undertakings.

(ii) On a 'need to know' basis as determined by the originating authority.

17. In order to implement these arrangements as effectively as possible, it is assumed that each authority may establish liaison officers at the comint centers of the other authority with such freedom of action as is agreeable to the host authority.

Brigadier General US Air Force, Acting Director of Intelligence, Walter R. Agee, to US Coordinator of Joint Operations, 7 June 1948, Top Secret, 'Proposed U.S.–Canadian Agreement', Director of Intelligence USAF HQ files, File 2-1200/2-1299, Box 40, RG 341, USNA.

2.5 **GCHQ and UK–US electronic intelligence, 1948**

Communications intelligence (or 'comint') was the collection of intelligence from communications signals. Electronic intelligence (elint) was the monitoring of non-communications signals, for example from radar and missiles, and was sometimes called 'noise investigation'. In 1948 elint was being brought within the growing body of Western signals intelligence agreements. At this time GCHQ was attempting to extend its control over elint, which was mostly conducted by service elements, such as special Royal Air Force (RAF) elint aircraft conducting 'Ferret' flights and RAF ground-based elint stations in Germany.

1. Colonel Marr-Johnson has approached the Coordinator with a proposal from his [British] superiors to initiate liaison on noise investigation matters. The proposed liaison would include the coordination of activities such as noise investigation or 'Ferret' operations and the exchange of relevant information. Such coordination and exchange would take place via Comint channels, as the above-mentioned activities are included in the Comint field insofar as the British are concerned. This proposal would in effect extend the present British–U.S. Comint collaboration to include [elint] countermeasures, intercept activities and intelligence.

45

2. Colonel Marr-Johnson indicated that certain Air Force officers had in the past attempted to establish contact with the British in regard to these matters but inasmuch as these officers were not cleared for Comint nor accredited as Comint representatives the British were unwilling to deal with them freely ...

J. N. Wenger, Captain, US Navy Coordinator of Joint Operations, to Colonel R. P. Klocko, US Air Force, CJO 0001922, 12 March 1948, Top Secret, Memo: 'British proposal for liaison on "noise investigation"', Director of Intelligence USAF HQ files, File 2-1100/2-1199, Box 40, RG 341, USNA.

2.6 Electronic intelligence and the Soviet Union, 1948

British electronic intelligence-gathering had continued without pause after the end of the Second World War, particularly from ground-based stations in Germany. Notwithstanding this, the summer of 1948 marked the launch of a greatly enhanced RAF programme of electronic intelligence-gathering around the perimeter of the Soviet Union by special 'Ferret' aircraft. The head of RAF intelligence, referred to here, carried the title Assistant Chief of the Air Staff (Intelligence) or ACAS(I).

... I now hand you four (4) sets of British 'Ferret' Flight reports to which A.C.A.S.(I.) refers. You may wish to note a slight inaccuracy in that the first Baltic Sea flights took place in June and July 1948 and not in May as stated in A.C.A.S.(I.)'s letter. The reports which I hand you herewith refer to these flights, also to the Adriatic flights in 1948 and Black Sea flights in September 1948, and the Baltic flights in November 1948.

Group Captain R. A. McMurtie of the British Joint Staff Mission Washington, to Chief, Air Intelligence Division, HQ USAF, Pentagon, Brigadier General Ernest Moore, 30 November 1948, Top Secret, Director of Intelligence USAF HQ files, File 2-8300/2-8399, Box 45, RG 341, USNA.

Signals intelligence

2.7 The Technical Radio Intercept Committee, 1951

By the early 1950s GCHQ gained full control of electronic and well as communications intelligence. A growing network of monitoring units were being developed with reports being routed to the Technical Radio Intercept Committee (TRIC). The importance to GCHQ of liaison with the United States, and the supply of technical equipment from the United States, comes through clearly in this American document. Commander Clive Loehnis, who appears below, became head of GCHQ in 1960.

FACTS AND DISCUSSION
2. At a meeting called by Capt. Gentry, acting in his capacity as Chairman of the Joint Countermeasures Panel of JCEC, the following people attended:

Capt. K.W. Gentry, USN [US Navy]
Cdr R.C. Sergeant, USN
Lt C.C. Andrews, USN
Maj. E.N. Jenkins, SC, USA [US Army]
Maj. S.D. Brown, USA
Maj. W.R. Harpster, USAF [US Air Force]
Cdr C. Loehnis, GCHQ (British)
Mr F.W. Smith, GCHQ (British)

3. Subject of discussion was exchange of raw data from non-communications listening efforts of various U.S. and U.K. agencies.

4. The following points were made during the discussion:

a. That GCHQ is entering the non-communications listening field. They will be responsible for transmission of information from the field to London.

b. New ground units, manned by Army or RAF personnel, will report through GCHQ to the Technical Radio Intercept Committee (TRIC).

c. TRIC will publish all reports of non-communications Intercept.

d. That present exchange of intercept data between U.K. and U.S. field units is satisfactory and will not be changed.

e. That exchange of raw intercept information is not satisfactory. U.S. Navy feeding logs to Royal Navy and getting only collated reports in return. That S/L Dunsford sends in extracts of air mission reports, but USAF representative with DSI [UK Directorate of

47

Scientific Intelligence, London] does not see raw data. He gets only published reports.

5. The following decisions were reached on the above points:

a. That exchange of raw intercept information must be kept to T.S. [top secret] crypto channels.

b. That Cdr. Loehnis and Mr Smith will attempt to see that TRIC passes raw intercept information to USAF and US Navy personnel in London.

c. That if U.S. Navy does not start getting raw data they will stop giving raw data.

6. Cdr. Loehnis and Mr. Smith requested information on procedure to follow for obtaining intercept equipment in the U.S. They were informed that U.S. Navy had authorised 6 AN/APR-9 receivers to be shipped to DSI, London for use on the expanded project.

Memorandum of a meeting held in the office of Captain Gentry (US Navy), 11 May 1951, Director of Intelligence USAF HQ files, File 2-900/2-932, Box 45, RG 341, USNA.

2.8 **Electronic intelligence at work, 1951**

This document gives a good picture of routine signals intelligence work against Soviet radars. It reveals the closeness of Allied co-operation in this field and the way in which different sources were combined to create an overall picture. Although this work was now controlled by GCHQ, the day-to-day business was a still a matter for the MoD's scientific intelligence elements and the Combined Signals Establishment at RAF Watton, which had pioneered this work during the Second World War under Professor R. V. Jones.

Room.727, D.S.I/1.

Dr. Blount,

I attach as you instructed notes on action taken regarding the Type 27 [a Soviet twin-engined light bomber].

2. I was informed this morning that the Americans had a Russian sergeant at Salzburg who had defected. He gave technical information about the Type 27, and said it had radar rear guns.

3. Photographs of the Type 27 have shown a bulge at the rear

which has excited our conjectures for some months. The bulge is not large, so that a radar of high frequency is to be expected. A range-only radar would be relatively simple, yet valuable.

4. Type 27 aircraft are known to be at Oranienburg, not far from A.D.I. Science Listening Station at Berlin. I have accordingly instructed A.D.I. Science to cover so far as possible the S.X.K.Q. bands from Berlin, and to give this priority.

5. Mr Garrard is now on his way to TRE, who have promised to provide some K – 9 equipment. He will return with it to-night.

6. C.S.E. Watton has agreed to provide some S & X band equipment. It will be delivered here to-night.

7. Major Farrior (A.D.I.Tech) has agreed to fly to-morrow morning to Germany. He will discuss at Wiesbaden the interrogation of the defector, and I have made available Flight Lieutenant Morgan whose Russian and radar knowledge should be invaluable, if Major Farrior finds it possible to get him an official invitation.

8. Major Farrior will fly from Wiesbaden to Buckeburg to-morrow afternoon, and will deliver to S/Ldr Ackernman the equipment mentioned above.

9. I have informed Sc. T.R.I.C. of this possible airborne radar.

Assistant Director of Scientific Intelligence (1), Dr J. A. Lees, to Director of Scientific Intelligence, MoD, Dr Blount, Top Secret, 5 May 1951, DEFE 40/26, PRO.

2.9 Relocation of British comint units in war, 1951

Britain and the United States had important reciprocal agreements for accommodating each other's comint units and permitting their continued operation if crisis or war required their evacuation. The American comint units on Cyprus, for example, were allocated emergency accommodation at British bases in Egypt. This document shows that in the event of war with Communist China, the British comint unit in Hong Kong would have gone to Japan. The value of Hong Kong as an intercept site, set against the background of the Korean War, is also clear.

1. In the event of emergency withdrawal from present location, United States is committed to providing relocation of British Hong Kong COMINT Unit on United States or United States controlled territory. This is in part quid pro quo arrangement in return for accommodation our units by British on UK or UK controlled territory plus others now in Europe. Current plans provide for relocating 7 such US COMINT Units to UK or UK controlled territory in event emergency relocation becomes necessary. One US COMINT Station already in UK and 1 other planned there plus 1 now in Asmara.

2. United States now receives full intercept output of Hong Kong Unit which is important and does not duplicate US effort. Present combined US–UK intercept facilities in Far East are far short of requirements. Considered essential full advantage be taken of British Unit and effort be made to relocate when necessary where interception will be most effective. This best achieved by relocation on Okinawa. Necessary detailed plans for relocation British Unit should be arranged accordingly by CINCFE.

3. British authorities will be responsible for evacuation of the Hong Kong Unit of 236 personnel from Hong Kong to Okinawa ...

US Joint Chiefs of Staff to CINCFE Tokyo, JCS 86211, Top Secret, 20 March 1951, FECOM Records, RG 4, Box 43 (Radiograms 30 June 1950 – 5 April 1951), Douglas MacArthur Memorial, Norfolk, Virginia. (I am greatly indebted to Matthew Aid for providing me with a copy of this document.)

2.10 UK–US communications security, 1952

By the 1950s Britain was increasingly aware that many of the machines that it used for enciphering communications, which were of Second World War vintage, no longer offered the desired level of communications security or 'comsec'. Financial constraints prevented the UK or the North Atlantic Treaty Organisation (NATO) from replacing these machines rapidly. The United States therefore offered assistance, allowing its cryptographic principles to be adopted by Britain and paying for the new machines operating on combined circuits carrying communications between the US, UK and NATO. A separate system was preserved by the United States for its own national communications. This US Joint Chiefs of Staff

(JCS) paper, with its message to the UK Chiefs of Staff, gives
an indication of the great complexity and cost of 'comsec' for
the Western Alliance.

REPORT BY THE CHAIRMAN, ARMED FORCES SECURITY AGENCY COUNCIL ...
THE PROBLEM
1. In the light of the memorandum by the Representatives of the British Chiefs of Staff, RHB 1/4 dated 4 January 1952 (Enclosure to J.C.S. 2074/11), to submit comment and recommendations on the security and replacement of the Combined Cipher Machine (CCM).

FACTS BEARING ON THE PROBLEM AND DISCUSSION
2. See Enclosure 'B'.

CONCLUSIONS
3. It is concluded that:

a. Complete replacement of the CCM, including those machines held by the North Atlantic Treaty Organization (NATO) forces, is necessary and should be accomplished before 1 January 1955.

b. Replacement by the U.K. and in NATO cannot be done without the provision of equipment by the U.S. It will be advantageous to the U.S. to promote adoption for U.K./U.S. and NATO communications of a crypto-principle used in Joint and inter-Service U.S. communications. This principle will be either the POLLUX principle or the BRUTUS principle. U.S. embodiments of both principles should be provided to the U.K. for service testing.

c. To insure availability of equipments as soon as possible, development of all necessary equipments, adaptors, and rotors for both POLLUX and BRUTUS cryptosystems should be expedited to the fullest extent. Service testing should include all equipment that might be required.

d. An accurate estimate of quantity of new equipments required, cost to the U.S., and a new target date for CCM replacement cannot be made until additional information is supplied by the U.K. Chiefs of Staff, and until it has been finally determined whether the replacement will be the POLLUX or BRUTUS cryptosystem.

e. The U.S. national security will not be endangered by the release of either the BRUTUS or POLLUX cryptosystem in either the AFSAM 7 or the AFSAM 47 [cipher machines].

f. The CSP 2900 [cipher machine] should continue to be reserved for exclusive U.S. use.

RECOMMENDATIONS
4. It is recommended that:
   a. The above conclusions be approved.
   b. The memorandum in enclosure 'A' be forwarded to the Representatives of the British Chiefs of Staff [British Joint Staff Mission Washington].

ENCLOSURE 'B'
FACTS BEARING ON THE PROBLEM AND DISCUSSION
1. Discussion by U.K. and U.S. cryptanalysts relative to the security of the Combined Cipher Machine (CCM) have been carried on since the CCM was first conceived early in World War II. The first official action on replacement of the CCM was taken by the U.K. Chiefs of Staff in a memorandum to the U.S. Chiefs of Staff in July 1949 (Appendix to Enclosure 'B' to J.C.S. 2074). Subsequent discussions resulted in the adoption of the 7-rotor BCM principle (assigned the designator BRUTUS and utilizing 26-point rotors), and an agreement that 1 January 1955 would be the target date for having it available as a replacement for the present CCM.

2. The BRUTUS principle was originally visualized as being embodied in adaptors which could be used with existing U.K. (TYPEX) and U.S. (CSP 2900) machines. In addition both the U.K. and the U.S. intended to use the BRUTUS crypto-principle in some of their new equipments. On the U.S. side this had been done in the case of the AFSAM 47 by incorporating the BRUTUS principle into the design of these machines. In the case of the AFSAM 7, an adaptor to convert the machine to BRUTUS is under development.

3. The original agreement to adopt the BRUTUS principle did not include its use in NATO as it was intended to continue the CCM for that purpose. The accumulation of previously known weaknesses and an additional insecurity recently discovered (Enclosure to J.C.S. 2074/10) point up the urgency of replacement of the CCM in Combined communications before the agreed target date of 1 January 1955 and require the extension of the replacement to NATO.

4. As an immediate alleviation of the insecurity in the CCM a procedural change was made which overcame the more recently discovered weakness. This procedure is unwieldy and time consuming and

does not correct many of the other insecurities present in the machine. As a next step in improving Combined and NATO communications the CCM is to be modified by a change in rotor-stepping action to a principle known as HERMES. A further development, the redesign of the rotors to permit the use of interchangeable and removable stepping rings, thus providing considerably more variability in the action of the machine, is being expedited by both the U.K. and U.S. to the fullest extent possible, and introduction of the new rotors is scheduled for 1 September 1953. Successful completion of this development should provide adequate security to Combined and NATO communications until the CCM can be completely replaced.

5. The U.K. Chiefs of Staff propose (Enclosure to J.C.S. 2074/11) that the ultimate replacement of the CCM be accomplished by the provision, by the United States of the cipher machines AFSAM 7 or AFSAM 47 to British Commonwealth and NATO nations on a free loan basis. They state that the BRUTUS adaptor for the TYPEX machine will not be ready before 1 January 1955, and that no suitable, new U.K. machine is sufficiently advanced in development to permit production within the next four years. The U.K. Chiefs of Staff further point out that the adaptor they have under development will be suitable for use only with the TYPEX. In this regard is also true that the U.S. BRUTUS adaptor for the CSP 2900 is unsuitable for use with other equipments, nor is there an adaptor which will change the present CCMs (SIGROD and CSP 1700 [cipher machines]) provided by the U.S. for NATO use to BRUTUS operation. Furthermore, these equipments do not now exist in sufficient quantities to satisfy the eventual Combined and NATO requirement; hence, some additional new and compatible equipments would be required if they were adopted for further use ...

US JCS decision on J.C.S. 2074/14, A Report by the Chairman, US Armed Forces Security Agency Council, on 'Security of the Combined Cipher Machine', 19 May 1952, Note by the Secretaries, Papers of the Joint Chiefs of Staff, 1951–3 CCS 311 (1-10-42) Sec.14, RG 218, USNA.

2.11 BRUSA and relay circuits between GCHQ and NSA, 1954

By the mid-1950s a vast network of comint communication relay centres was under construction, including one in Britain, superintended by the US Air Force Security Service. The burden of providing the increasingly expensive technical infrastructure fell primarily on the United States. This included the increased provision of land and sea cables, rather than radio communications, to provide better security against jamming and interception. However, this raised some problems in terms of past agreements between the US and the UK. The two documents below are an interesting example of GCHQ–NSA relations being governed, not just by the UKUSA agreement of 1948, but also by the pre-existing wartime BRUSA agreement of 1943.

1. In reference (a), certain requirements were expressed in relation to the plans of the American Cable and Radio Corporation to install a cable across the North Atlantic. The reference also indicates that operation of that cable is close to realization. Your statement of requirements in relation to this cable has been noted and will be considered in the military planning for the use of this cable ...

2. With regard to the need of the National Security Agency (NSA) for cable channels to replace some Service facilities now in use, continuing efforts are being made to improve the communications provided [to] your Agency. It is towards this end that efforts are being made to modify the arrangements resulting from the BRUSA Agreement [of 1943] so that the United States would have control of both terminals of the GCHQ–NSA communications ... Success in this goal coupled with other communications plans will permit a degree of flexibility necessary to provide adequate service.

3. The [US] Joint Communications-Electronics Committee (JCEC) and my office are aware of the vulnerability of radio communications to hostile jamming between North America and the orient. Because of this factor, increased emphasis is being placed on providing additional facilities to minimize this threat. Whereas the establishment of a trans-Pacific communications cable has not been disregarded in this matter, the high cost and lack of commercial interest in such an undertaking have prevented the initiation of such a project. Under these circumstances, numerous projects are being processed to provide additional radio facilities with the alternate routes potential resulting therefrom.

Memo from US Director Communications-Electronics, Major General R. V. D. Corput Jr., to Director, US National Security Agency, Lt General

Ralph Canine, 15 June 1954, DCEM 878, 'Trans-Oceanic Cables', Papers of the Joint Chiefs of Staff, 1954–6 CCS 334 NSA (7-24-48) Sec.12, RG 218, USNA.

In the reference, the views of the United Kingdom were expressed concerning a change in the agreement as to the operational responsibility for the London–Washington radio circuit. In general, the view expressed was to the effect that the United Kingdom did not agree to the U.S. Air Force operating both ends of the circuit. The reference also indicated that a meeting would be held in England in connection with a Centralised COMINT Communications Center (CCCC) some time in June of this year and that the London–Washington circuit could also be discussed at this time.

Captain W. B. Goulett (US Navy) for US Director Communications-Electronics, Major General R. V. D. Corput, to Director US National Security Agency, Lt General Ralph Canine, 1 June 1954, DCEM 865, 'Interim Outline Plan for Handling NSA and Individual Security Services Traffic', ibid.

2.12 **GCHQ and the Suez crisis, 1956**

The Suez crisis necessitated a greatly expanded British signals intelligence effort. This was provided by GCHQ in combination with its partners, the signals intelligence units of the three services. There were some notable successes which prompted the Foreign Secretary to congratulate them. The Director of GCHQ, Eric Jones, passed on these congratulations to units such as the Army's 2 Wireless Regiment and the RAF's 192 Squadron and 90 Group. There had also been shipborne signals interception by the Royal Navy.

Dear Jones,

Since the tension in the Middle East began to grow and particularly since Nasser's seizure of the Suez Canal I have observed the volume of material which has been produced by G.C.H.Q. relating to all the countries in the Middle East area. I am writing to let you know how valuable we have found this material and how much I appreciate the hard work and skill involved in its production. I would be grateful if you would convey to all those concerned my congratulations on the excellence of the results and my thanks for the great effort which they are making.

Foreign Secretary, Selwyn Lloyd, to Director of GCHQ, E. M. Jones, Top Secret, 20 September 1956, AIR 20/10621, PRO. (I am indebted to W. Scott Lucas for drawing this document to my attention.)

2.13 GCHQ and scientific resources, 1960

This memorandum by GCHQ, written in 1960, describes its own activities and the associated problems, stressing the steadily growing need for scientific and engineering resources in a field at the cutting edge of technology. It emphasised that this field now involved 'many problems on the edge of what appears to be possible'. The recipient, the Radar and Signals Advisory Board, was part of the Advisory Council on Scientific Research and Technical Development, working under the Ministry of Aviation.

2. The field of activity is extremely ramified [rarefied]. The technical content of the task is displayed by mentioning the main permanent activities of the organisation. Signals have to be heard, intercepted and recorded. There is a large and complex problem of data-processing before the recorded data can be analysed. Analysis is of several sorts – of the wave-form, of the information coding, the circumstances and the message content of the signals. It has to be seen whether Communications networks can be reconstructed by fitting together many scraps of information; whether Signals plans can be deduced, whether Ciphers can be recognised, isolated and broken. Non-Communications signals – radars, navigational aids, data transmissions and so on – present a range of problems very different from traditional communications. From all of these processes, directly and indirectly, arises a mass of information which has to be synthesized together with 'collateral' information in order to produce semi-finished intelligence. At all stages of this process there has to be a positive print taken from the negative and use made of the experience, critically and constructively, in order to enhance the security of British communications ...

4. The final point in this brief summary, which will particularly concern the Board, is that the whole activity has a large and steadily growing need of scientific and engineering effort if it is to continue. This is true in a number of fields – interception, data-processing, computing, instrumentation, security equipment. It applies to operational research, to applied physical research, to systems engineering, to equipment development, and to the fusion of human and automatic resources for the best development of complex resources in operation.

Memorandum to the Radar and Signals Advisory Board (A.C. 14896/ RSB.480), 'Government Communications Headquarters', from GCHQ, (GCHQ Ref. M/8087/100/1), 11 February 1960, WO 195/14887, PRO. (I am indebted to Rob Evans for drawing this document to my attention.)

2.14 Defection of NSA personnel, 1960

In 1960 two officials from the American equivalent of GCHQ, the NSA, defected to the Soviets. The United States informed its British signals intelligence partners and the usual 'damage assessments' were set in train. The advice offered to the Minister of Defence, reproduced here, is interesting. It suggests that GCHQ was making considerable headway against some Eastern Bloc communications by 1960 and that the West was increasingly dependent on this for its information. Because signals intelligence material was kept separate from other types of documents in the post-war period, and not usually included in policy files, examples of such material, other than VENONA, are not available. Accordingly, the exact nature of what the West was reading by 1960 remains unclear to historians at present.

MINISTER
Intelligence up to 26 August
Defection of U.S. personnel from N.S.A. (U.S. G.C.H.Q.)
The preliminary U.S. view is that if the individuals have really defected (which is not yet confirmed) we must expect severe, widespread and highly effective communications security countermeasures to be taken by Russia, with the result that we may be denied much of the intelligence which we are now producing. We can only

wait and see what happens, but sometimes things do not turn out as badly as feared.

Head of Joint Intelligence Bureau, General Kenneth Strong, to Minister of Defence, Harold Watkinson, 29 August 1960, Top Secret, DEFE 13/9 342, PRO.

PART II

SCIENTIFIC AND ATOMIC
INTELLIGENCE

By 1945 it was clear that the impact of science upon weapons and methods of war had been remarkable. British successes in this area owed not a little to the rapid development of scientific intelligence, especially within the Air Ministry, under Professor R. V. Jones. Entirely new fields, such as 'elint' (discussed in Chapter 2 above), had also been developed. But despite these successes the organisation of British post-war scientific intelligence was highly problematic and bedevilled by service politics. During 1945–46 this field was re-organised by a team headed by the naval scientist, P. M. S. Blackett. A committee system, modelled on the JIC, called the Joint Scientific and Technical Intelligence Committees (JS/TIC), presiding over separate service sections, was adopted. An alternative centralised model with a single Director of Scientific Intelligence was rejected.

But by 1949 Blackett's JS/TIC system had been abandoned as hopelessly cumbersome, and a single director appointed. Interminable arguments continued to rage about the extent to which scientific intelligence should be functionally re-organised, with inter-service sections looking at subjects of common interest such as radar, missiles etc. However, the three services wanted service sections, with specialists working much more closely with the operational and planning elements of each service ministry. In short, the natural growth of modern scientific intelligence was impeded by the same forces which kept the service ministries relatively strong and the MoD relatively weak, until the major re-organisation of defence in 1964.

As with so many aspects of intelligence during the Cold War, Germany was the front line for scientific collection. The major operational agency obtaining scientific and technical intelligence in Germany was the inter-service Scientific and Technical Intelligence Bureau (STIB), with over 500 staff. Its principal source of information was not Soviets, but Germans who had worked inside the Soviet Union on military projects immediately after the war.

The other source was Soviet defections, which are considered in this section because of their overwhelming importance for scientific matters. Good treatment of defectors was paramount if others were to be encouraged. A Soviet aeronautic expert, who defected, later became a lecturer at Cranfield and eventually secured a chair in aeronautics. Voluntary defection is often thought to be an entirely Eastern Bloc phenomena. In fact, defection by serving Western military personnel to the Soviets was not uncommon. In the 1950s alone, four RAF personnel defected. Flying Officer Anthony Maynard Wraight, who defected in December 1956, subsequently surfaced in Berlin, broadcasting to the West for the Soviets.

British scientific intelligence was also plagued by the artificial separation of atomic intelligence from other forms of scientific intelligence. This organisational model was adopted because it mirrored the American system, and was thought to facilitate co-operation. But the United States changed its own organisational pattern soon after 1945 and passed the McMahon Act in 1946, which outlawed the sharing of any atomic information, and thus the United States shared only limited atomic intelligence before 1957. In 1954, soon after the detonation of the first Soviet hydrogen bomb, British atomic intelligence was re-organised as a result of the Davies Report. Thereafter, it became a MoD responsibility directed by the high-level Atomic Energy Intelligence Committee, chaired by Sir Frederick Brundrett, the Chief Scientific Advisor. The day-to-day activities on atomic intelligence were placed under a major new division of the Joint Intelligence Bureau (JIB), which in turn would eventually become the Defence Intelligence Staff (DIS) in 1964. In the same year Britain became an operational part of the Ballistic Missile Early Warning System, a chain of radars that gave limited warning of missile attack, with the construction of a station on Fylingdales Moor.

Soviet strategic weapons developments constituted an almost impossible target for British and American intelligence, which both misplaced the date of the first Soviet atomic bomb by at least three years. The limits on co-operation hampered their efforts, but their main obstacle was the inaccessibility of high-security programmes located in Siberia. Britain knew even less about Soviet biological and chemical warfare programmes at this time. The only effective solution to this problem was the recruitment of one of the few Soviets who had knowledge in this area. Remarkably, one such individual, Colonel Oleg Penkovsky, volunteered his services in the late 1950s and became one of the most valuable spies recruited by the West. His information on Soviet intentions and upon the Soviet intercontinental ballistic missile programme proved useful during the confrontations over Berlin in 1961 and Cuba in 1962. Indeed, his information was so remarkable that his first overtures, made to the CIA, were regarded as implausible.

3

Scientific and technical intelligence

3.1 The JIC and German scientists, 1946

By 1945 it was abundantly clear that scientific developments in methods and weapons of war were of paramount importance. In several respects, Germany became the front line in the scientific battle between East and West. Firstly, British intelligence sought to identify key German scientists, in a wide variety of fields from rocket development to cryptography, in order to exploit their knowledge. Secondly, and somewhat later, they identified a wider category of scientists in an attempt to deny their knowledge to the Soviets. Thirdly, those Germans who *were* recruited into Soviet programmes subsequently proved to be an excellent source of information to the West on their return to Germany. The JIC paper below documents the shift in priority, from exploitation to denial.

MIGRATION OF GERMAN SCIENTISTS AND TECHNICIANS TO RUSSIA AND THE RUSSIAN ZONE OF GERMANY
3. We have examined in detail material supplied to us by Headquarters, Intelligence Division, Control Commission in Germany on the question of the migration of German Scientists and Technicians to Russia and the Russian Zone of Germany, and have come to the following conclusions:-

(a) There is evidence that the Russians have recruited German scientists and technicians in considerable numbers from all sectors of Berlin. Some of those are people whom we have interrogated or employed and whom we do not require further.

(b) There is no evidence of migration of significant numbers of scientists and technicians from the Western Zone to Russia or the Russian Zone.

(c) There is evidence that the Russians are attempting to recruit scientists and technicians from the Western Zone, and it is probable that they have an extensive organisation for recruitment.

(d) It is possible that during the coming winter the Russian attempts at recruitment may meet with more success than appears, on the evidence, to have been the case hitherto.

4. There are two categories of German Scientists and Technicians:-

(a) Those required specifically by us.

(b) The pool of Scientists and Technicians in Germany who, while not required by us, would nevertheless be a potential source of strength to the Russians.

Hitherto, we have concerned ourselves principally with those in (a). We consider, however, that every effort should be made to prevent the pool of scientists from becoming available to the Russians ...

... the present denazification policy as laid down by the Potsdam Agreement is being adhered to by us, thus debarring us from making use of scientists with nazi background. On the other hand, the Russians are ignoring this and offering employment to persons irrespective of their political history.

6. This movement, if unchecked, will increase significantly Russian war potential. We consider the most satisfactory ways in which it may be held in check are by:-

(a) Fostering research and technical development of a non-warlike character in the British Zone.

(b) The employment of German scientists within the Commonwealth, and in America and the American Zone.

It is relevant here to state that we have been unofficially informed that the United States authorities have just decided to remove to the U.S.A. about 1,000 German experts and families expressly to deny them to a potentially hostile power ...

JIC (46) 79 (0) (Final), 'Russian Enticement of German Scientists and Technicians', 21 August 1946, L/WS/1/992, IOLR.

3.2 TCS – the SIS scientific intelligence section, 1949

The centralisation of scientific and technical intelligence at Bryanston Square involved not only representatives from the three services, but also the Technical Co-ordinating Section

(TCS) of SIS responsible for the clandestine collection of scientific intelligence. The memorandum below is an interesting
example of SIS as 'consumers' of finished intelligence, and of
the dependence of SIS upon 'consumers' to help co-ordinate
their efforts with other 'agencies', such as GCHQ.

I. GENERAL.
The function of T.C.S. is the procurement of secret information which
is required by our Customers and which cannot be obtained by any
other means.

II. COLLATIONS AND BRIEFS.
1. It follows from paragraph I above that T.C.S. must be kept informed, not only in general, but in the maximum possible detail, of
Customers' requirements; they must also be kept informed from time
to time of the extent to which these requirements are being met or are
likely to be met by non-T.C.S. means. Account must be taken of the
fact that T.C.S. has no access to collated intelligence, except in so far
as it is supplied to us by our Customers, nor does T.C.S. undertake
any work of collation. Furthermore, T.C.S. does not, in general, have
access to any raw intelligence other than that produced by their own
sources.
    2. T.C.S. cannot set about its job efficiently unless, in regard to any
particular subject in any particular region, it has a reasonably clear
overall picture of what is at present known; for this picture we are
entirely dependent on our Customers, who not only do the work of
collation, but also have access to intelligence coming from Agencies
other than T.C.S. and to which T.C.S. has not direct access ...

Head of TCS, Alan Lang-Brown, to Chairman of JS/TIC, 6 September
1949, Top Secret and Personal, enclosing 'TCS/441', DEFE 40/26, PRO.

3.3 The JS/TIC, 1949

The organisation of scientific and technical intelligence
reflected the outcome of the P. M. S. Blackett Report in 1945,
and was controversial. One of the principal architects of
wartime scientific intelligence, R. V. Jones, was highly critical
of the Blackett system, which meant rule by a large

subcommittee of the JIC. In 1948 the rotation of its chairman had been suspended and a permanent chairman appointed to try and lend continuity to scientific and technical intelligence. In 1949 the decision was taken to appoint a single authoritative figure, Dr Blount, to the newly created post of Director of Scientific Intelligence. However, organisational problems and disputes continued to bedevil this complex area into the 1960s.

BACKGROUND NOTES ON JS/TIC

1. General. The Joint Scientific and Joint Technical Committees act as the Scientific and Technical advisers, respectively, of the Joint Intelligence Committee (J.I.C.) who serve the Chiefs of Staff and co-ordinate and control all aspects of Intelligence.

2. Organisation.

(a) The Joint Scientific Intelligence Committee (J.S.I.C.) is composed basically of the heads of the Scientific Intelligence Sections of the three Service Ministries, and the Scientific representative of the Secret Service ...

(b) The Joint Technical Intelligence Committee (J.T.I.C.) consists basically of the heads of the Technical Intelligence Sections of the three Service ministries and representatives of the Joint Intelligence Bureau and the Ministry of Supply ...

(d) Hitherto, and as a logical outcome of the constant relationship between Scientific and Technical Development, J.S.I.C. and J.T.I.C. have tended to work as one combined committee (J.S./T.I.C.), the Chairmanship being held in rotation by each Service for three months at a time.

8. Scientific Order of Battle Section. It became apparent to J.S./T.I.C. at a very early stage that Scientific Intelligence must be based on a comprehensive background knowledge of the leading personalities, institutions etc. in foreign scientific (and to a lesser extent technical) circles. J.S./T.I.C. have now therefore organised a small 'Scientific Order of Battle Section' (O.B.S.) ... directly controlled by Chairman J.S./T.I.C.

Memorandum by Chairman of JS/TIC to Director of Scientific Intelligence, Dr Blount, 6 September 1949, Top Secret, DEFE 40/26, PRO.

3.4 Scientific/technical intelligence at Bryanston Square, 1949

'Centralisation' was a matter of constant and often acrimonious debate. On the one hand, each service was anxious that
its own intelligence experts in this vital field should be close
at hand to inform all aspects of policy. On the other hand,
there was pressure to centralise and create an environment in
which experts from all three services could co-operate to
interpret intelligence on common problems, such as Soviet
guided weapons. The latter argument gradually gained superiority and the JS/TIC set-up at Bryanston Square to some
degree pre-figured the more integrated MoD structure that
would emerge in 1964–65. The structure in 1949 was set out
for the newly appointed Director of Scientific Intelligence in
this memo.

1. Each of the three Services has, under its Intelligence Director, a
Scientific Int. Section and a Technical Int. Section.

The Scientific Int. Sections of the three Services are located in the
J.I.B. buildings in Bryanston Square.

The Technical Int. Sections of the three Services are, in general,
located with their Ministries but those sub-sections which deal with
technical subjects which are closely associated with scientific development, are located at Bryanston Square.

(e.g. The Army Scientific Intelligence Section is M.I.16; the Techni-
cal Section is M.I.10. The former is located in toto in Bryanston Sq.
The latter has three sub-sections and has one of these (dealing with
Guided Weapons and Chemical Warfare) located alongside M.I.16.
The other two sub-sections remain in the main War Office buildings)
...

'Preliminary Notes for Dr Blount', by Colonel J. S. Neville, Chairman of
JS/TIC, 29 July 1949, Top Secret, DEFE 40/26, PRO.

3.5 The creation of the DSI organisation, 1949–50

Despite the physical centralisation of the scientific intelligence effort of the three services at Bryanston Square, problems persisted. There was duplication between service
sections and the sprawling JS/TIC resulted in weak direction.

By late 1949 the need for a properly integrated inter-service effort, with a permanent Director, was increasingly clear. The example of Kenneth's Strong's JIB, formed in 1946, a Whitehall inter-service intelligence organisation far ahead of its time, was influential. Service scientific intelligence sections were now formally abolished. But in practice the three new functional sections created in their place each had a predominant service interest. These were: DSI.1 looking at electronics, radar, aerodynamics and physics, headed by the RAF; DSI.2 looking at biological and chemical issues, headed by the Army; and DSI.3 looking at nuclear physics, naval issues and scientific order of battle, headed by the Navy. The Intelligence Unit of the Department of Atomic Energy was not drawn into the new DSI organisation in order to avoid disturbing 'the special relationship which exists between this Unit and its American counterpart'.

1. One of the main weaknesses in the present organisation of scientific intelligence, has lain, I believe, in the fact that the Joint Committees consisting of eleven members and representatives have endeavoured to direct an organisation of some 20 scientists and 40 technicians which included themselves ... it has not been able and is indeed unsuited because of its Service affiliations, to direct the long term study into pure scientific research, which ultimately is our key to the completely new weapons of warfare ...

2. Under the existing organisation there have been failures on many occasions for scientific intelligence to speak as one voice and this in itself has tended to weaken the authority of its pronouncements ...

4. Under the existing system each Service Scientific Section endeavours to cover as far as possible every field of scientific intelligence ... This results in a considerable duplication of work and the services of the scientific officers being used in the most uneconomical manner ...

6. Briefly it is suggested that the present JS/TIC organisation should be abolished and superseded by a Directorate of Scientific Intelligence organised on a functional basis, similar to the Joint Intelligence Bureau ...

Memorandum by Chairman of JS/TIC, Colonel J. D. Neville, 'Organisation of Scientific Intelligence: Deficiencies of the Present Organisation', (Draft) September/October 1949, DEFE 40/26, PRO.

3.6 **The position of DSI, 1954**

Bureaucratic infighting continued to characterise scientific
intelligence during the early 1950s. In 1954 the Chiefs of
Staff decided on a major review of this area and commis-
sioned the Brundrett Report into the Directorate of Scientific
Intelligence, and also the Davies Report into atomic intelligence. The recommendations of Sir Frederick Brundrett
accorded with the general drift towards a centralised MoD
that would emerge finally in 1964, but were implemented
only gradually because of their political sensitivity. Nevertheless, by the late 1950s JIB had absorbed atomic and scientific
intelligence. In 1964 JIB formed the core of the new Defence
Intelligence Staff in the centralised MoD.

... I have discussed the matter with the Chairman, J.I.C., 'C', and the
three Service Directors of Intelligence, the Director, J.I.B., and some
of the J.I.C. secretariat in addition to the late D.S.I.

2. It is extremely difficult to get any clear picture of the situation
because of conflicting views as to what happens at present. The one
thing on which everybody agrees is that the present arrangement is
not working as well as it should.

3. ... Intelligence nowadays is essentially a matter of team work
and any organisation which gives rise to jealousies between different
sections must, I think, be wrong ...

5. ... I believe that the subdivision of what may be called the service side of intelligence into scientific, technical and economic, or
whatever is the appropriate word to apply to the functions of the
J.I.B., is wrong and inevitably breeds trouble. I feel strongly that the
right solution is to bring all these activities into a single organisation,
which should be central in the Ministry of Defence, as a servicing
organisation for the J.I.C. I believe such an organisation would provide for the greatest economy of personnel and simplify the setting up
of suitable teams of the right mixture to deal with any particular
problem at any particular time. The organisation would take over the
functions of the present J.I.B. and the Department of Scientific Intelligence and absorb the technical sections of the Service Intelligence
Departments. It should be under the control of a very carefully selected senior service officer ...

6. ... the Service Directors of Intelligence would oppose the removal from their Departments of the technical branches at this

present time. For this reason, although I believe this is the final solution, it might well be desirable to let the matter grow rather than force it immediately ...

7. I do not, however, feel that this step in itself would be sufficient to ensure that adequate attention was given to purely scientific aspects at a sufficiently high level. For this purpose I would recommend that the post of D.S.I. [Director of Scientific Intelligence] itself should be removed from the joint organisation and replaced by the appointment in the Ministry of Defence of an independent senior scientist of the Chief Scientific Officer level to act as Scientific Adviser on Intelligence ...

Memorandum by Chief Scientific Adviser, Sir Frederick Brundrett, 'The Position of D.S.I.' (known as the Brundrett Report) annexed to COS (54) 70, 'Directorate of Scientific Intelligence', 2 March 1954, DEFE 32/4, PRO.

3.7 Missile intelligence and the Templer Report, 1961

In 1960 an enquiry by General Templer (another advocate of centralisation) into service intelligence recommended that all aspects of guided missile intelligence, including the Soviet missile 'order of battle', should be transferred from the service intelligence departments to committees under the JIB. The debate over this was heated and involved accusations that RAF intelligence in this area was subjective or 'slanted'. The Air Ministry responded by raising 'an Issue of Principle' – that of ministerial responsibility – and resistance on this basis continued into 1961. The point raised in the document below about the uselessness of the comparable American committee-based National Intelligence Estimates for policy purposes was a particularly strong one. The recognition by ACAS(I) that this was an issue of precedent was also perceptive. Yet the drift towards centralisation was irresistible, and would be completed with the creation of a centralised MoD in 1964.

1. The Chief of the Air Staff [CAS] has certain responsibilities laid upon him:-
    (a) Meeting the strategic air threat, from bombers and missiles, to this country.

(b) Maintaining the validity of the British nuclear deterrent.

(c) Preparations to penetrate the Russian defences and retaliate should this country be attacked.

2. Policy actions to meet these responsibilities must be based on a detailed analysis of Soviet offensive and defensive capabilities.

Because of the importance of this to all judgements and advice of the Air Staff the C.A.S. must have an Intelligence Staff in which he has full confidence. He must be able to appoint to this staff personnel of the calibre and qualifications which he may consider necessary at any time.

It would be quite unacceptable to any C.A.S. to base his policy and advice on a Committee estimate on which indeed his own staff may have to register a minority opinion ...

I am certain no C.A.S. would willingly launch his bomber forces against Russia unless the defences which they had to penetrate had been analysed and estimated with all the technical and professional skill available to the Royal Air Force. A 'committee' estimate with which the Air Force did not agree would never be acceptable as a basis for either preparation or operations ...

3. What is proposed by Field Marshal Templer is a 'Committee' system of threat assessment similar to the American system under which the Central Intelligence Agency hears the views of all departments and then amalgamates this into a National Intelligence Estimate.

The divergencies of views are such that this Committee estimate is of little or no use for policy decisions and recourse has to be made to the American method of Congressional Committees and lobbying ...

I consider that we should adhere firmly to the basic British system of departmental responsibility for missiles as we have done successfully in the past for other weapons.

... The acceptance of the Templer proposals on the other hand will perpetuate the difficulties which have arisen in the missile field and, by introducing the principle of 'centralisation' in Intelligence, will create a most undesirable precedent and departure from normal working principles.

Memorandum by ACAS(I), Air Vice Marshal Sydney Bufton, to Chief of the Air Staff, 'Templer Report: The issue of "principle"', Secret, 20 March 1961, AIR 8/1953, PRO.

4

Defectors from the East

4.1 TCS and the targeting of defectors, 1949

Defectors were one of the West's most promising sources of intelligence generally and were particularly important in the areas of science and technology. TCS, the section of SIS responsible for the clandestine collection of scientific intelligence, was anxious that its limited resources for this work should be properly targeted. Like many sections of SIS, it felt that consumers made unrealistic demands and were not always helpful in defining areas of priority, or identifying promising avenues to be pursued.

III. DEFECTORS.

1. We all agree that the best hope of progress in a number of fields lies in obtaining a flow of the right kind of defector: it is probably the case that, to date, the output of the relatively small number of defectors we have had compares very favourably with the value of intelligence from all other sources.

2. Defectors fall into two fairly clearly defined categories: -

(a) Those who, for personal reasons, backed perhaps by general propaganda from the West, make their own decisions to defect, and,

(b) targets deliberately selected by us in the light of their estimated intelligence value and subsequently enticed into defection.

3. To date, defectors have been confined to bodies falling more or less clearly into category (a) ...

... the principal difficulty we are up against, at present, is to recognise a target who will be of value should he defect and in this we require the help of Bryanston Square ...

9. We do not, of course, lose sight of the fact that in a defection there are always two factors, i.e. priority and opportunity, but the

first is under our control whereas the second is not. If, therefore, we are to work efficiently, we must know where we stand on the question of priorities. In the extreme case, it is now agreed that when the priority of an individual is sufficient, steps will be taken wherever possible, to create opportunity; so that on all counts priority is the first consideration.

Head of TCS, Alan Lang-Brown, to Chairman of JS/TIC, 6 September 1949, Top Secret and Personal, enclosing 'TCS/441', DEFE 40/26, PRO.

4.2 The handling of Soviet defectors and refugees, 1950

Defectors and refugees from the Eastern Bloc brought issues of intelligence-gathering and security close together. Defectors represented one of the best sources of intelligence on Soviet-controlled areas, but also posed an alarming security problem: they were in danger of being recovered forcibly by the Soviets or else might themselves have been planted by Soviet intelligence. The main defector battleground was Germany and Austria. Despite the importance of defectors, it had taken until the end of 1949 for the JIC to set out a general policy on this matter (JIC (49) 107 (Final)) and this was still being refined in 1950, as we see below. The most difficult issue was the cost of defectors' disposal (or re-settlement) after interrogation, which no service wished to bear. Parallel American efforts to achieve a centralised programme were dogged by the slow hand-over of defector activities from American service intelligence to an expanding CIA.

Soviet and Satellite Defectors and Refugees.
With reference to Minute 3 of JIC (50) 47th Meeting, I think that it would be of value to the Working Party on the disposal of defectors and refugees if the situation in Austria were placed before it ... the Colonel GS(I) [Austria] adds: -
'Our view is that in no circumstances should a Russian deserter be sent to a DP [displaced persons] Camp. DP camps are not secure and he would be an obvious target. He might be kidnapped, or even conceivably bamboozled by the visiting Russian Repatriation Commission to return to the Soviet held territory. That would be deplorable for two reasons:

(a) His lengthy interrogation and the circumstances of his deten-
tion (e.g. presence of other detainees) would provide the Russians
with intelligence.

(b) He would be 'persuaded' to make wild allegations about his
treatment and would be good propaganda to discourage other
would-be deserters to ourselves and to the Americans.

We should therefore welcome a general ruling that money for disposal would normally be authorised from the Secret Vote. While I
have referred here only to Russian deserters, it is possible that we
might also consider it most inadvisable to send certain Satellite deserters to DP Camps. Expenses involved in maintaining a normal
number of deserters can be borne by our local intelligence funds.
What cannot be met is expenditure of say £100 to £200 for disposal
of an individual.'

Arising from this comment, I feel that it might assist the Intelligence authorities in Germany or Austria, pending the Result of the
Working Party's deliberations, if it were agreed that money would be
found from the Secret Vote in any cases where the payment of fares,
e.g. to Australia, would solve a disposal problem, regardless of the
intelligence value of the individual. The expenditure would not be
great compared with the propaganda value of disposing of possibly
only a few by this means ...

Director of Military Intelligence, Major General Arthur Shortt, to Secretary JIC, 5 June 1950, Top Secret, WO 208/5015, PRO.

4.3 Operation 'Dragon Return', 1950

The most valuable form of defector from the East in the early
years of the Cold War was the German scientist formerly
employed inside the Soviet Union who had been allowed to
return to the Russian zone of Germany. The key to recruiting
these individuals was the offer of scientific employment away
from the drab conditions of Germany. This involved many
Whitehall departments, such as the Ministry of Labour,
which sought to find destinations for them. The overall programme was controlled by the Director of the Scientific and
Technical Intelligence Bureau, a key section of the ID CCG,
which employed many German, as well as British, personnel.
Most of these operations were straightforward defections.

More rarely, as this document reveals, individuals were persuaded to stay 'in place' for some time, on the basis of offers
of future scientific work in the West. This work was painstaking and dangerous.

1. 'DRAGON RETURN' as an Operation has been providing worthwhile results for some time. This brief deals with the phase of the
Operation resulting in September of a large group of scientists and
technicians who had been working in three main areas –
   (i) CHIMKI – Guided Missile research and development
   (ii) KUIBYCHEV – Aircraft research and development
   (iii) PODBERESJE – Aircraft research and development
Contact has been made under carefully-controlled conditions with
a cross-section of those Germans who have returned. This work is
complicated by the fact that we dare not show our hand nor let the
Russians realise just how valuable this security leak of theirs is to us.

2. On Guided Missile research and development a great deal of
valuable information has been obtained on the Russian exploitation
of German developments and their ability to produce original work
of their own. All this information is now being considered in relations
to the priority that we know STALIN put on the programme and preliminary assessments have been made by the Inter-Services Guided
Missile Intelligence Working Party in London [a working party of JS/
TIC]. The Anglo-American Working Party on Guided Missiles is also
being convened to see what assessments can now be made of Russian
potential in this field. On our preliminary information, the conclusions should be encouraging to us.

3. A good deal of information has also been obtained on the development of German work on advanced aircraft, particularly propul-
sion units ...

4. An operation, the ground work for which had been in process
for several years, took place over the weekend 2/3 December, 1950,
with magnificent co-operation from BAFO [British Air Forces of
Occupation], from which it was hoped to learn certain key information. These returned Germans are not allowed to move out of the
Russian Zone where they have their jobs and accommodation found
for them. In this case, STIB had developed contact with the circle of
friends of one of the returnees over a period and were able to arrange
for him to be contacted and introduced to a friend from his home city.
This friend was an officer of STIB. The possibilities of the returnee

obtaining an academic post in Western Germany were discussed and an arrangement was made for him, without compromising himself, to visit the West and discuss his academic future with a colleague of his former University professor. This colleague was also an officer of STIB.

5. Having arranged legitimate business in the Russian Sector of BERLIN over the weekend, contact was made with the first STIB officer and under an arrangement made for such contingencies, BAFO supplied a special aircraft to BERLIN at once. The returnee then spent the night in the British Zone in company with a former colleague and the second STIB officer, returning to BERLIN by an R.A.F. aircraft the following day so that he was able to resume his job without disclosing his connection with British intelligence. He is likely to be of further service to us in the future ...

Director, STIB, to Chief, ID CCG, 'Operation "Dragon Return" – Brief for Chief', STIB/7003/8033, 4 December 1950, Top Secret, DEFE 41/91, PRO.

5

Atomic intelligence

5.1 The JIC forecasts Soviet atomic developments, 1948

This single most important question to which British policy-makers desired an answer after 1945 was the speed of progress of the Soviet atomic weapons programme. On this issue the British and the Americans were spectacularly wrong. In 1948 the British JIC estimated that the most likely date for the first Soviet test would be January 1954. On this basis the British Chiefs of Staff concluded that the Soviets would be unlikely to contemplate risking war before the late 1950s, and attuned British armament programmes accordingly, placing a high proportion of their effort in the late 1940s into research and development, rather than short-term re-armament. The Soviet detonation of an atomic weapon in late August 1949 was a profound shock to them. The particular JIC paper cited below is of some importance. At seventy printed pages in length, and revised on an annual basis, it constituted a major reference point for British defence planning. Unlike most JIC papers, the revised version was usually presented to the Cabinet Defence Committee each year.

Special Weapons
54. *Atomic Bombs*.-The manufacture of atomic weapons demands not only a high standard of scientific knowledge and the application on a very large scale of difficult industrial techniques, but also the use of large quantities of uranium. The most reliable present estimate that can be made of Russian progress indicates that the limiting factor is their supplies of uranium. At the present time it is considered to be most misleading to attempt to forecast how much uranium will be available to any Russian project beyond January 1952 since this depends on two unpredictable factors:-

(a) the discovery within Russian-controlled territory of new high-grade deposits, which is believed to be unlikely, and

(b) the success the Russians will have in developing a practicable process for large scale extraction of the small percentages of uranium present in oil-shales, large deposits of which are available to them.

55. Existing estimates of the date when the Russians began their programme and of their ability to overcome the technological difficulties involved suggest that they may possibly produce their first atomic bomb by January 1951, and that their stockpile of bombs in January 1953 may be of the order of 6 to 22. Any subsequent production would be at the rate of 2 to 4 per cent per year on existing knowledge of ore supplies. These, however, will almost certainly alter considerably in the later 1950s.

56. These figures, however, are the maximum possible based on the assumption that the Russian effort will progress as rapidly as the American and British projects have done. Allowances for the probable slower progress of the Russian effort will almost certainly retard the first bomb by some three years.

57. On these assumptions it is improbable that the Soviet Union will have enough atom bombs by the end of 1956 to defeat the United Kingdom by this means alone. Even though the Russians may take a different view about the number of bombs required for this purpose, the defeat of the United Kingdom would still leave them with the greater problem of defeating the United States, which such an attack on the United Kingdom would involve. It is impossible at this juncture to add to this statement or to forecast the probable development in atomic weapons beyond 1956–57.

JIC (48) 9 (0) (Final), 'Russian Interests, Intentions and Capabilities', Top Secret, 23 July 1948, L/WS/1/1173, IOLR.

5.2 Sources of atomic intelligence, 1945–49

British and American estimates of the Soviet atomic programme were inaccurate partly because they tried to surmise it from the apparent general state of Soviet science, as displayed in open conferences and publications. The explosion of the Soviet bomb at the end of August 1949 prompted some reconsideration of this indirect approach.

3. The Russian atomic weapon provides a good illustration. D.At.En. [the Intelligence Unit of the Department of Atomic Energy] has exploited semi-overt means through contacts with nuclear physicists in most European countries, and the Russian leaders in the field are pretty well known. Yet the first information from Russia on the progress of the project was the explosion of the first bomb, and we were pretty widely adrift in our forecasts of when this would take place. In this case we should have got far better information from a messenger or labourer in the right place than from any number of Professors of Physics swanning round Europe, or even in Moscow.

4. I think it is vital to take every opportunity of pressing for authority to carry out active intelligence operations against Russia. Whether or not they are in fact practicable, if authorised, is a matter for M.I.6., but we must be very careful not to give the impression that there is any adequate substitute ...

Memorandum by the Assistant Director of Naval Intelligence (Science), G. Turney, 'Scope and Sources of Scientific Intelligence', 10 October 1949, Top Secret, DEFE 40/26, PRO.

5.3 The limits of atomic intelligence, 1951

In 1951 Commander Welsh, the head of the Atomic Intelligence Unit at the Department of Atomic Energy, gave a lecture to scientific and technical intelligence staffs at the MoD. He reviewed the British position frankly. Although some achievements had been made with the UK/US programme of long-range air-sampling of debris from Soviet tests (codenamed MUSIC), the key question about the scale of Soviet bomb production could not be answered by this means. He was not optimistic about the chances of a breakthrough.

...Gentlemen, the intelligence services are at war with Russia and we are losing heavily in the field in which I am engaged.

It is true that because of the nature of radio activity we are able to detect Russian test atomic explosions, but please do not let us deceive ourselves.

The fact that the Russians have made three tests is not by any means all that we want to, and indeed must know ...

Long distance detection techniques supply History *not* News.

Nothing is as stale as yesterday's newspaper.

What the J.I.C. want and what the J.I.C. demand is preknowledge of what are the enemies' intentions for tomorrow ...

What we do *not* know is the answer to the Chief's of Staff's all-embracing question:

'When will the Russians have a stock pile of atomic bombs which in their opinion is sufficient to justify the risk of open warfare?'

To answer this question we must find out with what type or types of bombs they propose to equip their armed forces, when and with how many.

What type of fissionable material are they manufacturing? What is their present stockpile, the different types and what is the rate of production of each and all of them? ...

In a previous lecture I told you that we believe the Russians must be manufacturing two types of fissile material, but we would like to know the exact location of the plants where those materials are manufactured. The location of these plants, while being important, is of course not the crucial information we require. What we want to know is the size of the plants and the rate of production ... Any agent, even of the lowest possible grade, who has had an opportunity of seeing such a plant would be able to give us very valuable information indeed ...

Lecture by Commander A. Welsh, 'Atomic Energy Intelligence', 1952, Secret, DEFE 41/126, PRO.

5.4 The Long-Range Atomic Detection Programme, 1951

British atomic surveillance flights consisted of aircraft with filters that picked up the airborne debris from Soviet atomic tests that were then subjected to scientific analysis. The value of this programme, codenamed MUSIC, came to be doubted by the British by the end of the 1950s. Like the British atomic bomb programme itself, some British atomic intelligence activities compelled the United States to co-operate in areas where they were initially unwilling to exchange information, as we see below.

1. The [US] atomic test to be conducted at Tonopah Gunnery Range, Nevada in the near future will introduce radioactive material into the air masses which may traverse eastern Canada and continue on across the North Atlantic past the British Isles. The British are known to be conducting extensive surveillance flights with airborne filters. It is understood that the Canadians have initiated a limited surveillance operation over Canada.

2. ... there is a major practical consideration involved in the possibility of misinterpretation by either of these two countries of the source of unusual radioactivity intercepted by their airborne surveillance systems. A subsequent inadvertent announcement to the press attributing this intercept to the U.S.S.R. or revealing the character of the U.S. experiment would be extremely unfortunate.

3. The erroneous assumption of the U.S.S.R. as the source would lead the British to faulty stockpile estimates. Publication of the character of U.S. tests would seriously compromise the AEC program. Finally, erroneous publication of the fact of another Russian A-bomb test might have serious international repercussions.

US Memorandum for Secretary Marshall from USAF Chief of Staff, General N. F. Twining, 23 January 1951, Top Secret, 'Subject: Item for the Combined Policy Committee on Area 5', Director of Intelligence USAF HQ files, File A201-A291, Box 35, RG 341, USNA.

5.5 Davies Report on atomic intelligence, 1954

In March 1954 the Chiefs of Staff considered the Brundrett Report on the DSI and the Davies Report on atomic intelligence. As a result, atomic intelligence gradually came under the aegis of the JIB at its Atomic Energy Intelligence Division, while scientific intelligence in general continued on its acrimonious path towards centralisation.

The Davies Report is discussed in a minute on COS (54) 70, 'Directorate of Scientific Intelligence', 2 March 1954, DEFE 32/4, PRO. The whole of this report is currently closed to public inspection under Section 3(4) of the Public Record Office Act.

5.6 **Warning of atomic attack, 1954**

In the first half of 1953, the JIC conducted a number of detailed studies of Soviet and Satellite war potential, and of probable Soviet strategy in the event of war between 1953 and 1956. These were difficult undertakings since the two vital missing elements in such appreciations were the JIC's uncertainty about the effects of an Allied air offensive on the Soviet ability to wage war and a lack of information about what the Soviets thought the effect of an Allied air offensive might be. Nevertheless, in 1954 they concluded that for the time being there would be adequate indication of a Soviet decision to attack because this could not be done with atomic forces alone. All this would change in the late 1950s with the advent of Soviet ballistic missiles (document 5.7), resulting in a radical reduction in warning time.

I attach a draft minute to the Prime Minister, enclosing an Intelligence Estimate. As you will see there is nothing to confirm the Prime Minister's suggestion that there has been a significant movement of Soviet forces out of Western Germany.

2. You will, I think, agree with the Prime Minister that, for the next few years, in view of their inferiority in atomic weapons to the United States, the Russians will be unlikely to launch an atomic attack without simultaneously attacking on the ground with the object of advancing rapidly into Western Europe; and that therefore we are likely to get some warning of attack. The Prime Minister placed great importance on this period of warning, as it would enable us to make further efforts to deter the Russians from attacking, and at the same time to alert our own forces, in particular the strategic air forces, anti-aircraft defences, and the Home Guard ...

Chief Staff Officer MoD, N. C. D. Brownjohn, to Minister of Defence, Harold Macmillan, 'Soviet Strengths in Western Europe', NCDB/M/329, Top Secret, 10 February 1954, DEFE 13/352, PRO. (I am indebted to Len Scott and Stephen Twigge for drawing this document to my attention.)

5.7 **Warning of atomic attack, 1956**

In 1956 the JIC reviewed the possibility of global war up to 1965 and the sort of warning that might be possible in the event of an attack by the Soviet Union. They concluded that the Soviet leaders clearly did not want war and that this was unlikely to change. They also believed that Chinese leaders wished to avoid war. If the Soviets did decide to attack, conventional preparations could be detected a month in advance. However, a nuclear surprise attack was a more likely option. This, they counselled, could be conducted against the UK from 1956 and might be possible against the United States from 1959.

WARNING OF ATTACK
Preparations for War ...
9.-(a) We think it more likely that the Russians would wish to achieve surprise for their nuclear air attack. At present the Soviet Long-Range Air Force would have to carry out an extensive and lengthy programme of construction, stockpiling and redeployment before it could undertake a large-scale attack on North America. They could, however, achieve surprise against the United Kingdom and the peripheral bases now.

(b) We believe the Russians will have the capability of mounting a large-scale surprise attack on North America from 1959 onwards.

Decision to Attack
10. We could be certain that a decision to attack had been made only if we succeeded in intercepting the decision. We have virtually no chance of doing this and we must, therefore, rely on interpreting the significance of military and other moves and preparations; in the event of a surprise attack we may never obtain such information.

Warning of Attack
11. We cannot expect to give the time of attack much in advance. At best we might get warning of the assembly or take off of enemy aircraft at or from their bases: but it is possible that the detection of those aircraft on Allied radar screens would be the only warning. At present, in the case of ballistic missiles, there would be no warning ...

JIC (56) 21 (Final), Appendix B, 'Likelihood of Global War and Warning of Attack', 1 May 1956, CAB 134/1315, PRO.

5.8 US–UK co-operation on atomic intelligence, 1950s

Between 1946 and 1958 UK–US co-operation in the atomic field was hampered by the American McMahon Act which forbade American citizens to transfer atomic information to other states. By 1953 the British were convinced that they had little to learn from the Americans on bomb production, but desired information on weapons effects from the very extensive series of American tests, and also proper intelligence co-operation on the Soviet atomic programme. Letters to Churchill from the Paymaster General, Lord Cherwell, show that, from 1953, there was a concerted British effort to restore atomic intelligence co-operation. This is also an example of the traditional role of the Paymaster General as the minister for co-ordinating intelligence services. Churchill had received assurances from Eisenhower on this subject at their meeting in Bermuda in December 1953, but the promised joint conferences on atomic intelligence were cancelled by the Americans. Further efforts were interrupted by the Suez crisis but co-operation was fully restored in 1957. This was finalised by Macmillan and Eisenhower in November of that year. In 1957 Admiral Strauss, the American official responsible for this, was rewarded with an honorary degree from Oxford University. Subsequently, a key vehicle for high-level exchange was the US–UK Technical Committee of Experts.

Though we exchange intelligence reports with the US on many aspects of Russian atomic bomb production detection we have hitherto been debarred from discussing with them the interpretation of the material collected concerning the nature of Russian atomic bombs. The reason for this bar was that the Americans considered that such discussion would inevitably reveal what they fondly imagined were the secrets of the design of their own atomic weapons.

I endeavoured to convince them in Washington that we had independently discovered most of the vital secrets, just as apparently the Russians have done. It would therefore be a great pity to jeopardise the prospects we might have of discovering what the Russians were

doing for fear we should tell one another what we both already knew.
I hope, in talking to Strauss, to drive home this argument ...

Cherwell to the Prime Minister, 1 December 1953, J138/5, Cherwell
Papers, Nuffield College, Oxford.

I am much disturbed by the delay in arranging for discussions between our intelligence people and the Americans about what the Russians have got in the way of atom and hydrogen bombs. As you will
remember both at Bermuda and later on in Washington, the President
and you agreed that nothing ought to be allowed to stand in the way
of getting as soon as we could the most accurate information as possible about the Russian situation ...

Cherwell to the Prime Minister, 19 January 1955, J146/31, ibid.

You will be delighted to learn that Admiral Strauss has played up very
well about our being allowed to monitor the series of highly interesting American explosions which are to take place in the next month or
two. I must confess I never thought the authorities in Washington
would approve his having agreed to this in Bermuda. But everything
is now in train and we are sending our aircraft to take part with the
Americans in collecting debris so as to be able to extract the maximum value from the data about Russian bombs which we collected
last year.

It seems to me that co-operation in intelligence, on which I set the
greatest store, is at last making definite progress. Now they realise
how much is known by many people about these matters ...

Cherwell to the Prime Minister, n.d. [late 1955], J146/1, ibid.

5.9 The problem of Soviet nuclear strategy, 1958

The JIC produced a number of 'standard' papers on important subjects which, although revised annually, tended to reit-
erate the same basic assumptions about the nature of Soviet

thinking. Major General Kenneth Strong, creator of the JIB, who superintended the JIB's Atomic Energy Intelligence Division, was alive to the potential dangers of this.

This paper is an annual exercise of the J.I.C. Its setting is global war and the unlikelihood of this is reiterated ...

5. J.I.C.'s efforts and expenditure produce much intelligence on the U.S.S.R., but there is scarcely any evidence as to how their leaders think or would act in given circumstances. For this reason, hypotheses are made which are repeated from year to year and, like advertisements, take root. This is inevitable, but we should not forget the lack of evidence and should keep open minds. Paragraph 3, for example, says that the Russian Leaders are reasonably certain that the West will not deliberately start war on them. Although I agree with this argument, it is equally possible that, imbued as they are with Marxist doctrine, they do not reject the possibility of some desperate American reaction during the next few years to the growing military and economic strength and widening political influence of the U.S.S.R. That the capitalist world might come to think that it is being overtaken by Communism and react desperately is a danger that they may feel they cannot discount. While, therefore, the West should maintain a firm and unambiguous position, we should remember how sensitive they are in this direction.

Note for Marshal of the RAF, Sir William Dickson, by Major General Kenneth Strong, head of JIB, summarising and commenting on JIC (58) 4 (Final) 'Soviet Strategy in Global War up to the end of 1962', Top Secret, 6 February 1958, DEFE 13/342, PRO.

5.10 **US–UK atomic intelligence co-operation, 1961**

By 1957 co-operation on atomic energy intelligence was fully restored. In the early 1960s British officials in the JIB's Atomic Energy Intelligence Division saw eye to eye with their opposite numbers in the CIA. However, agreement with the US JCS on strategic missile and bomber estimates was elusive.

We have received the latest U.S. National Intelligence Estimate on the Soviet Atomic Energy programme, covering similar ground to our own paper which was given a limited circulation last summer.

Our exchanges with our opposite numbers in the U.S. are now so good that for the first time for some years British and American estimates of the amounts of Soviet produced plutonium and U-235 are as nearly identical as it would be reasonable to expect. C.I.A. estimates the cumulative production of plutonium as 8.4 tons and of U-235 as 52 tons up to mid-1960; whereas J.I.B. estimated this as 8.5 tons and 50.4 tons up to the end of 1960. For some years past the C.I.A. estimate has been considerably greater than the British one.

However, our estimates of fissile material production for future years tend to diverge again ...

Head of JIB, Major General Kenneth Strong, to Minister of Defence, Harold Watkinson, 'The Soviet Atomic Energy Programme', 25 January 1961, Top Secret – UK Eyes Only, DEFE 13/342, PRO.

PART III

SERVICE INTELLIGENCE AND 'SPY-FLIGHTS'

The service intelligence departments, which were brought together to form the Defence Intelligence Staff (DIS) after the creation of the centralised MoD in 1964, represent the most under-studied aspect of British intelligence and security activity between 1945 and 1970. Dozens of books have considered the more famous espionage cases of the period, dwelling at length on figures such as Philby, Burgess, Blunt and Maclean, sometimes in almost mindless detail. Yet remarkably little has been written about the activities of British naval or military intelligence. The British Military Mission to the Soviet Forces in Germany, which constituted a source of valuable intelligence throughout the Cold War, only began to receive concerted historical investigation in the mid-1990s. The ID CCG, one of the largest British intelligence bodies of the early Cold War period, remains almost a complete cipher.

The most important development in the field of post-war service intelligence was the creation of the JIB in 1946. This body covered economic and topographical intelligence and was the first truly inter-service post-war intelligence organisation, inheriting work from wartime bodies such as the Ministry of Economic Warfare and the Inter-Service Topographical Bureau. Although the JIB sounded singularly unexciting, it was important in two respects. Firstly, it did a great deal of target intelligence during a period when strategic airpower was paramount. Secondly, centralisation was the growing trend, and although resisted vigorously by service chiefs, the JIB gained ground steadily. This could best be seen by the changes in scientific intelligence during this period (see above) and the JIB's acquisition of the crucial area of atomic intelligence in the 1950s. It was Kenneth Strong, the head of JIB, and a great evangelist of centralisation, who became the first head of the DIS in 1964. The example of intelligence, especially in scientific fields, added weight to the case for a centralised MoD in the 1960s.

Air intelligence has received considerable attention because of its political and diplomatic importance, and this area is now well understood. Aerial reconnaissance had made dramatic progress during the Second World War and its dividends informed the final stages of the war against Germany in astonishing detail. In the immediate postwar period, the most important aerial photographic intelligence of the Soviet Union was neither British nor American but German. The Allies captured large sections of the Luftwaffe's archive of aerial photography of the Soviet Union, some of which was snatched from under the very noses of the Soviet Army. An Anglo-American programme designed to share this photography and associated target traces, waggishly termed 'Operation DICK TRACY', ensured close co-operation from the outset.

Other factors reinforced UK–US co-operation. Firstly, the US Army Air Force was preparing to become the US Air Force, and was trying to build an intelligence organisation befitting a fully independent service. Assistance from British air intelligence was invaluable in this regard. Secondly, in the late 1940s the American State Department had forbidden overflights of the Soviet Union, whereas the Foreign Office had not. Washington was excited by reports of British overflights of the Soviet Union as early as 1948, and it was in this year that the RAF–USAF target intelligence agreement was signed.

The 1950s saw important co-operation over aircraft design and operational programmes. Electronic intelligence-gathering had already revealed the limited nature of Soviet air defences, while attempts at intelligence-gathering with human agents were proving disappointing. The result was a vast expansion of aerial reconnaissance over and around the fringes of the Eastern Bloc. High performance aircraft were essential to this process. In 1952, in a highly secret operation, American RB-45C Tornado aircraft were operating from RAF Sculthorpe with British crews and markings, but without registration numbers. 1953 saw the formal delivery of the long-awaited British Canberra PR3, the first RAF aircraft purpose-designed for aerial reconnaissance. One Canberra was damaged, but not destroyed, while examining a Soviet missile centre near the Caspian Sea in that year.

By 1956 the Americans had deployed the famous U-2 high-altitude lightweight aircraft, which was flown over the Soviet Union by both

British and American pilots in a CIA-managed programme in the late 1950s. In the same year, a less well known aircraft, an American-enhanced version of the Canberra, the RB-57D, was despatched to Germany. Unlike the lightweight U-2, this aircraft could carry a heavy payload of cameras and electronic monitoring equipment. By the late 1950s, the air around and over the Soviet Union was thick with surveillance aircraft of every type, with the British contribution overseen by the Joint Air Reconnaissance Intelligence Centre and the RAF's Central Reconnaissance Establishment at Brampton.

The golden age of aerial reconnaissance came to a dramatic end in the summer of 1960, with the loss of Gary Powers's U-2 aircraft over Siberia and the loss of an American RB-47 aircraft over the Barents Sea, which had been launched from Brize Norton airbase in Britain. Khrushchev exploited the U-2 shootdown with admirable skill. He refrained from revealing that the pilot, Gary Powers, had been captured alive, or that the pilot had failed to activate the U-2's self-destruction mechanism. Britain and the United States tried to pass these flights off as 'scientific investigations', only to be publicly confronted with material evidence to the contrary. The significance of this incident was not the loss of pilots or aircraft, for many aircrew, including six Britons, had already been lost in aerial confrontations with the Soviets. More significant were the political embarrassment and the resulting furore in the United Nations. Khrushchev withdrew from an East–West summit and scored a propaganda coup for the Soviet Union. Harold Macmillan, who had personally built the summit, found the episode painful and it had a profound impact upon the Prime Minister's attitudes to the risks of intelligence-gathering generally. British activities were curtailed and in September 1960 a stringent new UK–US agreement on American spy-flights to and from British bases was negotiated.

This episode also prompted Eisenhower to authorise the early American satellite reconnaissance programme in August 1960, inaugurating a new era of risk-free space-based collection, dominated by the United States. Britain, too, identified satellites as the way ahead. In the short term the RAF and the USAF turned to oblique photography of hostile areas, using vast cameras that weighed up to 2000 kg, to photograph objects at a distance of up to 60 miles, from the relative safety of border areas. The shoot-downs of 1960 also had their impact at sea. Britain all but abandoned aerial photography of the Soviet Navy, in preference for the expansion of a discreet programme of surveillance from British arctic trawlers. This continued until the loss of the arctic super-trawler, *The Gaul*, in mysterious circumstances in 1974.

6

Service intelligence

6.1 The JIB and targets, 1947

The JIB has often been dismissed as a dull section of the Whitehall intelligence machine which gathered information on topographical subjects, such as beach gradients, in its role as successor to the Inter-Service Topographical Bureau. But as early as 1947 its duties included helping with the preparation of target intelligence for atomic attacks on the Soviet Union. These reports were highly sensitive and it was rare for more than six copies to be produced. By the 1950s the JIB formed a growing nucleus of inter-service intelligence work on scientific subjects.

INTRODUCTION
The object of this paper, which has been prepared on request, is to indicate the main characteristics of Russian towns and to assess their susceptibility to air attack, particularly incendiary attack.

2. The scope of the paper is limited to towns of over 50,000 inhabitants that lie within 2,000 miles range of EAST ANGLIA, CAIRO or KARACHI. The limit of this range is shown on the accompanying map.

3. The paper is provisional and has been given a severely restricted circulation. It is based on the detailed examination of 5 specimen towns and a more general examination of many others. The conclusions reached can only be of a very general nature.

GENERAL
4. Out of 185 towns of over 50,000 inhabitants in the U.S.S.R. 150 (81%) are within 2,000 miles of EAST ANGLIA, CAIRO or KARACHI ...

GENERAL CHARACTER OF TOWNS
6. A compact centre with widely dispersed modern industrial suburbs
...

17. British visitors to MOSCOW, including members of a Civil Defense mission in 1941, agree as to the efficiency of fire services in that city, both of the regular fire-brigades, manned by a picked body of 5,000 men and adequately equipped, and of Civil Defense organisations during the war. Fire-watching, in particular, was far ahead of ours. The only inadequacy observed in 1941 was in static water supplies, in reserves of hose, and in the hand-pumps used by Civil Defense organisations. Although the Russians refused to admit inadequacy, they may well have profited by warnings. No information is available for other Russian towns.

CONCLUSIONS
18. The *centres* of Russian towns generally provide compact and flammable targets for incendiary attack, but, as large modern factories usually lie at a considerable distance from the town-centres and from each other, the bombing of the town-centres would not, in most cases, result in the destruction of the main factories. Nor would the workers of these factories necessarily be unhoused by the destruction of the town, because they mostly live in settlements adjacent to the factory in which they work. In these workers' settlements, the solidly-built houses are widely spaced, while the one-storey timber houses could be easily vacated and quickly replaced.

JIB Ref: 3/30, June 1947, MoD, Joint Intelligence Bureau, 'The Characteristics of Russian Towns as Targets for Air Attack', Director of Intelligence USAF HQ files, File 2-2001/2-2099, Box 42, RG 341, USNA.

6.2 UK–US co-operation and the German dividend, 1947

UK–US co-operation in the post-war period was not just the result of a well-established wartime relationship, but also of the need to combine their efforts to exploit the limited information available on the Soviet Union that was spread across the British, French and American zones of occupation in Europe.

... subject is project ABSTRACT

This project has been carried on in the Theater with the assistance of the British. To date 3 boxes of vitally important documents and cylinders containing the location of alleged burials of other documents and guided missiles equipment has been found in the British Zone [of Germany]. Further British co-operation is essential to the operation. Director of Intelligence here earnestly recommends furtherance of joint co-operation. Request authority to pursue the project on joint British-US basis.

[US] From CINCEUR Frankfurt to War Department, S-3827, 4 April 1947, Top Secret Top Priority, Director of Intelligence USAF HQ files, File 700/799, Box 38, RG 341, USNA.

6.3 **The ID CCG, 1947**

One of the largest British intelligence organisations in the immediate post-war period was the ID CCG. This interservice organisation, employing thousands of staff, began as a military organisation under Major General J. S. Lethbridge, but was gradually civilianised, not least through the recruitment of many Germans. Initially, it was preoccupied with post-war Nazi underground organisations which were targeted in 'Operation Nursery' and later 'Operation Selection Board'. By 1950 it had become a largely anti-Soviet organisation.

The main Headquarters of the Intelligence Division is within the Zone, with a small advance HQ in Berlin and a rear element in England ...

The Operations and Planning Branch ... is in fact responsible for directing and guiding intelligence activities throughout the Zone and to this end it is divided into several sections ... the chief interest of one section is the civilian internment camps. It runs a review and interrogation staff at each CIC which interrogates all inmates and makes a thorough assessment of their connection with the Nazi party, and of the degree of danger they might represent to security if released. It also prepares all documents required by the CCG review boards, which are the tribunals set up to divide Nazis into different degrees of guilt ...

Another section is responsible for political, social and industrial Intelligence. It deals with political trends, the study of political parties, and the chief personalities of each party. It evaluates reactions of the German population to the correct [current?] situation and the effect on general morale of measures taken by the occupying powers. It is also responsible for the vetting of important industrialists, and aspirants for high level posts in the German administration. It follows the course of German Youth Movements, Universities, Churches and Trade Unions, always with the intention of discovering or counteracting undesirable trends ...

A third section is responsible for combatting and studying all subversive activities of movements ranging from Nazi and militarists on the right to communism on the left. It is concerned with historical study of the German Intelligence service. In addition it co-ordinates the work of the intelligence teams along the demarcation line between the Soviet and British Zones ...

Finally there is the central Personality Index with its files and cards containing the records of thousands of Nazis and other subversive elements ...

There is another branch of Int. Div. which is organised in a semi-independent form – The Censorship Branch. This has a separate Headquarters in Herford and has three censorship stations, at Hamburg, Peine and Bonn. It censors a proportion of Civilian, POW [prisoners of war] and DP [diplaced persons] inter-zonal and international mail, and a small percentage of intra-zonal mail. In addition, monitoring of telecommunications is done at static units and by mobile vans spread throughout the zone ...

Monthly Intelligence Summary, January 1947, British Air Forces of Occupation, pp. 13–15, AIR 55/143, PRO.

6.4 Attempts to centralise service intelligence, 1950

In 1950, prompted by financial stringency, and also by the enthusiasm of Major General Kenneth Strong, head of the JIB, the Minister of Defence put forward plans for centralising the location of the three separate intelligence departments of the Army, Navy and Air Force. Although not explicitly stated, many saw this as pointing towards their eventual amalgamation. The three Chiefs of Staff resisted this bitterly, and the proposals were defeated for the time being.

PRIME MINISTER

Some little time ago I initiated some enquiries into the present Intelligence Organisation and General Strong prepared a note for me, of which I enclose a copy. It is, I think, an excellent statement, which you should see. I am arranging for his principal proposal for a geographical centralisation of the Intelligence Organisation to be examined by the Chiefs of Staff, though I am of course well aware that, in present circumstances, it may be very difficult to achieve.

In connection with this matter I made some enquiries about the present cost of the various Intelligence Organisations, exclusive of the Secret Service and the Security Service. The expenditure amounts to something over £3½ million of which the War Office account for £2,100,000, the Air Ministry £640,000, the Admiralty £575,000, while expenditure falling on the Ministry of Defence amounts to £225,000. If we could secure economies in these figures and an increase in efficiency at the same time by moving in this direction proposed by General Strong, I think we ought to do so.

I will keep you informed.

(SGD.) E. SHINWELL

MINISTER.

ORGANISATION OF INTELLIGENCE SERVICES.

... the Chiefs of Staff have examined the suggestion that the Intelligence Services might be housed in one building in the Whitehall area.

2. At present the Intelligence Departments of the Admiralty and War Office are accommodated in their main buildings. However, owing to shortage of accommodation the Intelligence Department in the Air Ministry is at present located in an office outside the main building. This arrangement has so far proved unsatisfactory even in peacetime.

3. The Chiefs of Staff emphasise the importance of ensuring that the intelligence, operations, planning, weapon development and training departments, etc., work in close liaison ...

5. The Chiefs of Staff maintain that if the present situation was reversed so that Intelligence Departments of each Ministry were housed in one separate building the work of their Ministries would

suffer greatly in peace; in war the result might be disastrous since intelligence must frequently be acted upon immediately and thus no measures which would cause any delay whatsoever can be accepted ... I suggest you will wish to endorse the views of the Chiefs of Staff.
(Sgd.) WILLIAM ELLIOT.

Minister of Defence, Emmanuel Shinwell, to Prime Minister, Clement Attlee, 22 June 1950, Secret, and MoD Chief Staff Officer, Air Marshal William Elliot, to Shinwell, 'Organisation of Intelligence Services', COS 1403/23/10/50, Top Secret, 21 October 1950, DEFE 11/349, PRO.

7

'Spy-flights' and aerial reconnaisance

7.1 USAF–RAF target intelligence agreement, 1948

This agreement was negotiated during the period April–November 1948. It was of immense importance in pointing the way to a substantial joint programme of overflights. It codified the British and American practice of almost free interchange of material and personnel relating to the sensitive subject of target intelligence. This included raw data, aerial photographs, finished target traces and also broader studies of subjects such as the physical and psychological vulnerability of the Soviet Union to bombing.

Dear Pendred,

You will be pleased to know that the USAF–RAF Joint Agreement on Target Intelligence has been approved by the Air Staff. As agreed, I am including a signed copy for your retention ... the agreement as now ratified provides a truly sound basis for the mutual exchange of target intelligence.

By now you have probably only had a limited opportunity to peruse the provisional target material which I forwarded to you through Group Captain McMurtie on 27 August 1948. I shall be interested in your personal evaluation of this material, as well as the comments of your staff, as soon as you have had a chance to examine the material carefully.

Sincerely yours, Cabell

Director of Intelligence USAF, Major General Charles Cabell, to UK Assistant Chief of the Air Staff (Intelligence), Air Vice Marshal L. F. Pendred, November 1948, Top Secret, and Appendix 'Target Intelligence', Director of Intelligence USAF HQ files, File 2-30003/2-3099, Box 42, RG 341, USNA.

7.2 British aerial reconnaissance over the Soviet Union, 1948

There are indications that Britain was conducting significant
aerial reconnaissance over the Soviet Union by 1948. This
mostly involved the fringes of the Soviet Union, but occasion-
ally important targets involved deep penetration, dependent
upon Middle East bases to achieve the required range. The
Soviet long-range missile testing sites on the shores of the
Caspian Sea represented one such target. At this time the
USAF was forbidden from conducting such operations.

It is understood that the British are or have been photographing the
south shores of the Caspian Sea. It is requested that we be furnished
at the earliest practicable date [with] film positives or duplicate nega-
tives and cover traces of such photography as they may have obtained
in the area.

BY COMMAND OF THE CHIEF OF STAFF:
[attached US] MEMORANDUM FOR THE RECORD

PROBLEM
1. To obtain new photo cover and traces produced by the British.

FACTS AND DISCUSSION
2. Commander Dibrell of Office CNO, Graphic Section, stated that
the British were taking photography of the southern shore line of the
Caspian Sea. This operation, conducted from Crete, is said to be
quite high level and that S/L Hutchinson probably had not heard of it.
Dibrell requested that we not ask Hutchinson but agreed that we
should query Harvey Brown in London ...

[US] Directorate of Intelligence to Lt Colonel Harvey C. Brown, United
States Air Attaché, American Embassy, London, England, 16 December
1948, Top Secret, Memo: 'New Photo Cover', Director of Intelligence
USAF HQ files, File 2-5000/2-5199, Box 43, RG 341, USNA.

7.3 Political clearance for aerial reconnaissance, 1950

From the late 1940s aerial photography was the main source
of intelligence on the development and expansion of the

Soviet Fleet. The potential for an 'incident' while conducting this sort of 'special reconnaissance' was clear from the outset and strict guidelines were laid down for clearance. During the late 1940s and early 1950s these flights were often cleared by the Foreign Secretary or the Prime Minister. Later, sensitive operations by submarine or aircraft could be cleared by the Permanent Under-Secretary of the Foreign Office.

We have recently been asked by Naval Intelligence to fly a special reconnaissance, as soon as possible, of Valona Bay (Albania) where the presence of two Soviet submarines has been reported.

2. It is hoped that only one flight will be necessary, but should the weather be unfavourable, a maximum of three might have to be carried out. The aircraft would be briefed to fly at 30,000 ft. and since the Albanians are not, so far as is known, equipped with modern interceptor fighters or early warning radar, the risk of interception is negligible, in fact it is unlikely that the presence of the aircraft would be detected.

3. The Foreign Secretary has approved the proposal for his part, and I also agree that this reconnaissance should be carried out, but I think it right to inform you of what is proposed.

4. I am sending copies of this minute to the Minister of Defence, and to the Foreign Secretary ...

Secretary of State for Air, Arthur Henderson, to Prime Minister, Clement Attlee, 17 March 1950, Top Secret, AIR 19/1107, PRO.

7.4 **Aerial reconnaissance and the Suez crisis, 1956**

Many of the demands made upon British aerial reconnaissance came in the context of the post-war insurgencies in Malaya, Kenya and Cyprus, and of episodes such as the Suez crisis in 1956. During the Suez operation, codenamed 'Operation Musketeer', this effort was controlled by the Joint Air Reconnaissance Intelligence Committee, Middle East. The work was mostly conducted by Canberra aircraft of No. 13 Squadron and by French RF-84s. The latter were simpler with fewer cameras, and so achieved a film development and initial interpretation time that was twice as fast as their more sophisticated British counterparts.

14. Daily reconnaissance was flown over Egyptian airfields, military targets, roads, railways, and canals for movement, special targets being Cairo Radio transmitters, radar sites, and parachute dropping zones. WADI HALFA, ASWAN and LUXOR were well within range of action of the Canberras from AKROTIRI [on Cyprus]. Two Canberras were shot at by fighters using self destroying ammunition which was presumed to be fired from the 37mm cannon in the Egyptian Mig 15. Syrian airfields were covered for the 1st time on the 31st October and from then on at frequent intervals. On 6th of November, one Canberra photographing the Syrian airfields was chased by Meteors with unidentified markings but managed to evade them and returned to base. Later on the same day, one Canberra failed to return from photographing RAYAK, ALEPPO and RACIND. Syrian radio claimed that the pilot and the navigator abandoned the Canberra after being shot at by Syrian fighters. The pilot and the navigator are still in a Beirut hospital with slight injuries, and the third member of the Canberra crew is known to have been killed when the aircraft crashed. On a later reconnaissance over Syria, Canberras were escorted by Hunters when withdrawing from targets and two R.F. 84 Fs were sent on each French mission ...

Memorandum by Squadron Leader R. H. B. Dixon, 'General Report on Reconnaissance Operations and Organisation leading up to and during Operation Musketeer', ATF/TS.26/36, 13 November 1956, Secret, AIR 20/9532, PRO.

7.5 Suspension of U-2 flights from British bases, 1956

The extent of political embarrassment that could be caused by bungled intelligence operations was underlined by the infamous Commander 'Buster' Crabb incident in April 1956 during the visit of Khrushchev to Britain on a Soviet cruiser. Prime Minister Anthony Eden certainly did not enjoy the massive press and parliamentary attention generated by the Crabb episode and launched a general review of the procedures for approval of all surveillance operations conducted against the Soviet Union from the United Kingdom. This review had important consequences for UK–US co-operation in the field of aerial photographic reconnaissance. Eden

banned U-2 flights from the UK. As a result, the first U-2
flight over the Soviet Union was flown from Germany, and
not the UK. Richard M. Bissell, director of the CIA's embry-
onic U-2 reconnaissance programme, recalls this.

My first trip was to the United Kingdom, where I met with Prime
Minister Anthony Eden and received his permission to base a squadron of three U-2s in a segregated hangar at Lakenheath ... Although
we were able to initiate a few practice overflights into Eastern Europe, an unfortunate incident altered the situation and adversely affected our ability to operate out of the United Kingdom. A soviet
cruiser docked in Portsmouth harbor while making a courtesy call,
and apparently a British frogman was dispatched to look at the sig-
nalling gear. A short time later his body was found floating in the bay.
There was a great deal of press attention and Eden's reaction was to
rescind authorization for the U-2s to fly over enemy or forbidden
territory from the United Kingdom ... the base was closed out rather
rapidly.

R. M. Bissell, Jr., *Reflections of a Cold Warrior: From Yalta to the Bay of
Pigs* (New Haven: Yale University Press, 1996), pp. 115–16.

7.6 Resumption of U-2 flights from British bases, 1957

In 1957, at the Bermuda Conference, Harold Macmillan
reversed Eden's decision of the previous year to halt U-2
flights from the UK. The context of these discussion at
Bermuda, which included tripartite systems for warning of
surprise attack and also strategic weapons, underlines the
extent to which aerial reconnaissance over the Soviet Union
and nuclear issues were closely integrated. To Eisenhower's
irritation, the fact that some of these subjects were discussed
at Bermuda was leaked in the British press (see below document 17.9).

At the Mid-Ocean Club
Bermuda
March 22, 1957

Dear Mr President,

At our talk this morning, you asked me to let you have notes on one or two of the subjects we mentioned. I now send you notes on the following subjects:

I.   AQUATONE
II. Tripartite Alerts Procedure
III. Nuclear Weapons for R.A.F. Bombers
IV. Nuclear bomb releases gear for R.A.F. bombers

Yours very sincerely
Harold Macmillan

The President of the United States

I. AQUATONE

At an earlier stage the United Kingdom Government felt unable to agree that bases in the United Kingdom should be used for operational flights for AQUATONE.

The United Kingdom Government are now prepared to allow bases in the United Kingdom to be used for operations of this nature, if that would be of advantage to the United States Government.

II. TRIPARTITE ALERTS PROCEDURE

An effective machinery should be established for the rapid exchange of intelligence between the Governments of the United States, Canada and the United Kingdom on any sudden threat of Soviet aggression against the NATO area. For this purpose a meeting between intelligence experts of the three Governments will be held in Washington immediately after the Bermuda Conference.

Prime Minister, Harold Macmillan, to President Eisenhower, 22 March 1957, DDRS 1997/743.

7.7 **The search for high performance, 1957**

In the early 1950s the RAF's main reconnaissance aircraft, the Canberra PR3 and PR7, were able to fly above the ceiling of Soviet air defences, to the exasperation of Moscow. However, awareness of Soviet progress in the field of anti-aircraft missile technology presented the RAF with serious problems in terms of the future of clandestine aerial reconnaissance over the Soviet Union. Although a few British pilots were soon to participate in the American U-2 programme, the British desired their own independent capability. By 1957 financial stringency had dashed hopes of a very high performance aircraft. Although an improved version of the Canberra (PR9) arrived in 1960, long-term thinking now focused on satellites.

Some months ago you asked us to look into the possibility of quickly converting a high performance research aircraft into a very high altitude reconnaissance aircraft for clandestine operations in the early 1960s.

2. Our investigation shows quite clearly that there is no possibility of any such short cut. As you know, the Mach 4/5 project, which was only at the Working Part level, has been cancelled by the Defence Review ...

4. You may remember at the end of 1955 the Long Range Reconnaissance Research and Development Working Party of the Ministry of Defence issued their report (DPP/P (55) 64) dated 5th November, 1955. They recommended that the most promising line of research and development for a future reconnaissance system was an orbiting satellite to carry optical reconnaissance equipment. They also recommended that a design study should be prepared for:-

(a) A rocket vehicle with equipment for long range oblique photography.

(b) An air launched, rocket powered manual aircraft with equipment for high altitude vertical and/or long range oblique photography ...

Memorandum by A/ACAS (OR), Air Commodore W. R. Brotherhood, to DCAS, 'High Performance Reconnaissance Aircraft', DCAS/3545/57, 31 July 1957, Top Secret, AIR 20/11406, PRO.

7.8 **Political clearance for 'special flights', 1960**

In the summer of 1960 the loss of two American reconnaissance aircraft, including the famous U-2 aircraft and captured pilot, Gary Powers, caused a huge diplomatic furore. It eventually resulted in the cancellation of an East–West summit. All this prompted discussions about how similar British 'special flights' secured clearance. The Foreign Office minute below sets out the procedure at that time.

Mr. Ormsby-Gore's assumption about the clearance of R.A.F. special flights is correct. In practice, a programme for R.A.F. special flights is submitted for the Prime Minister's approval six months ahead. Subsequently, each individual day flight has to be submitted for clearance by the Secretary of State, and each individual night flight for clearance by the Permanent Under-Secretary.

Minute by P. A. Wilkinson (FO), 22 July 1960, FO 371/173540, PRO.

7.9 **The Soviets, Britain and the RB-47/U-2 shootdowns, 1960**

In the summer of 1960 the Soviets shot down an American RB-47 reconnaissance aircraft over the Barents Sea. This had been launched from RAF Brize Norton in the UK. As with the recent loss of the Gary Powers U-2 aircraft over the Urals, the United States claimed that the aircraft was engaged in 'scientific research'. The UK chose to support this increasingly threadbare cover story, provoking a predictable Soviet response. Khrushchev eventually threatened the use of rockets against the UK bases of US reconnaissance aircraft. He was almost certainly unaware that some of the U-2 pilots were British.

... Instead of seriously weighing possible consequences, dangerous to the cause of peace and not least to Great Britain herself, with which the provocative acts of the United States are fraught; and instead of taking all measures within its power to put an end to such playing with fire the Government of Great Britain thinks only of how it can help the Government of the United States which is endeavouring to find a way out of its difficult situation by means of fabrications and unsubstantiated repudiation of the facts ...

  The Government of Great Britain, following the United States Government, asserts that the American aircraft RB-47 was shot down 'in international airspace' and even goes so far as to talk about an 'unprovoked attack' on this plane. The question arises on what basis does the British Government allow itself to come forward with these statements? Is it not clear to the Government of Great Britain that the Government of the U.S.S.R. itself, whose territory was violated by the American military aircraft starting out from Britain, has exact information regarding the place in which the aircraft, taken under the supervision of the Soviet anti-aircraft defence forces, violated the Soviet border, and where it was shot down after having ignored warnings?

By associating itself with the statement contained in the Note of the United States of July 13, the Government of Great Britain affixed its signature to the fabrication that the American bomber RB 47 was pursuing only 'lawful' aims – 'the study of electromagnetic phenomena'. As is known this 'explanation' is not original: it is almost an exact repetition of the methods by means of which the United States Government attempted at first to mislead world opinion after the destruction of the military spy-plane U-2 above U.S.S.R. territory ... But after just a few days, the State Department of the United States, and the Secretary of State Herter himself and President Eisenhower, driven into a corner by irrefutable proof of the pre-meditated violation by the American military aircraft of the border of the U.S.S.R. and the real objects of such violation, were forced to admit publicly that the previous official announcements from Washington on this subject were merely a false version intended to deceive the people of the United States ...

The Soviet Government has already warned the Government of Great Britain of the heavy responsibility which it takes upon itself in becoming party to the aggressive actions of the United States. The Government of the U.S.S.R. considers it necessary to again confirm its Note of July 11 and the decisive protest expressed in connection with Britain's providing territory for the carrying out of aggressive acts against the Soviet Union by American military aircraft. The Soviet Government expects that an end will be put to this. Otherwise it will take measures to ensure the security of the peoples of the Soviet Union by all means at its disposal.

Soviet government's Note of 3 August (in response to British government's Note of 19 July), 213/17 FO 371/173538, PRO.

7.10 UK–US discussions on the RB-47/U-2 shootdowns, 1960

During their meeting in September 1960, Macmillan and Eisenhower jointly reviewed both the scale of the aerial reconnaissance programme in international waters, and the nature of the cover stories used to disguise these flights. Their discussion was pragmatic and Macmillan did not reveal the depth of his anger and disappointment over the abrupt cancellation of the Paris summit, which had resulted from Eisenhower's refusal to apologise to Khrushchev over the U-2 incident.

Others present: Prime Minister Macmillan, Secretary Herter, Lord Home, Mr. de Zueletta, General Goodpaster.

... The Prime Minister next raised the question of reconnaissance flights that we both conduct of the periphery of the Soviet Union for intelligence purposes. He reported that agreement has been reached on procedures for consultation that have been under discussion, but the real question that remains is just what we should do in this program, what places we should go to, and what operation we should conduct there. On the one hand we do not want to permit the Soviets to drive us away from the free use of international waters and international air space, but on the other we must recognize that we are in a weak position when they can shoot our planes down over international waters and there is apparently nothing we can do about it. He suggested that the intelligence people of the two countries should get together on this. The President referred to certain rules he had put into effect after difficulties in the Far East, prescribing that the aircraft should keep a certain distance away from hostile shores at all times, and avoid direct headings towards critical areas within the Soviet bloc such as major cities, naval bases, etc. He said that his discussion of the matter with our people has disclosed that the information gathered is of great importance to our bomber planning. The Prime Minister asked that arrangements be made for Patrick Deane [sic] to meet with our people. He said there is also the question of what cover story we should use. He thinks it is foolish to say that we are conducting the flights for electro-magnetic research and thought it better to say frankly that they are for reconnaissance purposes. The President agreed, stating that when we tell what we are doing, we should simply say we are flying over the open ocean to see what the Soviets are doing that might have a bearing on military preparations – just as they do with their trawlers. The Prime Minister noted that the difference is they can shoot down our planes and conceal the facts as to location, etc., whereas if we were to do anything, our people talk so much that no details could be kept secret. (The President commented that the only regret he had regarding the U-2 is that the cover statement which was used did not fit the facts as they developed – on the assumption that the plane would be destroyed and the pilot probably lost.) The Prime Minister said he does not plan to make a public statement regarding the reconnaissance flights. If he is asked a question in Parliament – and he hopes he will be asked a question, preferably by some Communist-leaning member – he will simply say that he talked to the President about this matter, as he told the house he would, and what has been agreed upon has been satisfactory from a British standpoint.

Memorandum of Conference with the President, 22 September 1960, Secret, DDRS, 1997/1698.

7.11 Satellite reconnaissance and the Chinese atomic bomb, 1964

In late September 1964 the Director of the CIA, John McCone, toured NATO capitals, beginning in London, to brief premiers on developments in satellite photography and its implications. McCone informed the British Prime Minister, Sir Alec Douglas Home, of evidence that the Chinese atomic programme was making rapid progress. China tested its first bomb less than a month later on 16 October 1964. All this occurred in the wake of the Nuclear Test Ban Treaty of 1963 and pointed the way towards the growing use of intelligence satellites for treaty verification and counter-proliferation.

Mr. McCone said that he had come to Britain and was going on to other NATO capitals at the request of the President to bring the allies up to date about the results of satellite photography. He had given a presentation that morning to the J.I.C. and that afternoon to the Foreign Secretary, Defence Secretary and other senior civil and military figures. The effect of satellite photography had been that the United

States had almost complete coverage of the U.S.S.R and China and were now able to locate all missile sites inside these territories. United States assumed that the Soviet Union was able to do the same to the United States. Indeed, Mr. Khrushchev had said as much to M. Spaak [Belgian Foreign Minster] during a recent visit to the Soviet Union and had said that the time might soon come for Chairman Khrushchev and President Johnson to sit down together and compare photographs.

Mr. McCone went on to say that there was one surprise that they had received from their photographs of China. This was evidence of a nuclear test site nearing completion in North West China. From American knowledge of Chinese production facilities they had not thought that China had made so much progress. It might be that the test site was out of phase with the rest of the programme for Mr. Khrushchev had told Mr. Harriman at the time of the negotiations for the Nuclear Test Ban Treaty in 1963 that it would be 'some years' before China would be able to explode a nuclear device. However, the Soviet Ambassador in Washington had told Mr. Thompson about ten days ago that China might be able to explode a device at any time. In any case, according to the satellite photographs, the nuclear test facilities should be complete by the autumn.

The *Prime Minister* asked what effect a Chinese nuclear explosion would have on South East Asia. Mr. McCone thought that psychologically it would have a very serious effect, although militarily, it would be some time before China had developed a means of delivery.

The *Prime Minister* asked whether the Russians could afford to allow the Chinese to build up a nuclear potential. *Mr. McCone* replied that it looked as if they had no alternative. There was no move that they knew of on the part of the Russians to try and stop the Chinese. Indeed, within the last few days they had made an effort to get the Chinese seated within the International Atomic Energy Authority in Vienna ...

Record of a conversation between the Prime Minister and the head of the Central Intelligence Agency, Mr J. J. McCone [and also Sir Burke Trend, Mr Wright and the American Ambassador], at No. 10 Downing Street, at 3.30 p.m. on Monday, 21 September 1964, PREM 11/5197, PRO.

PART IV

MANAGEMENT

The new documentation released by the Waldegrave Initiative on Open Government has shed a great deal of light upon the management of British intelligence, including the system for approving operations. One of the obvious managerial differences between the British and American intelligence systems during the Cold War was a function of size. While both countries developed elaborate committee structures for this purpose, nevertheless, in Britain it remained possible for individual intelligence-gathering operations, for example by aircraft and submarines, to receive ministerial or even prime ministerial approval. In the United States the volume of activity made this increasingly impractical on a day-to-day basis.

It has often been remarked that the Cabinet committee system constitutes the engine-room of British government. This was especially true of intelligence management during the Cold War. The few attempts at overall enquiries and investigations into British intelligence, such as the Findlater–Stewart enquiry of 1945, and the Evill Report of 1947, seem to have been of little value. Specific enquiries such as the Brundrett Report on scientific intelligence and the Davies Report on atomic intelligence, both completed in 1954, had more impact. However, the key factor in re-shaping British intelligence has been constant incremental change, managed by committee, and especially the JIC.

The JIC was one of the most important legacies of the Second World War, ensuring a relatively integrated British intelligence community, rather than the coterie of separate agencies that existed in the 1930s. Beginning life as a lowly subcommittee of the Chiefs of Staff, by the end of the war the JIC had become the hub of a complex intelligence wheel. It not only formed the highest authority for intelligence assessment and interpretation, but it was also charged with making recommendations to 'improve the efficient working of the intelligence organisation of the country as a whole'. After 1945 the JIC continued to be chaired by the head of the Foreign Office Services Liaison Department, but it acquired new members. Its traditional stalwarts, the heads of the secret services and of the service intelligence departments, were joined by representatives from the new JIB, from scientific intelligence and from the Colonial Office. New regional JICs, such as JIC Germany, were also created in its image.

The JIC was a crucial nexus between the diplomats and the military, and it was not without friction. In 1944–45 they disagreed fundamentally about future Soviet intentions, and between 1945 and 1953 they argued about the extent to which the West should indulge in Cold War 'fighting'. This friction, together with a desire to emulate George Kennans's Policy Planning Staff in the United States, prompted the Foreign Office to create and *control* new mechanisms. The first new mechanism was the Russia Committee, formed in 1946, which claimed a role in co-ordinating assessments on the Soviet Union, as well as styling itself Whitehall's Cold War 'planning staff'. The former role was never convincingly carried off, while the latter was gradually occluded by the Permanent Under-Secretary's Department/ Committee (PUSD/C), created in February 1949.

The creation of the PUSD was a development of some importance in the management of British intelligence and indeed British overseas policy as a whole. It absorbed most of the critical planning and intelligence machinery of the Foreign Office, including the Services Liaison Department (SLD). By the 1950s, PUSD, SIS and the various propaganda organisations were very closely integrated and formed an inner circle of British foreign policy making. These organisations are not yet fully understood since some of the files of the SLD (1941–49) and PUSD (1949–) remain closed to public inspection. Nevertheless, it is clear that JIC and PUSD remained the key instruments for the routine management of intelligence, ensuring its smooth integration into the policy process.

Meeting less frequently were a host of Cabinet committees and subcommittees. On the intelligence services themselves, and dealing with matters such as annual budgets, the key committee was the Permanent Under Secretaries' Committee on Intelligence Services, consisting of the Permanent Under Secretaries of the departments who were the main consumers of foreign intelligence and chaired by the Cabinet Secretary. Enjoying a somewhat separate existence was the

Overseas Economic Intelligence Committee with its own arcane network of subcommittees on subjects like scientific development. Meanwhile security was superintended by an Ad Hoc Committee on Security consisting of ministers and chaired by the Prime Minister. Its *alter ego* was the Official Committee on Security, and below this were more specialised committees. For example, the Personnel Security Committee was concerned with positive vetting and the Security Committee – Policy and Methods had the mundane subject of the security of buildings, documents, filing cabinets and steel presses. Finally, in 1969 a new post of Cabinet Office Intelligence and Security Co-ordinator was created to help oversee this proliferating structure, which was becoming an impossible burden for the Cabinet Secretary alone. Sir Dick White, with unique experience as head of MI5 and SIS, was its first incumbent.

Any 'wiring diagrams' of this committee structure (and this volume intentionally shuns them) are bound to be misleading. The exact location of power and responsibility shifted in each administration, depending on the preferences of the Prime Minister and Cabinet Secretary. In the 1950s, in the wake of revelations about Soviet penetration, considerable emphasis was placed upon commissions and privy councillors, while the 1960s saw a re-emphasis on the traditional role of the Paymaster General as a senior ministerial figure with a watching brief for intelligence and security, in the stern form of George Wigg.

The manner in which this complex committee structure functioned also remains largely unknown to us. The related fields of signals intelligence, communications security and electronic warfare offer a good example. The received picture of management in this area is simplistic: namely that, after 1945, the Director of GCHQ was responsible to the senior Foreign Office official, while taking advice on priorities from the JIC. But in reality this field was governed by a intricate nebula of committees and subcommittees. By the early 1960s, a high-level body, the Official Committee on Communications Electronics, chaired by Captain Michael Hodges RN, superintended no less than six subordinate committees: the British Joint Communications-Electronics Board; the Cabinet Frequency Committee; the Electronic Warfare Board; the Joint Civil Service Telecommunications Committee; London Signals Intelligence Board (and below this London Signals Intelligence Committee); London Communications Security Board (and below this the London Communications Security Agency).

These, in turn, presided over important operational committees, such as the Technical Radio Intelligence Committee (TRIC). There were also the inevitable regional components, such as the Communications Security Committee, Middle East. It will be decades before the full records of this important network of committees are released, still less understood.

8

A world of committees

8.1 The JIC, 1948

This charter sets out the role and responsibilities of the JIC as revised in 1948. In 1955 its charter was reviewed again and a fifth responsibility was added in the area of Allied co-operation: 'To maintain liaison with appropriate intelligence and defence security agencies in the self-governing Commonwealth countries and the United States and other foreign countries, and with the intelligence authorities of international defence organisations of which the United Kingdom is a member.' Its membership was also expanded to include: Colonial Office, the Director of Scientific Intelligence, GCHQ, the head of JIB, and the Commonwealth Relations Office (the latter as observers only).

The Joint Intelligence Committee is given the following responsibilities:-

(i) Under the Chiefs of Staff to plan, and to give higher direction to, operations of defence intelligence and security, to keep them under review in all fields and to report progress.

(ii) To assemble and appreciate available intelligence for presentation as required to the Chiefs of Staff and to initiate other reports as the Committee may deem necessary.

(iii) To keep under review the organisation of intelligence as a whole and in particular the relations of its component parts so as to ensure efficiency, economy and a rapid adaption to changing requirements, and to advise the Chiefs of Staff of what changes are deemed necessary.

(iv) To co-ordinate the general policy of Joint Intelligence Committees under United Kingdom Commands overseas and to maintain an exchange of intelligence with them, and to maintain liaison with appropriate Commonwealth intelligence agencies.

JIC (48) 21, Charter for the Joint Intelligence Committee, 27 February 1948, L/WS/1/1051, IOLR.

8.2 Re-organising intelligence machinery: Germany, 1948

The JIC routinely conducted reviews of the co-ordinating machinery for the various British intelligence and security services, particularly in areas like Germany, where it was essential for many disparate elements to work harmoniously together. Economy, as ever, was a key consideration, as this document demonstrates.

1. GENERAL

In agreement with the Military Governor and Commander in Chief and with the Chief of Intelligence Division Germany, a delegation of experts representing the Joint Intelligence Sub Committee will visit Germany in January, 1948.

The Delegation will examine the existing machinery for providing the intelligence required, both in Germany and in London and in the light of the necessity to reduce establishments.

2. OBJECT

The object of the Delegation will be to examine and report to the Control Commission and to the Joint Intelligence Sub Committee in London on the organisation of, and the methods employed by, all intelligence bodies in Germany. The Delegation's report will be designed to enable the Joint Intelligence Committee to advise the Control Commission in Germany and parent ministries in London of the means by which :-

(a) the existing flow of intelligence required in London can be maintained or improved.

(b) the requirements of the intelligence organisations in Germany can best be made.

(c) penetration by hostile agents can best be combatted.

3. COMPOSITION
The Delegation will be composed of :-
Mr. W.G. HAYTER Foreign Office (Chairman) [chair of the JIC]
Col. R.H. QUILL Admiralty
Brig. C.E.R. HIRSCH, War Office
Gp Capt E.E. BRODIE Air Ministry
[line deleted under Section 3(4), presumed SIS representative]
Mr D.G. WHITE MI5
Lt Col E.C.W. Myers JIB
Lt Col P. GLEADELL (Secretary) [and Secretary of JIC London] ...

'Draft Terms of Reference for the Joint Intelligence Delegation to Germany', Appendix 'A' to HQ.INT.DIV/JIC/7053/10, Top Secret, 6 January 1948, DEFE 41/70, PRO.

8.3 The rise of PUSD, 1949–52

In the 1940s the Foreign Office's SLD formed the crucial nexus between the Foreign Office and the Chiefs of Staff and its head served as the chairman of the JIC. But in 1949 SLD was absorbed into the newly formed and increasingly powerful PUSD. The role of the Foreign Office's Russia Committee in intelligence assessment and co-ordination role regarding the Soviet Union was also gradually eclipsed by the rise of the PUSD which absorbed some of its functions in 1952. By the mid-1950s, the term 'PUSD' was synonymous with intelligence in Whitehall.

(b) Contacts with the Chiefs of Staff and J.I.C.
It will be seen that in the previous terms of reference [for the Russia Committee] the following sentence appeared : – 'The Committee will maintain close contact with the Chiefs of Staff and J.I.C. with a view to co-ordinating intelligence and estimates of Soviet intentions at every stage'. It is proposed to omit this sentence from the new terms of reference since it would seem that effective liaison in this is now maintained through the Permanent Under-Secretary's Department in the first instance.

Foreign Office memorandum, 'Russia Committee Reorganisation', 13 November 1952, RC/62/52, FO 371/125005, PRO.

Management

8.4 The PUSD, 1949

In February 1949 Sir William Strang, the Permanent Under-Secretary at the Foreign Office, set up the Permanent Under-Secretary's Committee (PUSC) to consider long-term questions of foreign policy. He also created a supporting Permanent Under-Secretary's Department (PUSD), which absorbed central planning and intelligence machinery. H. N. Brain, the last head of the SLD, became the first head of PUSD. In the 1950s additional machinery was created, including the Planning Department. However PUSD, with its brace of little-known subcommittees, remained the control centre for special activities, with some personnel seconded from SIS. Little has been written on the British overseas policy machine in this period.

The Department which, for want of a better name, is called the Permanent Under-Secretary's Department. This is the department which maintains liaison with the Chiefs of Staff, which represents the Foreign Office on the Joint Intelligence and Joint Planning Staff subcommittees of the Chiefs of Staff, and which coordinates the exchange of scientific information. It collates departmental briefs for the use of Foreign Office representatives at international conferences and collects material for speeches by ministers.

Lord Strang, *The Diplomatic Career* (London: Andre Deutsch, 1962), pp. 87–8.

8.5 The JIC in the 1950s and the 1980s

The work of the JIC in peacetime was largely routine. Much of it involved either the preparation of weekly reports, or the revision of annual reports on subjects which did not change dramatically from year to year. However, the JIC was a successful war-proven instrument with which most were reluctant to tamper. Although it was brought within the Cabinet Office in 1957, its chairman remained a Foreign Office official. One elaboration in the JIC system was the creation of working parties to review specific subjects and geographical areas, known as Current Intelligence Groups. Otherwise the

JIC's workings remained little changed until the Franks Report reviewed Britain's intelligence organisation after the Falklands War. Thereafter, on Lord Franks's recommendation, JIC chairmanship became a full-time job held by a Cabinet Office official. The memoirs of the Director of Scientific Intelligence between 1952 and 1954 recount the experience of JIC meetings in the 1950s.

Apart from occasional highlights ... proceedings on the Joint Intelligence Committee were routinely dull. We met every Thursday morning, when one of the weekly reports submitted to us was the 'perimeter review', which surveyed incidents all around the Warsaw Pact perimeter to see whether there had been any movements which presaged an impending Russian thrust. The idea was worthy enough, but I felt there was a danger that we could get so 'acclimatized by slow change' that we might fail to spot a stealthy build-up by the Russians in which there was no great change in any one week ...

To emphasize the 'Joint' approach, JIC procedure was for the signatures of all directors to appear on all the important reports, even when some of the directors had not been personally concerned. There was even one instance when a report appeared over the signatures of three officers when none of the signatories had either seen the report or been consulted about it. Clearly the Whitehall organization had slipped far from its wartime tautness.

Only a minority of the members of the JIC had been selected on their past achievements as intelligence officers ... I had to record that 'too much time and effort was dissipated in the JIC machine', with its 'dangerous system which may plunge a man with very little of the right background into a position of the highest responsibility in intelligence, and which will almost certainly remove him again as soon as he is beginning to learn his job' ... the ponderous nature of the JIC procedure showed up in the Falklands affair. The Franks Committee inquiry into the amount of warning the JIC had before the Argentinean invasion found that the JIC organization 'was too passive in operation to respond quickly and critically to a rapidly changing situation which demanded urgent attention'.

R. V. Jones, *Reflections on Intelligence* (London: William Heinemann, 1989), pp. 26–8.

8.6 The JIC and the Red Book, 1966

In October 1966 the JIC reviewed its system for acquainting Whitehall with current developments, which is set out usefully below. The result was that the Red Book was divided more clearly into Part I, of interest to senior policy-makers, and Part II, which was more detailed and did not go automatically to ministers. More specific assessments were also circulated. The Grey Book, a weekly review of intelligence and codeword supplement, was abolished. The Prime Minister's private secretary was one of a number who requested these changes.

JIC CURRENT ASSESSMENTS
The Joint Intelligence Committee wishes to review its present practice with regard to current intelligence assessments. These are at present issued in the following forms and circumstances:-

(a) *Special Assessments*. These serve two main purposes:

(i) To review situations of importance to HMG in which there has been some important new development.

(ii) To sum up a developing situation at some point at which we believe it might be useful to policy makers to do so.

(b) *Weekly Survey of Intelligence (Red Book)*.

Issued by the 5 p.m. Home Service Messenger delivery round each Thursday, this is designed to bring to the attention of Ministers, Chiefs of Staff and senior officials interdepartmentally agreed assessments of the current intelligence available to HMG. It is divided into two parts:

Part I. Developments of major importance and those likely to involve the use of British troops or to effect major British interests.

Part II. Intelligence notes on other important developments.

An abridged version is sent to HM The Queen.

(c) *JIC Notes*. These are rather longer (up to 2 to 3 pages) summarising and commenting on current intelligence on particular, often detailed, subjects. These are designed for the working level and not for Ministers.

2. The Committee's information is that the special assessments and notes are meeting the need for which they are designed, but they would welcome any comments or suggestions from users.

3. Although the Red Book does not always live up to its aims, it

should avoid repeating information already known from the press or the ordinary Whitehall telegram distribution, except where it is necessary to correct the information available from these sources or to form a judgement about some aspect of it.

4. The draft Red Book is agreed interdepartmentally at meetings which bring together those within the Foreign Office, the Commonwealth Office, Defence Intelligence Staff and the collecting agencies who are concerned with the interpretation of events in the particular part of the world concerned.

[six lines deleted under Section 3(4)]

5. The JIC would like to know:

(a) Whether the Red Book is in fact of use to the recipients.

(b) Whether it would be of more use to Ministers and other senior recipients if the JIC were to decide to circulate important items separately.

(c) What value if any, senior users derive from part II of the Red Book.

6. I should be most grateful for your views ... I should, however, make it clear that the present enquiry does not cover JIC's output of medium- or long-term studies, a subject which the Committee proposes to consider separately.

Yours ever

[Name deleted under Section 3(4)]

JIC to A. M. Palliser, Private Secretary to Prime Minister, 31 October 1966, J 337/6, PREM 13/1343, PRO.

PART V

SECURITY

The central element in the provision of security in Britain after 1945 was MI5, often referred to as the Security Service. During the election campaign of June 1945 there had been an irascible exchange between Churchill and Attlee over the dangers of the creation of a post-war 'Gestapo' in Britain. Attlee's initial approach to MI5 reflected this concern for restraint and constitutionality, with the appointment of an outsider as its new Director, and no thoughts as to an extension of its powers or responsibilities.

Attlee's desire for restraint was gradually eroded. In 1946 and 1947 high-profile espionage cases in Britain, Canada and Australia suggested a concerted Soviet secret service effort. Added to this was a wave of industrial action in Britain, culminating in the Dock Strike of 1949, which Attlee was increasingly disposed to explain in terms of malignant orchestration. Meanwhile, the United States withheld full exchange of information, awaiting evidence of improved security. In the background were accelerating security problems in the colonies, with heavy demands being made on MI5 by riots and insurgencies in Palestine, the Gold Coast and Malaya. Finally, 1950 and 1951 were characterised by the shocking cases of Klaus Fuchs, then Guy Burgess and Donald Maclean, revealed as the result of the VENONA decryption effort against Soviet communications. Attlee's hopes of avoiding some sort of security purge had now been fatally undermined and positive vetting was introduced as the last act of the outgoing Labour government in October 1951.

MI5 has traditionally been portrayed as a domestic security organisation, but after 1945 its officers often found themselves serving overseas. They assisted with a huge effort to expand and retrain colonial security forces, notably the Police Special Branches in the colonies, and also in countries that had recently achieved independence.

They served as the main nodal point for security intelligence exchange with other colonial powers, for example the French and Belgian security services in Africa. They also worked to ensure regional security service co-operation under the auspices of new defence organisations such as the Baghdad Pact. Within NATO, Britain undertook the sensitive responsibility of co-ordinating its security policy.

Increasingly, MI5 found itself working in collaboration with other organisations, both governmental and non-governmental. By the 1960s, much of the overseas work of MI5 was superintended by the Cabinet Counter-Subversion Committee, which surveyed a broad range of activities from security to propaganda to economic development, and was empowered to deploy 'special funds' in crisis areas. MI5, at home and abroad, worked increasingly closely with propaganda organisations on counter-subversion. The revival of the Irish Republican Army (IRA) as a significant problem in the late 1960s and 1970s further blurred the distinction between domestic, colonial and foreign issues, but MI5 regarded this area as matter for the police and the army.

The period 1945–70 also saw the continual growth of the security staffs and responsibilities of other Whitehall departments. As early as 1947, small Cabinet subcommmittees had been looking at subversion and had embarked on a limited programme of 'negative vetting'. This meant looking at people who were already on the files of Special Branch and MI5. Their concern was to try and transfer communists and fascists away from secret work, focusing primarily on scientists, and the numbers were very small. Positive vetting was introduced in late 1951 and became gradually more rigorous; by the 1960s huge numbers of staff had to undergo this process. At GCHQ alone, this amounted to over 10,000 people. This presented serious political and administrative problems, and also a vast backlog of routine security work that was never quite overcome.

9

MI5 (the Security Service)

9.1 From war to peace in MI5, 1945–46

The early post-war period was characterised by a deep suspicion of security agencies. This was not just a manifestation of the new Labour administration. It also reflected a wider public wish to escape the suffocating blanket of security that had existed during wartime.

And all the while MI5 remained my boss.

I was no longer an executive so I never went to head office to look at the files ... Despite this minor role I was still able to observe the mood of MI5; and the impression I had was that counter-espionage was in the doldrums. There was little to do. The ham fisted attempts of the Germans to plant agents in Britain had been successfully dealt with. Why should anyone believe it possible that the Russians could do any better? At the end of the war there were only two or three people in the Russian section of MI5 ...

I believe that one of the reasons for the MI5 failure after the war was due to over-sensitiveness. There was a strong undercurrent of prejudice against MI5 in many prominent circles, and it showed itself in a curious way. People would proclaim that they were being persecuted by MI5, and gained prestige by so proclaiming. 'My telephone is being tapped ...'

D. Tangye, *The Way to Minack* (London: Michael Joseph, 1968), pp. 141–3.

9.2 **MI5 in the Middle East and Far East, 1950**

MI5 maintained offices in the Middle East and the Far East
where they were responsible for security in British colonial
territories. SIS (or MI6) was responsible for active counter-
espionage in neighbouring non-British territories. In practice,
these duties overlapped to such a degree that MI5 and SIS
tended to combine their regional counter-espionage operations into one office. In the Far East this office was known as
Security Intelligence Far East (SIFE), whose head gave this
presentation.

It is the Far Eastern office of the Security Service – otherwise know as
MI5. We work very closely with our sister service MI6, and in fact
their section which collates information to back their offensive operations against subversive elements and hostile intelligence, is now to be
integrated with SIFE under the overall control of H/SIFE. Otherwise
the difference between MI5 and MI6 is namely that they are the spies
and ourselves the 'spycatchers' ... In explaining our methods it is important to understand that we are not purveyors of intelligence in the
sense that information is procured in its raw state for consumers. We
ourselves are consumers and we depend for our information on agencies such as MI6, the Foreign Office, friendly foreign intelligence
services, the British Colonial Police and of course, Military Attachés.
Collation of this information allows us to direct the security effort
generally and advise on preventative measures. Our role is advisory
rather than executive, although in certain circumstances our field representatives may be required to assume direct control over a case.
This applies particularly to Counter-Espionage which involves the
defection, control or liquidation of enemy spies ...

'Lecture on SIFE', by J. P. Morton, head of SIFE, Appendix E, Report of
Far East Military Attaché's Conference, GHQ FARELF, Singapore,
21–23 March 1950, WO 208/4835, PRO.

9.3 **Growing security problems in Austria, 1951**

By 1951 it was increasingly clear that, with the expansion of
espionage activity by Eastern Bloc services, the numbers of

Communist agents on the ground in Germany and Austria was now vast. In 1951 two spy-rings involving over 100 agents had been uncovered in Austria and some British NCOs had been sentenced for selling information. The temptations were considerable, since the sum of £4,000 had recently been offered for mundane documents relating to a training exercise. Although not strictly the responsibility of MI5, whose remit covered British territory only, there was increasing pressure on an over-stretched service to provide specialist advice to the military authorities.

One of my officers has recently returned from a short tour of Austria and Trieste. As you will know, M.I.6 recently lent you an officer to carry out certain interrogations in Austria which revealed certain attempts at penetration of B.T.A. [British Troops Austria] by the Czech I.S. [intelligence service], and great activity among the large number of small-time agents in that area. My representative is strongly of the opinion that the [British Army] Field Security organisation, with their limited resources and lack of experienced and fully qualified personnel, have only scraped the surface of the problem, and that, although no actual cases of penetration have come to light in Trieste, there is every reason to suppose that similar activity prevails there to that which has come to light in Austria.

The great ease with which agents can move from the Russian Zone into Austria and Trieste leaves little room for doubt that this area is a danger spot of the first order and that, as a field for counter-intelligence, it should be given high priority.

I realise that you are suffering as much as anyone from shortage of officers, and possibly your charter does not now permit you to function openly in these countries, but I should be grateful if you would give consideration to the possibility of supplying the commanders in B.T.A. and BETFOR with assistance by more frequent visits by an M.I.5 officer who would be able to put and keep himself completely in the picture and give professional advice to the security authorities on the spot. It would, of course, be ideal if a D.S.O. [Defence Security Officer – the term for a resident MI5 officer] could be appointed for the area.

Director of Military Intelligence, Major General A. C. Shortt, to Director of MI5, Sir Percy Sillitoe, MI1(E)/1884/3, Secret, October 1951, WO 216/951, PRO.

9.4 The MI5 'charter': the Maxwell-Fyfe directive, 1953

Until 1951, the Director-General of MI5 was directly responsible to the Prime Minister. Thereafter, MI5 was placed under the Home Secretary. Sir David Maxwell-Fyfe, Home Secretary at the time, chose to issue a directive to the Director-General of the MI5, setting out its role and responsibilities. Prior to the 1989 Security Service Act, the organisation had no standing in law, and so this directive served as its 'charter'. It makes clear that MI5 officers were mere civil servants and did not enjoy any 'special powers', for example the power of arrest, in contrast to police officers.

(1) In your appointment as Director General of the Security Service, you will be responsible to the Home Secretary personally. The Security Service is not, however, part of the Home Office. On appropriate occasions, you will have right of direct access to the Prime Minister.

(2) The Security Service is part of the Defence Forces of the country. Its task is the Defence of the Realm as a whole, from external and internal dangers arising from attempts at espionage and sabotage, or from actions of persons and organizations whether directed from within or without the country, which may be judged to be subversive of the state.

(3) You will take special care to see that the work of the Security Service is strictly limited to what is necessary for the purpose of this task.

(4) It is essential that the Security Service should be kept absolutely free from any political bias or influence and nothing should be done that might lend colour to any suggestion that it is concerned with the interests of any particular section of the community, or with any other matter than the Defence of the Realm as a whole.

(5) No enquiry is to be carried out on behalf of any Government Department unless you are satisfied that an important public interest bearing on the Defence of the Realm, as defined in paragraph 2, is at stake.

(6) You and your staff will maintain the well-established convention whereby Ministers do not concern themselves with the detailed information which may be obtained by the Security Service in particular cases, but are furnished with such information only as may be necessary for the determination of any issue on which guidance is sought.

MI5 (the Security Service)

Lord Denning's Report, Cmnd 2512 (London: HMSO, 1963), para. 238.

9.5 **MI5, communism and the trade unions, 1956**

The extent to which the Communist Party had infiltrated
various unions and might be responsible for industrial unrest
was a question which preoccupied Labour and Conservative
administrations equally between 1945 and 1970. The Cabinet paper referred to below on this subject is still closed to
public inspection. But the discussions that flowed from it
illustrate the extent to which ministers, leading trade unionists and MI5 co-operated closely to take discreet counter-
action.

This is an interesting paper by the Security Service, and I thought that
you and some of your senior colleagues should see it for two reasons:-

(a) It shows that, contrary to popular belief, the Communist Party
as such has not yet adopted a policy of promoting strikes or fostering
industrial unrest.

(b) It shows how near the Communist Party have come to success
in their first policy of capturing a dominating position on the Execu-
tives of the Unions.

2. So long as Communism is a legitimate political party, Government agencies cannot be overtly used to counter the threat at (b)
above. Nor can the Conservative Party take much effective action,
overtly, against it. The best defence is to ensure that responsible people in the Trade Union movement are alive to the threat and are organising themselves to meet it. And, from that point of view, the
creation of this new organisation 'I.R.I.S.' [Industrial Research and
Information Service] is a most welcome development.

3. At this morning's meeting you will doubtless ask the Minister of
Labour what he knows about this new organisation. Despite its creation, I still think it would be worthwhile for the Minister of Labour to
discuss this problem privately with selected leaders of the Trade Union movement, as suggested in paragraph 4(b) of my covering note. In
the past, officials of the Ministry of Labour have been most reluctant
to advise their Minister to touch anything of this sort. They are, as
you know, imbued with a laissez-faire philosophy and are, in particular, frightened to death of doing anything which might be thought to

impair the impartiality of their Minister as a 'conciliator' in industrial disputes. But this particular problem – of preventing Communists from capturing key posts in the Unions – is nothing whatever to do with conciliation functions; and the health of the Trade Union movement is a matter which the Minister of Labour can properly show an interest. I should be interested to know what attitude the present Minister of Labour takes to this problem. I hope very much that he may be willing to do what he can to assure himself, in private conversations, that responsible Trade Union leaders are taking adequate steps to meet this threat. And I think myself that he could go further and ask whether there is any help which Government could give them, unobtrusively, in this struggle.

[With Eden's approval, the Minister of Labour held a meeting with Sir Vincent Tewson, Sir Tom Williamson and Mr Heywood on 5 July 1956, at which they discussed portions of the Security Service paper. The trade unionists pressed in particular for government help in proving that Communists were cheating in union elections and the minister thought that this was one of a number of areas where the Security Service might be able to offer effective help.]

Minute by the Cabinet Secretary, Norman Brook, to Prime Minister, Anthony Eden, 'Communism and the Trade Unions (Gen. 526/1)', 30 May 1956, PREM 11/1238, PRO.

9.6 The IRA, 1966

By 1966 concern about the IRA was gradually increasing in Whitehall and appeared regularly on the agenda of JIC meetings. MI5 were preoccupied with the Cold War and did not, at that time, consider it a matter for them. But the Chiefs of Staff were anxious that the right organisation was set up to handle 'up to date information on the IRA threat'. They opted for a 'special organisation' within the MoD's Defence Operations Centre for this task.

AIR MARSHAL MAGUIRE, Deputy Chief of the Defence Staff (intelligence) said that he had discussed his note at a meeting of the Joint Intelligence Committee (JIC) that morning. In the course of considering how best the information on IRA activities could be handled and passed to the operational branches of the Services, the wider application of a similar organisation to serve Whitehall had been considered. The Director General of the Security Service [Martin Furnival Jones] was of the opinion that IRA activities constituted a 'law and order' problem and were not a security one. Crimes arising would be dealt with by the normal processes of law and the correct channel for assessment was through the Special Branch. The Home Office representative had agreed that the Central Current Intelligence Plot (CCIP) would be set up by the Special Branch.

The view of the JIC at the moment was that we had not arrived at the stage for a Current Intelligence Group (CIG) to be set up, and action would lie between the Special Branch and local police forces with Special Branch keeping the CCIP.

In discussion, the following points were made:

a. Although accepting the views of the JIC ... it was important to get early and adequate information on these aspects.

b. Intelligence should be fed into a central cell in the MoD and it was suggested that the Defence Operations Centre (DOC) was best equipped for this task ...

COS (66) 15th meeting, Confidential Annex, (2) 'Irish Republican Army Threat', 17 March 1966, DEFE 4/197, PRO.

9.7 **MI5 and electronic bugging, 1966**

By April 1966 the Postmaster General, Tony Benn, had become increasingly concerned about the threat of electronic eavesdropping posed by a new generation of 'microbugs' facilitated by transistors and miniaturisation. Somewhat to his surprise, he was informed by civil servants that his own department had licensed their use by private detective agencies. However, his hopes for new legislation in this area posed complicated problems.

This afternoon Ryland and Lillicrap [senior civil servants] came and we had a long discussion about eavesdropping and the new menace of microbugs. I want a select committee to sit on this but apparently the Home Office are worried that if a select committee is set up, it will lead to awkward questions about the devices used by the security services. This seems to me just making a monkey out of the House of Commons and trying to preserve secrecy over an important area of public interest for one particular reason ... For my part I want regulations making it an offence to eavesdrop using radio microphones or to intercept telephone conversations and listen to and record them. But I can see that I shall have some difficulty about this. No doubt every other department will brief its Minister against me and I daresay I shouldn't carry this through a ministerial committee.

Tony Benn, *Out of the Wilderness, Diaries 1963–1967* (London: Hutchinson, 1987), diary entry for Tuesday 9 April 1966, p. 403.

9.8 **Electronic bugging and foreign diplomats, 1967–68**

MI5 and SIS were separated more by geography than by function. Much intelligence-gathering against foreign diplomats in London was conducted by MI5, albeit there was inter-service co-operation. Technical surveillance of visiting dignitaries and delegations seems to have been fairly routine. A frequently alleged example is surveillance of the delegations attending the Lancaster House talks on the future of Rhodesia in 1979. Two diary entries by Tony Benn, reproduced below, the first as Postmaster General, the second as Minister of Technology, show that ministers routinely received this material. The second diary entry also underlines the importance that Britain has long attached to economic intelligence, which is rarely discussed in the literature.

Monday 6 February 1967
Premier Kosygin's visit to Britain [Soviet Premier] ... I might add here that the security services bugged Kosygin during his visit. I know this because I got a mysterious memorandum from the security services, reporting something they had picked up on tape that Kosygin had said about Pompidou. I didn't find it very useful, as it happened, except that it indicated how very close Kosygin and Pompidou were, due to de Gaulle's Eastern policy.

Monday 14 October 1968
Had lunch with Klaus von Dohnanyi [the German Secretary of State

for Economic Affairs] at Admiralty House. The security services had given me a secret note on what he had said, namely that he thought the Germans would assign leadership to us on the multi-role combat aircraft so long as we went in on Airbus. It shows the security people are always at work, even on our alleged allies.

Tony Benn, *Out of the Wilderness, Diaries 1963–1967* (London: Hutchinson, 1987), p. 488; and, *Office Without Power, Diaries 1968–72* (London: Hutchinson, 1988), p. 106.

10
Moles and defectors from the West

10.1 The Igor Gouzenkou case, 1945–46

During the war some Soviets officials with knowledge of the extent of espionage against the West had defected, only to be met with official disinterest. In late 1945, when Igor Gouzenkou, a cipher clerk working for Soviet military intelligence (GRU) at the Soviet Embassy in Ottawa, defected with considerable information about Soviet espionage in the West, he too was initially regarded as an unwelcome embarrassment. However, his information pointed the way to the first 'atom bomb spy' to be exposed, the British scientist Dr Alan Nunn May. A public enquiry followed in Canada in 1946. More importantly, many in London saw this episode as confirming the need for a harder line on communism. MI5 officers despatched to Canada were instructed to press for tough action. In London, the Foreign Office Russia Committee was instructed to prepare a special study of the Gouzenkou case and decided to acquire 400 copies of the Canadian 'blue book' report on the Gouzenkou case to alert Whitehall and Westminster to the dangers of Soviet activities.

[The Gouzenkou case reveals ...]

(a) The uncanny success with which Soviet Agents were able to find Canadians who were willing to betray their country by supplying secret information to a foreign power.

(b) The Soviet Government worked almost exclusively through the Communist Party and by means of Communist cells.

(c) That the Soviet Government paid special attention to subjects affecting the post war defence of Canada, the US and the UK, and that they were successful in getting substantial quantities of very secret information about Radar, Asdic and new types of explosives and propellants in addition to atomic energy.

Minute on the Gouzenkou case from Neville Butler to the Permanent Under-Secretary, Sir Orme Sargent, 10 August 1946, N10/992/10772/38, FO 371/56912, PRO.

10.2 **Herbert Morrison and the Gouzenkou case, 1946**

In Whitehall opinion varied as to the nature of Britain's long-term response to the Gouzenkou case. The Secretary of State for the Dominions, Viscount Addison, believed that enough fuss had been made. The Home Secretary, Herbert Morrison, believed further action should be taken to highlight its importance. In November 1946 he was still pressing the matter on the Prime Minister, Clement Attlee. He suggested that the BBC produce a programme on the subject and that the Trades Union Congress (TUC) and the Labour Party distribute books on the subject. Questions were arranged in the House of Commons to generate press interest. At this time plans were under way for an anti-Soviet propaganda (see below document 13.2) section. However, the Chairman of the Labour Party declined to assist and the Cabinet would not authorise an energetic propaganda offensive against the Soviet Union until early 1948.

I have had some correspondence with Addison and McNeil on the question of securing further publicity for the contents of the Report of the Canadian Royal Commission on the spy case. It seems to me that in view of their sensational and dramatic character they have received extraordinarily little attention here and that the public have hardly begun to believe what happened in Canada and the implications for us.

More emphasis might be laid on the fact that Zabotin [a GRU officer and Gouzenkou's immediate superior] was particularly instructed to collect information on the post war defence plans for Canada, the UK and the USA (c.f. p. 619 of the Report), and also on the allegations that the Soviet Government was secretly preparing for a 3rd World War (p.638/39). A further point to which it would, he suggests, be worth drawing attention is that the Russians discouraged certain selected sympathisers among certain categories of the popula-

tion from joining the Communist Party openly (p.69). In fact they
were instructed to keep their membership of the Party from the
knowledge of their acquaintances who were themselves members ...
    ... There would be scope for an abridged version of the Report:
indeed it could be quite a thriller with plenty of human interest. We
should perhaps approach the TUC ...

Home Secretary, Herbert Morrison, to Prime Minister, Clement Attlee,
28 November 1946, N15403/10772/G38, FO 371/56913, PRO.

10.3 Australian leaks and the formation of the Australian Security Intelligence Organisation, 1949

One of the first leaks of classified information to the Soviets
to be identified after the war was from the Australian Department of External Affairs. This included some of the earliest
anti-Soviet planning documents prepared by officials working under the British Chiefs of Staff. This news, provided by
the VENONA codebreaking effort (see document 2.2 above),
had a profound effect upon UK–US–Commonwealth relations. The United States, already nervous about security
because of the arrival of new members such as India and Pakistan, whose security was unproven, decided to place a security 'embargo' on Australia and reduced the scope of defence
co-operation with the Commonwealth generally. This was
especially unwelcome for Britain, which was attempting to
restore its nuclear relationship with the United States.
Accordingly, in 1949 the British Prime Minister, Clement
Attlee, despatched the head of MI5, Sir Percy Sillitoe, to
investigate. He was accompanied by Roger Hollis, the head
of MI5's C Branch, who stayed on to help set up the Australian Security Intelligence Organisation (ASIO), an Australian
equivalent to MI5. However, despite Attlee's efforts, American concerns were not easily placated and in 1950 the security 'embargo' on Australia had been only partly lifted.

Dear Mr President,
    You may remember that in January of this year we exchanged Top
Secret and Personal letters on the security situation in Australia. Subsequently you invited Sir Frederick Shedden of the Australian De-

fence Department to visit Washington for discussions with your Secretary of Defence. In anticipation of this visit in May, I am anxious you should know that I have in the meantime received most reassuring reports from Australia.

In the past three months the Government has taken certain definite measures to improve the security situation, the most impressive and comprehensive of which has been the creation of a new Security Service. In selecting as its first Director General a Judge of the Supreme Court of South Australia, the Australian Prime Minister has given a clear indication of the importance which he attaches to the establishment of adequate security machinery. Mr. Justice Reed, who acquired considerable experience of security problems during the war, has already assembled a nucleus of hand-picked men and started work. The new Service has been given a satisfactory charter and ample resources. While it will be closely linked with other Civil and Service security authorities and able to improve security throughout the whole Australian Government Service, its sources of information and records will be entirely within its own control. Thus it will henceforth be possible for highly confidential and delicate investigations to be undertaken.

I hope you will agree with me that in taking the above steps the Australian Government is displaying firm determination to improve security in Australia. Throughout the past months, officers of the British Security Service have been aiding and advising the Australians towards this end and it is from their reports to me that I have felt able to send you this encouraging account. Sir Frederick Shedden will doubtless be able to add much more to what I have said. My hope is that he may be able to restore the old confidence which existed between the United States of America, Australia and ourselves over the handling of defence secrets of all kinds.

Clement Attlee to Harry S. Truman, 4 April 1949, Personal, PSF Subject File (A-Attlee) Box 170, Harry S. Truman Memorial Library, Independence, Missouri.

10.4 **Kim Philby and SIS–CIA co-operation, 1949**

In the literature on Soviet 'moles', Kim Philby and Donald Maclean still vie for the dubious honour of the most

135

damaging Soviet agent within British government. This document illustrates the sort of routine access that Kim Philby enjoyed on succeeding Peter Dwyer as head of the SIS station in Washington in late 1949, where his principal duty was to liaise with his American counterparts in the CIA. Philby was dismissed in 1951 because of his association with the proven Soviet agent, Guy Burgess, but the case against Philby remained uncertain until 1963. The confirmation that Philby was a Soviet agent was a most profound shock to some of his colleagues in SIS and the CIA.

MEMORANDUM FOR THE RECORD:

1. A conference was held at 1530 in General Anderson's office 16 November to discuss the proposed Central Intelligence Agency radio base in the United Kingdom. The following were present:

CIA
Admiral Hillenkoeter [Director, CIA]
Col. Rob Schow [Assistant Director for Special Operations]
Mr Franklin Lindsay
Cmdr. Johnson (CIA Communications)
Mr Orwin (CIA Communications Engineer)
Lt Col. R. Ellis
BRITISH
Air Vice Marshal Edward Barker Addison (Chief Signals Officer, RAF)
Group Capt. Bell (RAF Staff)
Mr Peter Dwyer (British Emb.) [Head of SIS station]
Mr Philby (British Emb.) [Head of SIS station designate]
U.S. AIR FORCE
Maj. Gen. S. E. Anderson
Col. O. L. Grover
Lt. Col. J. A. Kelly

2. The CIA proposes to establish a radio base in the United Kingdom for intelligence purposes. The station is to be established, operated, financed, and manned by CIA personnel, logged as an RAF radio station, and the U.S. Air Force in the United Kingdom to be used as security cover for this operation. They further stated that this project had been informally cleared by all interested (U.S. and U.K.) agencies ...

5. Air Vice Marshal Addison, Chief Signals Officer of the RAF, agreeable to the project in principle, is returning to London within the next two or three days. He stated he would contact the appropriate persons in the Air Ministry and will then advise the Director of the CIA as to the proper procedure to follow in order to obtain formal approval of this project. Further, he will contact General Johnson, Commanding General of the Third Air Division, to acquaint him with the purpose of the operation.

Memorandum of a conversation by the Chief of the USAF Psychological Warfare Division, Colonel O. L. Grover, 17 November 1949, Programmes of Special Interest No. 1 England, RG 340, USNA. (I am indebted to Len Scott and Stephen Twigge for drawing this document to my attention.)

10.5 **Maclean and Burgess: a damage assessment, 1955**

This US JCS document reviews the impact of major defections four years after the event. It illuminates the difficulty of assessing the impact of the more famous defections upon the Western intelligence community. Much of the literature points to an intense climate of mutual suspicion which imposed restrictions on co-operation, but elsewhere, as this document makes clear, there seems to have been little real action or concern.

1. Attached is an Enclosure which is a copy of a memorandum on the above subject from the Acting Deputy Director of Intelligence of the Joint Staff.
   2. I am concerned with the security implications connected with this matter and feel that the JCS should discuss the problem in the near future. It is apparent that the circumstances surrounding the defection of these individuals were known to certain U.S. officials in 1951. Yet, if faced with the question in 1955, we could show little or nothing in the way of positive action which has been taken either to correct past mistakes or prevent future repetition of these mistakes. Recent renewal of interest in these defections raises the possibility that we might soon be faced with answering such questions.
   3. I recommend that the enclosure be shown to each Service

Secretary.
(Sgd)ARTHUR RADFORD

Memorandum by Chairman of the US JCS, Arthur Radford, for General Twining, General Taylor, Admiral Burke, General Sheperd, 26 October 1955, CM-221-55, 'National Security Implications Resulting from the Defection of British Diplomats, Donald Duart McLean [sic] and Guy DeMoncy Burgess', Papers of the Joint Chiefs of Staff, 1954–6 CCS 325 (6-4-46) Sec.14, RG 218, USNA.

1. A study of the available information on the two British diplomat defectors, Donald Duart McLean and Guy Frances DeMoncy Burgess, has been made with a view toward estimating the national security implications arising from their defection to the Soviets.

2. In their youth and through college, both men knew each other, both had decided leftist inclinations. It is believed that they were actually recruited by the Soviets at this time, and were trained for the espionage job they were to do later. Of the two, McLean appears to have had access to very nearly all sensitive material in the British Foreign Office from the time he entered there until his defection. Burgess on the other hand appears to have been in and out of foreign office work and by comparison had only limited access to sensitive material. However, he appears to have had complete control of McLean so, together the two were a formidable, unsavoury, team.

3. McLean entered the British Foreign Office October 11, 1935, remaining in London until September 24, 1938. At this time he was sent to the Embassy in Paris until June 18, 1940, after which he remained in London until May 1, 1944. At this time, he was placed in the Embassy in Washington where he remained until September 1, 1948. From November 6, 1948 until May 1950, he was in Cairo, Egypt where an alcoholic breakdown occurred. He returned to England and resumed duty as head of the American Department of the Foreign Office in London in October 1950 until his disappearance, 25 May 1951.

4. Burgess was a History Professor at Cambridge 1934–1935. From 1935–1938, he was with the BBC working with anti-nazi propaganda. From 1938–1941, he was with Section MI-6 of British Intelligence, 1941–1944 another tour with the BBC, 1944–1948 Foreign Office working primarily in the private office of Minister of

State, Hector McNeil. From 1948–1950 he was in the Far Eastern Department of the Foreign Office after which he was sent to the British Embassy in Washington still in Far Eastern Affairs. He was sent back to England on May 1, 1951 for reprehensible conduct and was notified he was finished in the Foreign Office. On May 25, 1951 he defected to the Soviets in company with McLean.

5. From these two career sketches it is apparent that McLean was the one with access to almost all sensitive information. During his tour in Washington, McLean was occupied with problems of postwar policy to be followed in Germany, France, Belgium and Holland. He represented the Embassy on matters dealing with the political aspects of Atomic Energy and attended all US/UK/Canadian discussions concerning cooperation between these countries, arrangements for raw materials, future production, etc. He was head of the Chancery Section of the Embassy and had access to all incoming and outgoing communication as well as supervision of the Code Room of the Embassy. After his lapse in Cairo, 1948–1950, he resumed the same type of duties in London from October 1950 to May 25, 1951.

6. From the date of defection until now, periodic out-bursts against the British Foreign Office have appeared in various organs of the British press. It has been determined that these two men definitely went over to Russia and are still there. Our FBI evaluates both men as Soviet Espionage Agents. They probably operated in that capacity throughout their time in public office and were apparently protected by others in even higher places, some of whom are alleged to be still occupying key positions.

7. Evaluating the available data on the activities of these two men the following conclusions are drawn:

a. Both Burgess and McLean were Soviet agents for many years prior to their defection. They were apparently protected from exposure and dismissal for a long time by other highly placed officials in the British Government, particularly in the Foreign Office.

b. McLean had access to practically all high level plans and policy information that were Joint US/UK/Canada projects. As Code Room Supervisor, he naturally had access to all U.K. diplomatic codes and ciphers as well as the opportunity to scan all incoming and outgoing communications.

c. In the fields of US/UK/Canada planning on Atomic Energy, US/UK postwar planning and policy in Europe and all by-product information up to the date of defection undoubtedly reached Soviet hands probably via the Soviet Embassy in London.

d. All U.K. and possibly some U.S. diplomatic codes and ciphers in existence prior to 25 May 1951 are in possession of the Soviets and of no further use.

8. Insofar as U.S. security implications are concerned it would appear that very nearly all US/UK high level planning information prior to 25 May 1951 must be considered compromised. Rather than attempt an estimate of how much damage has been done, it might be more profitable to quietly enquire into just who may be taking the place of these two men in the apparatus at this time. It is inconceivable that the pipeline dried up and operations stopped on 25 May 1951. It may be more appropriate to assume total compromise as of the defection date and continue the enquiry into present and future of Joint US/UK projects.

Enclosure: Memo from Colonel Robert Totten, USAF, Acting Deputy Director of Intelligence of Joint Staff, to Chairman, JCS, 18 October 1955, 'National Security Implications Resulting for the Defection of British Diplomats, Donald Duart McLean and Guy DeMoncy Burgess', ibid.

10.6 **Defection, diplomacy and the Geneva Conference, 1954**

Defectors from both East and West often appeared to be of greater importance for their role in the propaganda war than for the secret information that they brought with them. High-level discussions about the wider consequences of defector policy for East–West relations often accompanied decisions in this area. Here, in 1954, the Prime Minister led discussions about policy on Nikolai Khokhlov, an MVD [later the KGB] assassin who had defected to the West, complete with his unpleasant equipment, an electric pistol that fired special cyannide-tipped bullets. The meeting also considered the expulsion from Britain of two Soviet attachés for espionage. The propaganda advantages of publicising these issues had to be balanced against the danger of damaging the forthcoming Geneva Conference, of which Churchill and Eden had high hopes. It is worth comparing this episode with events in 1960 when, to Macmillan's irritation, revelations about the loss of an American U-2 spy-plane destroyed a superpower summit in Paris (documents 7.9–11).

The meeting was called to consider:

a) Mr Selwyn Lloyd's minute of 29 April about the visit of Khokhlov to this country.

b) Mr Nutting's minute of May 1 suggesting that Khokhlov should give a Press Conference.

c) Sir Ivone Kirkpatrick's minute of May 1 about the proposed expulsion of two attachés at the Soviet Embassy.

The Prime Minister said he took an unfavourable view of the Khokhlov affair. There was no full corroboration of Kholhkov's statements as to his motives and intentions, and there was a serious danger that the proposed Press Conference would make a hero of the traitor and would engender anti-Russian feeling at a time when such feeling would be disadvantageous to our policy and to the international security we were seeking. The Foreign Office representatives said that this was the fifth defection of a member of the N.V.D [sic] in the last two months and that, despicable as they may be, it was important to encourage further would be defectors to come over to the Western Powers in order to undermine the Soviet Spy System and to obtain information about possible traitors who might still be working in the British Services.

Although Khokhlov's idea to mobilise democratic public opinion to save his wife (which the Prime Minister thought was tantamount to arousing anti Russian hate) was a forlorn hope, to allow him to have a Press Conference would demonstrate to would be defectors that we did not treat such people inhumanly.

The Prime Minister said that, if as a matter of policy we wanted to stir up anti Russian feeling, there was no shortage of material, but he thought it would be a wrong policy at the present time especially during the Geneva Conference. If the whole matter were referred to the Foreign Secretary, and if Mr Eden pressed for the proposed action to be taken, he would be prepared to reconsider his attitude; otherwise he was totally opposed to any Press Conference. He would agree in any case to the expulsion of the Russian attachés, but thought that should be postponed as long as possible without the facts leaking to the Press through police officers who knew about them. [They had been caught attempting to recruit serving British officers for espionage purposes.]

It was agreed:

1) To expel the Russian attachés at a date to be arranged by Sir Ivone Kirkpatrick after he had consulted the Police Authorities.

2) To abandon, without consulting the Foreign Secretary [Anthony Eden], the proposal that Khokhlov should have a Press Conference.

Record of a meeting of the Prime Minister, Winston Churchill, with the Under-Secretary of State for Foreign Affairs, Anthony Nutting, and officials Sir Ivone Kirkpatrick and John Rennie, 1 May 1954, PREM 11/773, PRO.

10.7 **Philby, Burgess and Maclean, 1963**

In 1963, when Kim Philby fled to Moscow and his real allegiance was finally established, there was widespread indignation. Many had not been informed of the long-term suspicions of MI5, and of some in SIS, that it was Philby who had tipped off Burgess and Maclean, allowing them to escape the enquiry that was closing in on them in 1951. Philby had left SIS in 1951, but had maintained an informal association into the 1960s. In 1963 Herbert Morrison was one of those supremely indignant about how little he had been told. He sought and obtained a memorandum from the Foreign Office outlining the pattern of events during his short tenure as Foreign Secretary in 1951.

Burgess and Maclean

Mr Herbert Morrison MP became Foreign Secretary in March 12, 1951. At this time an investigation by the Security Service had been going on for over two years into a leakage of information to the Russians which had taken place in Washington in 1944 and 1945.

By mid-April 1951, investigations had reached the stage at which D.D. Maclean had come under suspicion, though he was not the only possible candidate. On April 17, Sir William Strang explained the background to Mr Morrison and told him of the decision, taken at a meeting held the previous day, that the Security Service should investigate Maclean's past history and associations and his present activities. Mr Morrison agreed with this course of action.

On May 25 Sir William Strang submitted to Mr Morrison a summary of the facts in the case and a proposal that Maclean should be interviewed by the Security Service between June 18 and 25. Mr Morrison agreed to the proposal that Maclean should be interviewed. On the same evening Maclean and Burgess left England.

On May 29 Mr Morrison was told that Maclean had disappeared.

Philby
We have no indication that Mr Morrison was ever told, while Foreign Secretary, that Philby was suspected of having tipped off Maclean. Nor was the financial settlement made to Philby when he resigned in July 1951 mentioned to Mr Morrison.

Foreign Office to Herbert Morrison, 19 July 1963, with enclosed memorandum, Burgess and Maclean file, 8/5, Morrison Papers, British Library of Political and Economic Science.

10.8 The escape of George Blake, 1966

George Blake was an SIS officer convicted of espionage for the Soviet Union in May 1961 and sentenced to forty-two years imprisonment. He escaped from Wormwood Scrubbs Prison in October 1966 and made his way to Moscow via East Germany. The account of the subsequent meeting held by the Prime Minister, Harold Wilson, reproduced below, indicates the nature of the procedures adopted by SIS when Blake was first identified, and the sort of cross-party consultation that had, by then, become fairly routine in security matters.

George Blake
The Prime Minister invited Sir Dick White to explain the relevant security considerations. *Sir Dick White* said there were two main aspects. First, the security and vital interests of the State. In this respect he felt on completely firm ground in saying that Blake had no access to information affecting the security of the State since September 1960: and indeed very little information of that nature before that date. His escape could therefore cause no further damage in this respect, and it was fair to say that he had equally done little harm before he was caught. Secondly, Service Security. Here again there were two aspects :-

    (a) Damage to personnel security for members of the S.I.S. This had been carefully assessed when Blake was caught and the Service divided into 3 categories. Those in the most sensitive category who had certainly been identified through Blake's disclosures would never be transferred again into positions where they would be vulnerable to Soviet intelligence and a number of them would in any case be gradually withdrawn from the Service as opportunity occurred. In respect of those in other categories, this aspect would be constantly in mind in relation to their future availability, even those in the least sensitive category would never be posted anywhere where the Russians might be a danger to them.

[Sub para. (b) deleted and retained under Section 3(4).]

Sir Dick White said that it might be argued that the interrogation to which Blake had been subjected might be of value to the Russians by giving them an indication of the direction in which the questions had been pointing. Blake had been interrogated by S.I.S. 42 times. He had been entirely free and frank in his replies; and had made it clear that he had passed to the Russians as routine any information, written or oral, which came into his possession ...

The Prime Minister said that the escape also involved Blake's use against us in a politically embarrassing sense, e.g. on the analogy of the Penkovsky Papers, but his was not of course a security point. *Sir Dick White* said that the Russians might be more likely to try to exploit his escape to damage Anglo-American relations in the intelligence field. Their constant purpose, in the furtherance of their own interest, was to drive a wedge between us and the Americans on counter-intelligence work. Any Soviet success here could be damaging to us. But we had briefed the Americans since Blake's escape in order to minimize any risk of this. Sir D. White was still inclined to doubt whether the Russians had got Blake. Whereas Lonsdale had refused to answer interrogation, Blake had admitted everything very fully. There was not therefore any very strong Soviet obligation to him. They might conceivably give him some money and leave him to work out his own future ...

On 31 October 1966 the Prime Minister, Harold Wilson, received the Leader of the Opposition, Edward Heath, accompanied by Sir Alec Douglas-Home in his room at the House of Commons. Also present were the Foreign Secretary, George Brown, and the head of SIS, Sir Dick White, who addressed the meeting, PREM 13/952, PRO.

11

Positive vetting and official secrecy

11.1 Security and the problem of European co-operation, 1948

Although the United States increasingly came to regard the British as a security risk, both the British and the Americans regarded their European allies as worse. France and Italy were seen as especially problematical. In the late 1940s the Communists had come close to forming a government and some departments were considered to be heavily penetrated by Soviet agents. The issue of how to exchange information with the French, especially in the context of a tripartite Anglo-American-French command like Supreme Headquarters Allied Powers Europe (SHAPE), was a vexed one. The views of the British Chiefs of Staff are outlined below.

II. CURRENT CONSIDERATIONS
3. The British Chiefs of Staff conclude in the case of France, because of extensive penetration of the political system by Communists, a natural garrulous tendency in the French character, a certain decline of moral standards in Europe, a French lack of security consciousness, and the possibility that present ministers may be replaced by less reliable persons, that any staff talks that may be held with France can be considered secure only if information is issued for the personal use of the officers concerned and may be delivered orally by them only to their immediate superiors provided it can be guaranteed those superiors are not Communist or fellow travellers. The Navy is estimated most secure, the Army less secure, and the Air Force, being most heavily infiltrated, less secure.
4. It is concluded by the British that Communist penetration in Holland, Belgium and Luxemburg is negligible, and that security arrangements within those Governments and Armed Forces are reason-

ably satisfactory with the qualifications that security regulations within the Belgian Armed Forces could be improved, civilians employed at lower levels of the Netherlands War Ministry are not entirely reliable, and security generally in Luxemburg is probably of a low order.

5. There is a danger that should these countries hold staff talks with France they may pass classified information to the French which they have received from the British.

Memorandum from General Cabell, USAF Intelligence, to General Spaatz, US StrategicAir Command, 26 March 1948, Top Secret, Memo: 'SecurityAspects of Possible StaffTalks with France (TABA), Belgium, Holland and Luxemburg (TAB B)', Director of Intelligence USAF HQ files, File 2-1200-1299, Box 40, RG 341, USNA.

11.2 Positive vetting, 1951

Very limited security screening was introduced by theAttlee administration with some reluctance in 1947 in the face of problems relating mostly to government scientists who were communists. Several related issues increased the pressure: revelations about Communist penetration in Britain, Australia and Canada; worries about the security in the New Commonwealth states; and problems persuading the United States to exchange information on atomic weapons. In October 1951, in the last days of the Labour government, and as a result of requests from American atomic energy officials, Clement Attlee rather reluctantly agreed to a more rigorous system which became know as positive vetting.

(3) General Morgan said that the thing which bothered him most about his set-up was the security situation. He indicated that the Government's decision regarding revised security procedures which was made as the result of the recent U.S.–U.K. security talks in London has not yet been implemented because the Cabinet has not yet given final approval. He explained that the contemplated changes had important internal political potentialities, and gave his private opinion that nothing would be done before the elections. He was, however, optimistic that no matter which Party wins, the situation would be very quickly cleared up after the elections are over ...

Memorandum of a conversation by the Counsellor of the American Embassy in the United Kingdom (Penfield), with Lt. General Sir Frederick Morgan, British Controller of Atomic Energy, Top Secret, 9 October 1951, *FRUS*, 1951, Vol. I, *National Security Affairs, Foreign Economic Policy*, pp. 774–5.

11.3 Churchill and Soviet bugging devices, 1952

Between 1950 and 1952 a number of Soviet 'bugging' devices were discovered in British and American official buildings. On 14 October Churchill wrote to the Minister of Defence: 'This is most important. It shows how far the Soviets have got in this complex sphere. Please keep me informed.' An active programme of research into defensive security measures and also 'bugging' techniques for Britain's own offensive use then ensued.

In July 1950 the Air Attaché in H.M. Embassy in Moscow, while testing a wireless receiver, heard the voice of the Naval Attaché, who was in a nearby room, on the loudspeaker. Nothing could be found in the Naval Attaché's office, and the general opinion was that the Russians had installed a portable radio controlled transmitter, which they had succeeded in removing before it could be found.

2. In January 1952 a similar occurrence took place in the American Embassy in Moscow ... action (with a special British detector) resulted in the discovery ...

6. M.I.5 are considering what should be done in the case of certain particularly important rooms here.

[4 lines retained under Section 3(4)]

Current Investigation

8. At the request of the Joint Intelligence Committee, Sir Frederick Brundrett [Chief Scientific Adviser] is co-ordinating technical investigations in this country. The security authorities of the Foreign Office are carrying out the immediate investigation into apparatus of the type discovered in September.

9. Either independently or as a result of the original occurrence in 1950 at least three separate scientists in this country have developed miniature devices which would transmit voices in the room in which they are. All the devices are different in principle from that discovered in Moscow.

10. The major steps in the investigation are:-

(a) consideration of all the Moscow incidents in the light of the discovery of the object in September and the work done in this country, to ensure proper defensive action is taken:

(b) consideration of the prospects of developing devices suitable for offensive action by ourselves ...

MoD memorandum, 'Russian Eavesdropping', enclosed in Morrison (MoD) to Prime Minister's Private Secretary, John Colville, Top Secret, 13 October 1952, DEFE 13/16, PRO.

11.4 Positive vetting and the Foreign Office, 1955

> Although the practice of positive vetting was introduced in 1951, there were a number of problems and loopholes that were only gradually tightened. As the memoirs of the head of the Foreign Office Security Department make plain, the main impediment to the positive vetting programme was its huge cost, and this remained so into the 1960s.

So here I was Head of Security Department. It was by no means looked upon as a plum post in those days: indeed many members of the Service looked upon it with contempt and derision. Several of my colleagues in the Office wondered what I could have done to deserve so degrading a post ...

Largely because of the defection of Maclean and Burgess the Security Department had instituted 'positive vetting'. This complicated procedure involved the vetting of all Foreign Office members at home and abroad, whether administrative, executive or clerical. All had to nominate two persons, not members of the Service, and these were interviewed by members of the Security Department. The interviewers were all former members of the Diplomatic Service, mostly retired Ambassadors. They then gave me a report on each case, but as the Treasury would allow us only five men for this task I got at best only ten reports a week, often less. At that rate vetting all the members of the Diplomatic Service would take years. The system was also flawed in that those being vetted could nominate their own referees ... many of [the referees] protested to us and their members of Parliament at being interrogated by 'snarks' on the background and integrity of

148

their friends. So 'positive vetting', though largely effective, was in many cases a farce ...

... I went to see the Permanent Under-Secretary, the redoubtable late Sir Ivone Kirkpatrick, and told him of my fears that the Office would come in for adverse criticism in parliament when our very slow rate of positive vetting became an issue, as it was virtually certain to become. Sir Ivone had a most disconcerting and unnerving way of dealing with his problems: he took off his spectacles, chewed the ends of them and gazed quite expressionless at his interlocutor. This could go on for as long as a minute and it seemed on that occasion that it lasted not a minute but an hour. I had no idea what his reaction would be. At last he spoke: 'Of course we need many more staff on positive vetting. But the Treasury will not pay for one more than we have now. We have to manage with what we've got. Now your reaction, it seems to me, is that we should try to speed up ... But if you hasten the procedure and it happened that someone got through the net, everybody including the Opposition in the House would blame us, you and me, for taking insufficient care and being too haphazard in our methods: I do not want us to have to accept blame which rightly falls upon the Treasury ...'

So we carried on at the old pace. Far from making any inroads into the huge backlog, we were hardly able to keep abreast of the new intake into the Service and thus the number not yet vetted went on increasing ...

Sir Arthur de la Mare, K.C.M.G., K.C.V.O., *Perverse and Foolish: A Jersey Farmer's Son in the British Diplomatic Service* (Jersey: Le Haule Books, 1994), pp. 99–100.

11.5 **The nature of 'security risks' at GCHQ, 1957**

This document, produced by the Treasury for the Cabinet Personnel Security Committee, reveals the range of non-political characteristics regarded as rendering an individual a 'security risk' in 1957, albeit expressed in somewhat coy language. It also demonstrates the special nature of security problems at GCHQ, where the usual practice of transferring an individual to less sensitive work was rarely an option. The reality of these problems was revealed at Cheltenham more than a decade later by the Geoffrey Prime case.

1. The problem of the removal or dismissal of civil servants who are a security risk but not on grounds of Communist or Fascist associations was considered by the Committee twelve months ago (S(PS) (55) 8 and the Minutes of the Second and Fifth Meetings S(PS) (56) refer).

2. This problem is particularly acute in the G.C.H.Q., where there are very few non-secret posts to which an individual could be transferred.

3. The main difficulty arises in devising a suitable procedure to remove a civil servant from a P.V. [positive vetting] post on grounds of character defects alone, when there are insufficient grounds for making a disciplinary charge.

4. Some examples are: -

(a) schizophrenics, where the chance of recovery is problematical and the chance of a relapse equally problematical, although the man is not blameworthy and no charge can be made against him in this respect;

(b) where a man is living a very shady existence but has not been brought to Court: in these cases the information is confidential to the police;

(c) suspected homosexuals about whom there is no direct evidence on which to base the charge;

(d) cases of financial difficulties because of matrimonial entanglements;

(e) where a person has religious convictions, e.g. Jehovah's Witnesses, which require him to owe no allegiance to the Crown or to the temporal Government and may, in fact, require him to fight against both.

5. In most Departments the solution might be to transfer the civil servant to non-secret work; but this is seldom possible in the G.C.H.Q. because there are so few of these posts and almost all of them are in the lower grades. Moreover, the specialist training given to G.C.H.Q. staff more often than not makes them unsuitable for transfer to another Department. There is therefore no alternative to dismissal. But as in the majority of cases no case has been proved against the individual concerned, such action may be considered to be undesirable.

6. The Committee are invited to discuss this problem.

S.(P.S.)(57)(23), 'Civil Servants as security risks on other than Communist or fascist grounds', Note by the Treasury, 26 April 1957, Top Secret, CAB 21/4530, PRO.

11.6 **The political impact of security scandals, 1963**

Harold Macmillan's government was jeopardised in its last year by security scandals. The case of John Vassall, a Soviet spy in British naval intelligence, new revelations about Philby's treachery and, most importantly, the 'Profumo scandal' combined to suggest high-level cover-up and incompetence in the security field. In June 1963 John Profumo resigned as Secretary of State for War, after admitting intimacy with Christine Keeler, who had a simultaneous relationship with the Russian assistant naval attaché in London, a fact Profumo had previously denied. Macmillan claimed ignorance about the matter. Christine Keeler received a prison sentence, and her associate, Dr Stephen Ward, committed suicide before the judge could pass sentence. By June 1963, President Kennedy concluded that, as a result of Profumo, Macmillan was finished. This underlined the serious political dangers presented by such cases, aided and abetted by the rise of the tabloid newspaper, and this probably prompted the incoming Labour administration of 1964 to take a more conservative line on security matters.

Eyes only for President and Secretary of State ...
The Prime Minister is under heavy attack. On Monday next he must make the most difficult speech, followed by interrogation, of his long career in the House of Commons.

It is evident, although I must interpose the caveat that a foreigner is a mediocre judge of British behaviour, that in six days the standing of the Prime Minister has undergone a marked diminution. The reasons are not difficult to define.

In the Profumo case, the continuance of that now ruined man in Cabinet office, and his solemn denial to the House of any physical intimacy with Miss Christine Keeler, has given weight to alternative charges against the Prime Minster (1) that he was in collusion with Profumo in the telling of a palpable lie, or (2) that through naivete or stupidity, as well as because of an indolent disregard, or neglect of the warning of British security services, he took a personal assertion of innocence as an accepted fact. The counter argument of uncritical reliance on the word of a colleague and a friend is of little public avail in this connection.

I think few people believe that Macmillan, whose private integrity has not been questioned, would have connived at a clumsy attempt to avoid an almost inevitable disclosure if he had known that Profumo had lied. Nor would it consort with the character of the PM to have done so.

The second charge is more serious ...

No matter what tribunal or special committee may be appointed to review the security aspects of this affair, the UK people, their appetite for sensations already whetted by partial revelation, may reach, if subjected to further shocks, a determination to force out the existing head of government. There are constitutional and traditional impediments to accomplishing this with celerity, but once confidence has been too greatly undermined in rulers, ways of dismissing them are usually devised ... A sacrifice is increasingly demanded here, and the appointed lamb for the altar is the Prime Minister, who must already have appreciated the sad truth that no ingratitude surpasses that of a democracy.

Meanwhile, the lurid details of the involvement of degraded personalities like Dr. Ward, Miss Keeler and other nymphs, fan the popular imagination, inciting both meretricious and wholesome indignation in the public, who feel betrayed by dereliction in official circles ...

It is ironical and sad that la Keeler, who was led by the sleazy Dr. Ward through London streets, harnessed to a dog collar, might occasion the demise of a government. Her frank predilection for her 'hairy chested Russian', her laments for her beloved Profumo, who was less fortunate than her lucky Jamaican lover, do not create the image of a sensitive individual.

No one suspects at worst the Prime Minster of other than gullibility, or stupidity. He must, however, bear the burden of leadership, and concomitant criticism and atonement.

Telegram from the American Ambassador in London, David Bruce, to President Kennedy and Secretary of State, 15 June 1963, *FRUS* 1961–63, Vol. XIII, *Western Europe and Canada*, pp. 1132–4.

11.7 Cabinet secrecy and the thirty-year rule, 1965

In 1965 the Prime Minister, Harold Wilson, proposed that internal government documents, including Cabinet minutes and memoranda, should be released into the public domain after thirty years. But the new Public Record Office Act that eventually flowed from this had exception clauses, including Section 3(4), which in practice allowed government departments to retain sensitive material at will. Much of the material reproduced in this book was considered too sensitive for release at the thirty-year point and was withheld for a longer period.

Harold had a proposal to relax the fifty-year rule about the publication of Cabinet documents into a thirty-year one: said it would be good for our 'liberal image'. Dick [Crossman] supported vigorously, quoting the outrageously one-sided nature of the present position whereby former Cabinet ministers, with the approval of the PM, can scoop the pool lucratively with their memoirs at any time, *e.g.* Lord Avon. I discovered that an official secret is what we say it is. Ex-Cabinet ministers *are* bound by the Official Secrets Act but a current PM is free to decided what 'secrets' to reveal at any time. With typical establishment caution the Foreign Secretary wanted forty years, supported by Jim Callaghan, but the liberal image won, backed by supporting noises from [Anthony] Crosland and me.

B. Castle, *The Castle Diaries, 1964–1976* (London: Macmillan, 1990), entry for Thursday 5 August, p. 29.

11.8 **GCHQ security, 1966**

Positive vetting was introduced for government officials with access to sensitive material by the Attlee administration. The scope and scale of security measures in government departments was gradually increased during the 1950s and 1960s, with wider and wider categories of personnel being subjected to positive vetting. This was a reaction to the long stream of revelations about Soviet penetration – for example the public revelations about Kim Philby after his decamp to Moscow in 1963. In 1966 the Paymaster General, George Wigg, was asked to conduct a review of security in the Diplomatic Service, GCHQ and the Ministry of Defence. A section of the report dealing with GCHQ is reproduced below. It underlines the main impediment to implementing intensive security in large areas of government – its high cost. The presence of George Carey-Foster as Security Adviser to GCHQ in the 1960s is surprising since he was not regarded by everyone as an effective figure during his previous service as head of the Foreign Office Security Department, 1947–54.

Government Communications Headquarters

13. Although G.C.H.Q is a department of the Foreign Office and its Director is administratively responsible to the Permanent Under Secretary, it is autonomous to a considerable extent. The responsibility for security rests with the Director under the Permanent Under-Secretary. The Department operates in a highly sensitive field and the security problem is a serious one.

14. The Department is directly responsible for some 8,000 of the 11,500 concerned with Signals Intelligence (SIGINT); the remaining 3,500 are Service personnel for whom responsibility rests with the Service Departments. About half of the 8,000 are at Cheltenham (and a small London office); the other 4,000 are scattered at listening stations at home and abroad. With the exception of a very few officers, e.g. ancillary staff (616), all the staff are now positively vetted. The Department has its own team of Investigating Officers (twenty-one in number). Vacancies for Investigating Officers are normally advertised though contact is maintained with the Foreign Office from which some new recruits have been obtained. A number of the present team have been recruited from retired Cheltenham police officers; this has been found to be advantageous since the majority of G.C.H.Q. staff at Cheltenham are recruited locally and a considerable knowledge of the background and circumstances of the staff has been acquired by these retired police officers ...

16. As in the case of the Diplomatic Service a backlog of positive vetting has built up; and, like the Diplomatic Service, this backlog could be ascribed to particular circumstances. Of the total of 1,731 post requiring P.V. [positive vetting], 1,000 were brought into the total in 1961 when G.C.H.Q decided to P.V. all its Radio Operators, and during 1964 and 1965 G.C.H.Q took on approximately 3,000 staff from the Service Departments. In the latter case the P.V. of 1,360 had not been completed. The number of posts for which P.V. had not been started at 30th June, 1965 was nearly 700.

It was hoped that the backlog would have been cleared by the end of 1965 and the number of Investigating Officers was increased from twenty-one to twenty-five for this purpose. The elimination of the backlog was not, however, achieved ...

18. At my request the Director of G.C.H.Q. considered measures for effective monitoring within the Department. This was not any easy question because of the particular circumstances which prevail there.

Three separate types of classified papers are involved:-

(a) First, certain intelligence papers originate from G.C.H.Q. and are circulated in the form of top secret documents to several Government Departments [i.e. the intelligence product]. These papers are protected by special procedures which are administered by Communications Intelligence Security Officers (COMSOs) in each Government Department which receives the material. These officers are briefed by and remain in constant touch with G.C.H.Q. The procedures governing the handling of these papers conform to the general doctrine laid down by the Ministerial and Official Committees on Security. But they are more stringent than normal security arrangements: they are prepared in G.C.H.Q. and are based on the U.K./U.S.A. SIGINT agreement and take account also of current and relevant U.K. security regulations. They are submitted to the Security Sub-Committee of the London Signals Intelligence Committee (L.S.I.C.); they then go to the L.S.I.C. and finally to the London Signal Intelligence Board for approval. The principles on which they are based are approved by the Prime Minister at the time of issue. The current regulations were issued in June 1960. I am not entirely satisfied that these regulations should be promulgated without first being approved by the Ministerial Committee on Security and I have taken this point up with the Treasury.

(b) The second category of papers are registered papers received and produced by G.C.H.Q. in the normal conduct of business [i.e. policy and administrative documents]. All these papers are subject to registry or other control and easily lend themselves to monitoring checks. Spot checks are, therefore, easy during the normal working day but if a monitoring system is to be effective it must provide for checks without warning out of working hours. The Department has given very careful thought to the type of monitoring scheme which could be introduced. They have borne in mind the recommendation in the Security Commission's recent report about the desirability of spot searches of staff leaving buildings. They have considered whether this should be done but they reached the conclusion that it should not. One important factor in arriving at this decision was the effect that such an arrangement would have on staff morale. There are other practical difficulties, particularly in that the layout of the site at Cheltenham does not readily lend itself to such a system ...

(c) The third class of paper, which is probably peculiar to G.C.H.Q., consists of a large amount of top secret material which is generated in specialist branches of a number of divisions. This working material [i.e. that generated by cryptanalysts in breaking ciphers], most of which never leaves the branch, is not known to exist except among those officers who generate or work on it. It is not capable of being spot checked and for its protection the Department has to rely on the security arrangements within each branch, backed up by those of the headquarters as well as on the Department's personnel security. These arrangements consist of night checks to ensure that papers are locked away, security patrols, late leaving and abnormal attendance, e.t.c., checks ...

20. Following an invitation from the Director I spent a day at Cheltenham on 6th June during which I had further discussions with several of the staff. I am generally impressed with the Department's attitude towards their problems and with the readiness with which the Director is willing to examine such points as I have raised. There are one or two areas which I think require further study and these are being looked at. The main vulnerable area seems to me to be the number of ancillary staff (e.g. cleaners, labourers, etc.) who are not subject to P.V. At June, 1965 these totalled 616; since then, however, it has been decided that the 136 industrial labourers should be P.V'd. The total non-P.V. posts have therefore now been reduced to 480. The Director will examine this further with a view to the subjection of further ancillary staff to the P.V. procedures.

21. I have absolute confidence in the Director's attitude to security and his ability to grapple with both overall policy and day-to-day problems which arise. There is no one I have met who has impressed me more as being at grips with security matters. The thought, however, constantly comes to mind as to what would happen if the Director became ill and his influence and drive were lessened, for the Security Adviser (Mr. Carey Foster) does not arouse similar confidence. After careful consideration I therefore asked Mr. Palliser to obtain from the Foreign Office a paper giving their view of the situation; this is attached. To sum the matter up, it looks as if the Security Adviser works better at home than he does on the racecourse, an

expression which I shall be happy to explain if its meaning is not clear
to you. You will notice that in paragraph 5 of the note it is stated that
the Director has no one within G.C.H.Q. whom he could appoint
now to the post of Security Adviser. The question to which I continually return is whether the situation will be the same at the expiration
of Mr. Carey Foster's contract in March, 1968. Has not the time
come to think very seriously about Mr. Carey Foster's successor and
if there is no one inside G.C.H.Q. should we not look outside the
organisation and start to train a successor, for March 1968 is not
much more than eighteen months away?

Paymaster General, George Wigg, to Prime Minister, Harold Wilson,
enclosing 'The Organisation of Security in the Diplomatic Service and
Government Communications Headquarters', 17 August 1966, PREM
13/1203, PRO.

11.9 **The D notice affair and cable interception, 1967**

On Tuesday 21 February 1967, the *Daily Express* ran a story
entitled 'Cable Vetting Sensation' by the journalist Chapman
Pincher. This exposed the time-honoured practice whereby
commercial cable companies allowed government to see all
overseas telegrams. Subsequently photographs were published showing how bags of telegrams were routinely
collected from the companies in unmarked GPO cars and
Ministry of Works vans, inspected and quickly returned. Such
stories had hitherto been prevented by a press self-censorship
system in which newspapers respected 'D Notices', asking
them not to publish stories on defence-related issues which
might be prejudicial to national security. This system was co-
ordinated by the D Notice Committee, whose secretary was
Colonel Lohan. A public furore ensued and an enquiry was
held by Lord Radcliffe which focused on the D Notice system. The enquiry showed that the system had broken down
because the secret services were unwilling to brief Colonel
Lohan properly. The affair was also symptomatic of a sea
change in public opinion. Press and public were increasingly
reluctant to avoid discussion of secret service matters, a trend
accelerated by the publication of Kim Philby's memoirs the
following year. Westminster and Whitehall were also deeply
divided over the issue of what should enter the public

domain. This is illustrated in the minute from Harold Wilson to the Cabinet Secretary, Sir Burke Trend (who took a special interest in secret service matters), reproduced below. This discussed the recommendation of an inter-departmental committee that none of the Radcliffe Enquiry's report should be published (instead, a slim white paper was published in June). The last two paragraphs were added in Wilson's own hand.

My inclination now is to wash my hands of the whole affair and let the [official] machine decide how this should be handled. Indeed I feel I have now no alternative. Once an inter-Departmental Committee has produced a unanimous Report of this kind, on which Departmental briefs will be based, I could only secure the publication of the evidence by making clear to all my well-briefed colleagues that I must insist on publication. I have no doubt that I could be successful, but I have to reckon with the comments which will appear under the signature of a number of political journalists about the disagreements which I overrode. So probably the right thing for me is to accept that now this Committee has reported, the issue is closed ...

I should not propose to take any further Official advice on how I should address the House of Commons, either in my statement on publication, or in the Debate which follows. For the advice I received on February 21 has proved somewhat counter-productive so far as I am concerned. Once we reach the stage of a Debate, I feel my duties must be to the House of Commons. I feel I should give the House of Commons a full and frank account of what has taken place, as I see it ... qualified only by my overriding duty to see that nothing affecting security is made available to them ...

Further, I have to give the House the answer to the big question raised by Radcliffe in his Report, which I have now for the first time read. This is the question why, as Radcliffe feels and as we all now agree, the Secretary of the [D Notice] Committee, who ought to be sufficiently trusted to have all the necessary information, even on the most secret issues, made available to him, was not trusted on this issue? You and I know the answer and, since this is so germane to the main conclusions of the Report, I see no reason why the House should not know it ... While, however, the House cannot be made privy to the greater part of the evidence of the Director of G.C.H.Q., I think one part of his evidence is so relevant that I could not in honesty withhold it. That was the statement of the Director when he made it clear that the Secretary of the [D Notice] Committee could not have been told about these highly relevant issues because he had not undergone the appropriate security procedures. The House, of course, may well ask why, as I did.

There is also the statement of the Director of the Security Services to Lord Radcliffe ... that, whether or not he enjoyed the confidence of the Press, the Secretary did not enjoy the confidence of Whitehall.

... in the political phase, I handle the matter in whatever way seems right to me and ... I do not seek or ask advice. If I therefore withdraw from intervention at this stage, I shall be somewhat intolerant of intervention by the Official machine once we move into the political phase. I can assure you I shall consult the Paymaster General [George Wigg], whose concern for security matters is beyond all doubt. Indeed I feel that after nearly three years of Parliamentary silence he might well wind up the Debate, since I trust his judgement implicity on this matter ...

In other words, Burke, I know when I'm beat, provided the last battle is fought under my direction.

But I want you to be absolutely clear that whatever disagreements we have had – and I respect your motives and concern for my interests as you do mine – this whole sad episode will make no difference whatsoever to our relationship on other and far more important matters.

Prime Minister, Harold Wilson, to Cabinet Secretary, Sir Burke Trend, Prime Ministers' Personal Minute No. M63/67, 29 May 1967, Top Secret and Personal, PREM 13/1818, PRO.

11.10 **Operation FOOT: the expulsion of 105 Soviet intelligence officers from Britain, 1971**

In May 1971 Britain decided to take action to reduce the substantial and expanding nature of Soviet intelligence activities in the United Kingdom. The numbers of Soviet diplomats in London was very large, twice the number of British diplomats in Moscow; moreover, the staffs of organisations such as TASS and Aeroflot had mushroomed improbably. This combined contingent hid at least 120 Soviet intelligence officers and possibly as many as 200. It was decided that this represented an intolerable threat and 105 persons were expelled or denied visas for re-entry, an all-time world record. This matter was co-ordinated by the PUSD of the Foreign Office and discussion there centred on how to handle this without completely disrupting Anglo-Soviet relations. Moscow was shocked and KGB and GRU operations in London never recovered.

The documents released on this subject do not indicate why action had not been taken in previous years or why this matter suddenly caught British attention in early 1971. The primary motivation was in fact information from a number of defections, notably the defector Oleg Lyalin in the spring of 1971, a KGB officer in London, giving unprecedented detail of KGB operations in the UK. The main emphasis of Soviet espionage in Britain was upon scientific and technical intelligence. However, Lyalin belonged to a special war and crisis contingency section of the KGB, and his work was mostly identifying strategic installations for demolition and lists of key figures for assassination. It is not unlikely that some of those British officials discussing Operation FOOT were on these lists.

Soviet Intelligence Activities in the United Kingdom
Sir Denis Greenhill [Permanent Under-Secretary] ... Was it agreed in principle that the Russians must be cut down to size?

... *Sir Martin Furnival Jones* [Director of the Security Service] emphasised the weight of the Soviet attack. In the last fifteen years there had been evidence of penetration of the Foreign and Commonwealth Office, the Ministry of Defence, the Army, Navy, and Air Force, the Labour Party, Transport House and the Board of Trade. It was difficult to say exactly how much damage was being done. But it was equally difficult to believe that the Russians maintained such a large establishment at no profit. At least thirty or forty Soviet intelligence officers in this country were actually running secret agents in government or in industry. *'C'* [Sir John Rennie, head of SIS] agreed.

... *Sir Thomas Brimelow* [Deputy Under-Secretary] HM Ambassador in Moscow doubted if the game was worth the candle, and had suggested that our future partners in the European Economic Community might react badly. Sir Thomas Brimelow did not find these views convincing. We were open to public criticism for tolerating Soviet activities on their present scale for so long. It would be better to achieve reduction without a major row, but this would probably be impossible.

4. *Sir Burke Trend* [Cabinet Secretary] asked whether the Russians would not increase their 'illegal' operations [activities by those without diplomatic immunity] if we cut down their 'legal' residency, and consequently create greater problems for us. *Sir Martin Furnival Jones* said that this would be difficult, as 'illegals' were much more difficult to run, and could not themselves actively recruit ...

10. *Sir Burke Trend* said that we still had to consider whether the game was worth the candle. Sir Denis Greenhill agreed that we were particularly vulnerable to commercial reprisals and general beastliness. But he did not think the Russians would go so far as to break off diplomatic relations ... *Sir Martin Furnival Jones* said that, if we removed the 100 identified intelligence officers, it would take the Russians a very long time to repair the damage. He also pointed out that HM Commercial Counsellor in Moscow had expressed the view that our commercial position might be rebuilt within eighteen months to two years.

11. 'C' said that our allies in Western Europe, far from viewing our action badly, would probably welcome it. It was clear that the French were concerned about the numbers of Russians in their country. They might emulate our action ...

14. On timing, *Sir Burke Trend* said that it would be better to carry out the operation during the [parliamentary] summer recess ...

Record of a meeting in the Permanent Under-Secretary's Office on Tuesday 25 May 1971, at 3.30 p.m., Top Secret, reprinted in G. Bennett and K. A. Hamilton (eds), *Documents on British Policy Overseas Series III, Volume I, Britain and the Soviet Union, 1968–72* (London: HMSO, 1997), No. 66, pp. 339–43.

12
Intelligence and the 'end of empire'

12.1 The transfer of intelligence machinery, 1948

A key British activity associated with the end of empire was the transfer of the more secretive instruments of the British colonial state to post-independence governments. In many Asian and African countries, British intelligence staff stayed on for a while.

VI. PAKISTAN
2. Security organisation and efficiency.
The Pakistan Deputy Chief of Staff (who is British) has recently secured the approval of the Pakistan Government to the establishment of a Joint Counter-Intelligence Bureau, under the Joint Services Director of Intelligence, the main object of which is to ensure Service security, and of which a British Officer has been appointed the first head. On the civil side the Director of the Intelligence Bureau is a very experienced officer. He is intimate with his Prime Minister and has undoubtedly succeeded in convincing him as to the importance of security. He has recently visited the Security Service in London and impressed all he met with his grasp of the subject and his efficiency. He has agreed in principle to an exchange of Security Liaison Officers and when this has been effected it should lead to improved security. He is handicapped by lack of senior and experienced staff but such staff as he possesses is considered to be reliable.

Report by the Security Service: 'Security in the Dominions', Appendix A, JIC (48) 127 (Final), 'Disclosure of British Military information to Commonwealth Countries', 17 December 1948, Top Secret, Guard, L/WS/1/1074, IOLR.

12.2 **Intelligence and the Malayan Emergency, 1948–57**

In 1957 the Director of Military Operations (Malaya) reviewed the history of the Malayan Emergency and attempted to distil some lessons. His main conclusion was the importance of a Police Special Branch of adequate strength and quality to be able to predict future problems arising from subversion. 'Whatever this may cost', he advised, 'it will avoid far greater cost and danger later.'

Intelligence

53. In his first report on taking over the appointment of Director of Operations in April 1950 General Briggs wrote, 'unfortunately our Intelligence organisation is our "Achilles Heel" and inadequate for present conditions, when it should be our first line of attack ... We have not got an organisation capable of sifting and distributing important information quickly.' In May 1950 a Federal Joint Intelligence Advisory Committee was appointed to examine means of strengthening the Intelligence and Police Special Branch organisation and in August a Director of Intelligence was appointed. Efforts were made to recruit in the United Kingdom candidates for commissions who had experience in the Indian and other police forces. But it was over a year before an adequate number of trained officers were engaged for the Special Branch with an increment of Military Intelligence Officers to assist them ...

96. The Police Intelligence system (Special Branch) in Malaya has not only charted nearly every member of the enemy army, but has brought about the great majority of contacts resulting in eliminations. This has only been achieved where it has been possible to post really good men to Special Branch and to avoid unnecessary reposting; and also by integrating suitable Military Intelligence Officers into Special Branch. As with civil officials, quality and continuity in Special Branch has declined during the past year, though the Federation Government has recently given over-riding priority to money and manpower in an attempt to put this right. The control of militant Communism, before, during or after an armed revolt, will not be achieved unless such priority is given to Special Branch for suitable men, and the terms made generous enough to attract them. If necessary, posts must be filled through secondment from Army or other sources. There is no comparable investment against Communism.

Report by Director of Military Operations (Malaya), R. H. Bowen, 'Review of the Emergency in Malaya from June 1948 to August 1957', WO 106/5990, PRO.

12.3 **Malaya: Templer and centralisation in the 1950s**

In October 1960 the retired Field Marshal Templer, architect of victory in the Malayan Emergency, made a brief visit to Vietnam at the invitation of President Diem. He held a three-hour discussion with Diem and also met members of the US Military Aid Advisory Group. As well as setting out Templer's security approach in Malaya, this document underlines Templer's national and international prestige. This prestige lent force to Templer's recommendations for the reorganisation and centralisation of aspects of intelligence in the UK during the 1950s and 1960s. It also contributed to the demand for British security advice in developing countries during the 1960s and 1970s.

4. M. Diem is a great talker and the difficulty of getting any idea across to him is to choose the right moment to interrupt the discursive monologues to which he is prone. Field Marshal Templer decided to give him no time to get going but to seize the initiative right at the start ...

5. Field Marshal Templer then described the circumstances in which he was nominated High Commissioner after the assassination of his predecessor. Sir Winston Churchill, he said, had sent for him and looked him over for three days before deciding to appoint him. He travelled home with Sir Anthony Eden. They stopped for dinner in Montreal where a ninety-three year old Canadian statesman gave him the following advice. 'After you have been fourteen days in Malaya, type out for yourself not less than three nor more than five principles of policy. Keep one copy yourself and put the others in four separate banks. Then never in any circumstances deviate from them.'

6. At the end of his first fourteen days in Malaya, Field Marshal Templer said, he typed out the following:

(a) By every means – social organisation, improvements, information services – seek to gain the hearts and minds of the working population.

(b) At each centre, on each level establish an intelligence set-up consisting of a military officer, a policeman and a civilian administrator under the orders of the last named. If any of them fails to cooperate, throw him out.

(c) Pay particular attention to the junior officers in the Army, Police and Home Guard. It is Captains and Lieutenants – not Generals – who are in contact with the population.

7. At this stage the President took up a pad and wrote down Field Marshal Templer's three principles and he continued during the interview to take notes of what his visitor said. The Field Marshal next expanded on the need for a unified system of intelligence, both in the provinces and at the centre. When he arrived in Malaya, there had been two Army, one civilian and several political intelligence organisations. Such organisations must all be unified under one man who could be trusted. The President asked who he had been. The Field Marshal said that it had been an Englishman who had been seconded by the Security Service. It was still an Englishman but in six months' time it would be a Malay ...

[Paragraph 11 withheld under Section 3(4)]

12. Field Marshal Templer's opening statement took about forty minutes and my United States colleague tells me he has hitherto never known the President to take notes. The fact that it was possible to speak to M. Diem for forty minutes without being interrupted has indeed created a minor sensation among my colleagues here ...

British Ambassador in Saigon, H. A. Holler, to Foreign Secretary, Lord Home, Secret, 5 November 1960, No. 56, FO 371/159673, PRO.

12.4 General Templer's report on colonial security, 1955

In 1954 the Minister of Defence raised the problem of colonial security services as a generic issue, pointing out the heavy drain imposed on resources by the major counter-insurgency campaigns in Malaya and Kenya. He argued that a structure consisting of good intelligence, efficient security forces and well-trained colonial troops could have nipped such problems in the bud, and suggested a small committee to examine appropriate reforms to create this. In the event General Templer, flushed with successes in Malaya, was tasked to produce a report on the subject for the Cabinet Committee on

Colonial Security. Templer's Report confirmed what the Minister of Defence suspected and, despite the looming election, a number of the recommendations were acted upon. Colonial security was a matter of constant attention between 1945 and 1970, with cost, as this document makes clear, forming a major restraint on action.

General Templer has now finished his report on Colonial Security for the Committee on Security in the Colonies. This Committee has ceased to exist because Lord Swinton was its Chairman (not as Secretary of State for Commonwealth Relations but in his personal capacity) and I understand that Sir Norman Brook is proposing to wait until after the Election before putting up proposals for reinstituting it. Meanwhile the Colonial Office proposes to implement such of General Templer's recommendations as they can agree with other Departments.

General Templer's Report is long, but I think it would repay reading in full at your leisure. Meanwhile his introduction (Flag A pages 9–12) gives a summary of his proposals and you may wish to read this and also passages on Cyprus (Flag B) and Hong Kong (Flag C) now.

General Templer recommends more money for Intelligence and Police in the Colonies and a reorganisation inside both colonial administrations and the Colonial Office to ensure that Intelligence is properly collated and that the Police are well organised. He also proposes changes to the armed forces (mainly the Army) in the colonies which would involve handing them over to local control, but reducing their size and in particular cutting down on units such as artillery which are no longer useful in the atomic age. He estimates his savings from military reduction at £3.08 million, and the cost of his proposals for extending the Police and Intelligence Services at about £250,000 (capital sum) and about £70,000 (recurrent). The picture which General Templer paints of the present system of collecting and using Intelligence and of organising the police forces is certainly frightening.

Private Secretary, Philip de Zuluetta, to Prime Minister, Anthony Eden, 13 May 1955, PREM 11/2247, PRO.

12.5 **Cyprus and EOKA, 1958**

Despite the lessons learned repeatedly about the importance
of intelligence during more than a decade of post-war insurgencies, and Templer's report in 1955, the events in Cyprus in
the late 1950s still found the authorities initially unprepared
in this respect.

Intelligence.
Our overriding need now is a first class man to organise and co-ordinate intelligence (see my telegram No.1935). We have always been
weakest on the intelligence side and our effort against EOKA [Greek
Cypriot underground movement] cannot be fully effective until all
intelligence work is pulled together and given better central direction.
The Director of Operations very rightly gives this top priority and I
greatly hope that a man of the highest calibre can be found to take
charge of our intelligence organisation with the least possible delay.

Police.
We shall be submitting to you shortly two proposals for reinforcing
the police first in the Gazetted Officers ranks ... and second in the
cadre of interrogators working under the Special Branch ...

Political Warfare.
... I must frankly say that those which have had experience of successful activity of this kind in such places as Malaya and Kenya have not
been able to give us much practical assistance in our unique circumstances here.

Special Operations.
I shall reply to you separately on the question ...

Anti-Assassination Measures.
I shall report separately on new measures we are taking arising from
the EOKA murder of civilians ...

Governor and Commander-in-Chief, Cyprus, Sir Hugh Foot, to Colonial
Secretary, Alan Lennox-Boyd, No. 1966, 9 November 1958, Secret,
DEFE 13/97, PRO.

12.6 **The Cabinet Counter-Subversion Committee, 1964**

The Cabinet Counter-Subversion Committee was set up in 1964. Its remit was: 'To keep under review threats and potential threats by subversion, to British interests overseas; and, where necessary, to recommend and co-ordinate action to combat such threats.' Although it met only quarterly, its industrious Regional Working Groups met much more frequently. Its purpose was to address the advance of Communism in under-developed areas, particularly those areas in transition from Empire to Commonwealth status. Counter-measures took the form of economic and technical assistance, military and security advice, information and cultural activities including sponsored visits, administrative and educational training and what they described as 'other activities of an unattributable and covert nature'. By 1965 it was chaired by Sir John Nicholls of the Foreign Office and attended by a wide variety of officials from interested departments including MI5 and SIS – usually represented by Sir Dick White in person. The section below reporting the activities of one of its Regional Working Groups is typical.

XII. MAURITIUS AND THE SEYCHELLLES

23. *Mauritius*. The Working Group met on 25th January. They noted that considerable progress had been made on the subjects taken up at the previous meeting, notably the Premier of Mauritius had been indoctrinated on the Security Intelligence System; that following on the Deputy Chairman's meeting with the Governor last Autumn, special additional I.R.D. [propaganda] material had been sent to the Governor by the Colonial Office on Subversion through the Trades Unions in Africa and the N.C.N.A. [National Council on Native Affairs]; further action was in train to scrutinise the character of communist literature imported into Mauritius; and that the Services Community Relations projects we making progress. The Security Service have decided to introduce regular quarterly liaison visits to Mauritius. The Colonial Office informed the meeting about the prospects of constitutional talks later in 1965 and possible political and communal reactions arising therefrom.

24. *The Seychelles*. The Colonial Office Security Intelligence Adviser reported his impressions of his visit last Autumn. These highlighted the need for strengthening the Police Force, the re-establish-

ment of the Special Branch, as well as Economic and Social Development, particularly communications (an airfield). He described the activities of the two political parties and the problems arising from the American presence in the islands (e.g. the tracking station in Mahe) ...

SV (65) 9, 'Report on the Activities of Working Groups and Ad Hoc Meetings', 18 May 1965, CAB 134/2544, PRO.

PART VI

SPECIAL OPERATIONS AND 'BLACK' PROPAGANDA

A multitude of special operations units were formed on an extemporary basis during the Second World War. Some, like the Special Air Service (SAS) and the Special Operations Executive (SOE), scored notable victories. However, it is not widely realised that, at the same time, these 'private armies' were losing the bureaucratic battle in Westminster. Ill-disposed by nature to regulations and procedure, they had irritated established Whitehall departments and theatre commanders alike by pursuing what seemed like a separate foreign policy. The related area of propaganda also witnessed distasteful squabbling over rights and authorities. Eden's straightforward answer, articulated early in the war, was for the Foreign Office to take full control of all unconventional and para-political activities, but his senior official, Sir Alexander Cadogan, resisted the idea that they become a 'department store', responsible for such 'fantastic' things. Having alienated those in high places, in the winter of 1945–46 the SAS, SOE and the Political Warfare Executive (PWE) were all dissolved and their expertise dispersed, with limited attempts to preserve their unique skills.

Yet as early as May 1946, these capabilities were being revived. Within the Foreign Office, several officials who had been seconded to work with SOE and PWE during the war were increasingly convinced that these instruments were well-suited to prosecuting the Cold War, although the Cabinet remained unconvinced until 1948. The military were, if anything, more enthusiastic. Senior special operations figures who had retired, such as Sir Colin Gubbins and Fitzroy Maclean, pressed for revival, taking their own steps to ensure that personnel with 'special skills' could be recalled at short notice. The increasing pace of counter-insurgency in the colonies also saw a revival of such units, often on an *ad hoc* basis, to carry out unattributable activities.

171

By 1948 Britain had moved on from the idea of a mere defensive-offensive Cold War strategy and had committed herself to the idea of liberating some of the satellites of the Eastern Bloc. This commitment was not unqualified and Britain saw herself as singing a descant to a much better resourced American programme. These Western attempts at special operations, or in American parlance 'covert actions', in Communist countries were disastrous. The thorough Communist penetration of operations in places as far apart as Albania, the Ukraine, Poland and the Baltic states is now well known. Attempts to encourage dissent in Communist China were no more successful. Efforts in this field were further undermined by squabbling amongst the irascible exile organisations and the Allied secret services who tried their best to control them. Significant guerrilla campaigns were waged against the Soviet Union in the Ukraine and the Baltic states into the early 1950s, but they do not seem to have owed much to Western assistance. Knowledge about the existence of Western liberation efforts clearly had an impact on Stalin's already paranoid mind, but its precise effect on Soviet foreign policy has yet to be assessed.

Britain's disillusionment with 'Cold War fighting' had less to do with operational failure and more to do with the twin surprises of the Soviet atomic bomb in 1949 and the Korean War in 1950. 'Hot war' now seemed much closer and by the early 1950s Britain had come to view 'liberation' as dangerously provocative. These fears were underlined by American contingency planning for special operations on a massive scale in a future 'hot war' with the Soviet Union, and a vast expansion of US Special Forces in the 1950s. By contrast, Britain's special operations capability during this period grew only slowly, with the burden of responsibility being gradually passed from SIS to a revived SAS by the 1960s. The issue of how such wartime activities might be dealt with in areas controlled by multinational commands such as NATO was a perennial and thorny issue.

In direct contrast to this rapid disenchantment with Cold War 'fighting', Britain's attitude towards special operations in the Third World was marked by enthusiasm. The joint Anglo-American operation to instal the Shah in Iran and to reverse the nationalisation of the Anglo-Iranian Oil Company in 1953 was of British inspiration. Britain was increasingly favourable towards the American-inspired operations against President Sukarno in Indonesia, launched in part from Singapore in 1958. Meanwhile Harold Macmillan compared

Eden's obsession with 'getting Nasser down' with the charade of repeated American attempts to deal with Castro from 1959. In the 1960s SIS and the CIA were jointly involved in Africa. These operations in the Third World, despite their mixed record, were considered by London to be broadly more promising than intrusions into the Eastern Bloc.

The most significant development in this field was probably the effective revival of PWE, the wartime propaganda organisation, in 1948, in the form of the Information Research Department (IRD) and at least half a dozen associated bodies. These departments worked closely with the CIA and discreetly influenced British groups and movements in a manner which is still not fully understood. The deployment of IRD in a domestic context, sometimes with MI5, underlined the clear recognition that the clandestine Cold War was now a struggle between societies not states, and had no respect for the traditional Whitehall boundaries between home and overseas affairs.

13
Clandestine or 'black' propaganda

13.1 The 'Soviet Campaign Against this Country', 1946

By the spring of 1946 senior Foreign Office officials perceived an aggressive Soviet campaign against Britain. The tone seemed to have been set by Stalin's strident 'election speech' which forecast confrontation with the West. They character-ised this campaign as composed of economic warfare, propaganda and subversion, identifying the Soviet creation of international federations and world front organisations as an especially alarming aspect. The memorandum below reviewed all this and suggested a new British strategy of 'defensive-offensive'. This led to the creation of a new Foreign Office 'Russia Committee' and eventually to a semi-clandestine propaganda department. The paper below was written by Christopher Warner. In 1945 Warner had wished to give the Soviets the benefit of the doubt. His new tone underlines how far Foreign Office attitudes had travelled in less than two years.

... In other words, the Soviet Union has announced to the world that it proposes to play an aggressive political role, while making an inten-sive drive to increase its own military and industrial strength. We should be very unwise not to take the Russians at their word, just as we should have been wise to take *Mein Kampf* at its face value ...

4. The Soviet Union is no doubt war-weary, and, as the Soviet lead-ers have proclaimed, wants a prolonged peace to build up her strength. But she is practising the most vicious power politics, in the political, economic, and propaganda spheres and seems determined to stick at nothing, short of war, to obtain her objectives ...

We must therefore study this Russian aggressive policy as a whole in all its different manifestations, and not only make up our minds what measures we should take to defend ourselves against the Soviet Union's present manoeuvres, but also try to foresee the future development of her campaign against us and how we can meet it. We should also consider whether, in some directions at least, we should not adopt a defensive-offensive policy ...

Another question which requires study is the Soviet Government's clever trick of securing the creation of international federations of various kinds and arranging that the executive functions should be controlled by Communists. Examples are the World Federation of Trade Unions, the recently created World Youth and International Women's Federations. There is obviously an almost limitless field for the repetition of this trick ...

'The Soviet Campaign Against This Country and Our Response to It', memorandum by Christopher Warner, 2 April 1946, Top Secret, N5169/5169/38, FO 371/56885, PRO.

13.2 **The call for the revival of covert warfare, 1946**

By May 1946, as a result of discussion of Warner's memorandum (above) the Russia Committee was created to co-ordinate a British response. It delegated Ivone Kirkpatrick to draw up plans for a propaganda counter-offensive which would involve the BBC, Chatham House and the Press. Kirkpatrick drew on his own experience as wartime controller of the BBC European Service, which worked closely with the wartime SOE and PWE. The Permanent Under-Secretary, Sir Orme Sargent, approved his plan, but it was vetoed by the Foreign Secretary, Ernest Bevin, who was not enthusiastic about an anti-Communist campaign, and called instead for a positive projection of British virtues. Kirkpatrick's plans were revived in response to the formation of the Soviet Cominform at the end of 1947. They received Cabinet approval in the first week of January 1948.

The Secretary of State's paper (DPM (46)13 of 23 April 1946) contained the following passage.

'If this picture is accepted – and the accumulating evidence of Soviet actions and publicity is overwhelming – we have no choice but to immediately defend ourselves in every possible way and everywhere, and our defensive measures must include doing our very best to counter the Soviet Government's policy and propaganda as described above. This could be done by developing our own propaganda to this end, directing our campaign against Communism as such (which we should frankly expose as totalitarianism) rather than against the policy of the Soviet Government'.

The Prime Minister has approved the paper. Mr Harvey's Committee then asked me to convene a working party to consider ways and means of implementing the Secretary of State's recommendation on propaganda ...

We have a good analogy in our very successful campaign during the war directed towards stimulating resistance movements in Europe. The V sign was emblazoned all over the world. But at the same time we acted. We parachuted men, money and arms into occupied territory. We were not inhibited by fear that the Germans would find out what we were doing, or that they might react or that we might be criticised. Propaganda on the larger scale was co-ordinated with our policy. The result was a success.

Memorandum by Ivone Kirkpatrick, 22 May 1946, P449/1/907, FO 930/ 488, PRO.

13.3 Before IRD: the Cultural Relations Department and cultural warfare, 1946

The battle for control of international organisations, trade unions and the media is often considered to have been the preserve of IRD. In reality the Foreign Office's struggle to oppose Communist influence in national and international organisations began before the creation of IRD, indeed even before the end of the Second World War. It involved many different departments, some of which remain almost unknown. Among these is the Cultural Relations Department, which undertook sensitive work in this area, such as attempting to reduce Communist influence in the National Union of Students (NUS). The struggle for influence over the mind of youth accelerated in the late 1940s and eventually led the Foreign Office to help create the World Association of Youth. This was a 'spontaneous' rival to the Soviet-controlled front organisation the World Federation of Democratic Youth (WFDY).

1. An International Student Congress has been planned to take place in Prague from 18th to 31st August next. It is known to be Communist inspired. The National Union of Students which is also under strong Communist influence, has been invited by the conveners to 'co-ordinate' a British delegation. The Foreign Office have refused an application from the N.U.S. for financial assistance ...

10. Since the Congress will lay plans for the establishment of a World Student Federation to be affiliated with the W.F.D.Y. we have no motive for wishing a British delegation to attend it unless the delegation will fight, in the unfavourable conditions expected, against the attempt that will certainly be made to promote Communist ideology under the pretence of voicing the needs of the students of the world. Moreover, the delegation 'co-ordinated' by the N.U.S. who have nominated to it at least one Communist member of their Executive Committee – the lady who they also chose as one of their two representatives on the British Youth Committee that is to work with the W.F.D.Y. – is, to say the least, unlikely to oppose the prevailing opinion very stoutly. On the other hand, it would be difficult to engineer a change in the composition of the delegation ...

... Enquiries are on foot about the management of the N.U.S.: whether besides the Secretary and the Executive Committee there exists a governing body, and whether any of this personnel might be induced to work for the creation of a body of opinion within the Union to balance the extremists. As regards publicity, it has been suggested that a Parliamentary Question might be inspired and that some newspapers might be interested in showing up the real purpose of the congress. If adequate publicity were assured, it might strengthen the hand of the moderate element in the executive. Such publicity would not presumably conflict with the Secretary of State's rejection of proposals for a full-dress anti-Communist campaign.

Memorandum by the head of the Cultural Relations Department, William Montagu-Pollock, 'British Participation in an International Student Congress to be held in Prague in August', 28 July 1946, Secret, W8195/524/G50, FO 371/54788, PRO.

13.4 **The creation of IRD, 1948**

In early January 1948 Ernest Bevin presented Cabinet with important aspects of his future foreign policy. This included a firmer line on ideological competition with the Soviet Union, expressed as British social democracy, and also more broadly as the values of Western civilisation. He also proposed a 'small' section in the Foreign Office to take the propaganda offensive – the IRD. This was to be funded through the Secret Vote in the same manner as SIS, GCHQ and MI5. The Cabinet gave its approval to this organisation, but it did not remain small.

Soviet propaganda has, since the war, carried on in every sphere a vicious attack against the British Commonwealth and against Western democracy ... Something far more positive is clearly now required. If we are to give a moral lead to the forces of anti-Communism in Europe and Asia, we must be prepared to pass over the offensive and leave the initiative to the enemy, but make them defend themselves ...

... to oppose the inroads of Communism, by taking the offensive against it, basing ourselves on the standpoint of the position and vital ideas of British Social Democracy and Western civilisation, and to give a lead to our friends abroad and help them in the anti-Communist struggle.

2. The only new machinery required would be a small Section in the Foreign Office to collect foreign information concerning Communist policy, tactics and propaganda and to provide materials for our anti-Communist publicity through our Missions and Information Services abroad ...

In general we should emphasise the weakness of Communism rather than its strength. Contemporary American propaganda, which stresses the strength and aggressiveness of Communism, tends to scare and unbalance the anti-Communists, while heartening the fellow travellers and encouraging the Communists to bluff more extravagantly. Our propaganda, while dwelling on the Russians' poverty and backwardness, could be expected to relax rather than raise international tension.

CP (48) 8, Memorandum by the Foreign Secretary, Ernest Bevin, 'Future Foreign Publicity Policy', 4 January 1948, CAB 129/23, PRO.

13.5 **IRD and the Labour Party, 1948**

One of the most important aspects of the work of IRD was the development of reliable conduits for its material. IRD wished for its material to appear in non-governmental publications, but without its governmental authorship being acknowledged. Accordingly it employed collaborators in political parties, trade unions and many types of non-governmental organisation to distribute its material. The two most important conduits for IRD material were probably the TUC and the Labour Party's International Department. The latter was headed by Denis Healey, who worked closely with key Foreign Office figures such as Leslie Sheridan, Adam Watson and Christopher Mayhew in this task. As a result, approximately half of the papers in the surviving archive of the International Department appears to be of IRD or similar origin. Once this material was forwarded on from the Labour Party its origin was not revealed.

PR 182/57/913   NOTE
The attached material on 'Some Facts about Communism and the Freedom of the Press' is for the use of Missions and in particular Information Officers as seems best to them. It may be passed confidentially or informally without reserve to editors, etc. as a factual statement, or it may be used as the basis for written up material or features for issue by Information Officers, if they consider that is the best way of handling it.

   This covering note must be detached from any copy of the material before it is passed beyond confidential office use.
   INFORMATION RESEARCH DEPARTMENT
   FOREIGN OFFICE 10th April 1948

Preface Note to IRD materials, 10 April 1948, Box: Anti-Communist propaganda, 1947–50, Labour Party International Department, National Museum of Labour History.

13.6 **Semiotic warfare, 1948**

This document, which survives in the archives of the International Department of the Labour Party, is a useful example of the increasingly co-ordinated British propaganda effort, of which IRD formed the centre. It underlines a major problem faced by Western propaganda agencies: namely trying to compete with the centrally organised and monolithic Soviet apparatus, while employing Western resources which were, by their nature, pluralistic and inimical to any central control or effective steering, and therefore difficult to marshal.

The persistent use of particular words or phrases to convey a meaning is an elementary step in any organised publicity. In the present battle for world opinion, which has unfortunately been thrust upon us by Soviet policy and propaganda, it is essential that we should have recourse to this technique. It has, of course, long been used by Communist propaganda, in the case of words like 'imperialism,' 'colonialism,' 'reactionary,' 'war-mongering,' and even the appropriation of the word 'democratic,' with outstanding and dangerous success.

In order to concentrate and sharpen our publicity about Communism it is important that a number of words, crystallising the judgements or information which we wish to convey to world opinion, should be used extensively, and that other descriptions and variations should be avoided as far as possible.

Below is a list of words which have been carefully considered at official and ministerial levels ...

THE REVOLUTION BETRAYED This phrase and concept is particularly useful for European audiences on the fringe of communism against whom our publicity must be especially directed. It crystallises the criticism to which the Soviet system must and should be exposed from the extreme Left and the most humanitarian viewpoint.

THE STRANGLING OF ART AND SCIENCE This is an issue which we must do our utmost to keep alive and on which fresh material is daily reaching us from Moscow. It is of great importance to convince the 'intellectuals' they would have no freedom of expression under Communism and would be expected to produce only work in tune with the Party line and 'popular democratic' idiom.

FORCED LABOUR This is an issue on which the Russians are particularly vulnerable and have no effective answer. In order to get the idea across to the public it is essential to build up the names of one or two well-known camps until they are as familiar as Dachau or Belsen. Karaganda, the remote coal-mining region in central Asia which is worked almost entirely by forced labour, is considered the most promising name to use in this context. It is, moreover, the name most familiar to the Russian public.

Words which should be avoided

COMMUNIST This word is not considered suitable because of its vague attraction for many waverers. Insistence upon it, moreover, is not necessary.

RED This is liable to cause confusion with Socialist Parties and tends to be used as a term of reactionary abuse.

TYRANNY This word is not as effective as dictatorship.

SLAVERY This is a difficult accusation to substantiate, but 'the new serfdom' might be useful.

STALIN The figure of Stalin himself should not be built up on the analogy of Hitler, as great efforts are made by Soviet propaganda to run him into a popular and friendly figure with the masses. It is, however, important to explode the fallacy that Stalin is a benevolent realist who is prepared to over-rule the rasher and more intransigent decisions of his subordinates and with whom one can talk peace with a reasonable chance of success.

PR 704/G, 'Memorandum on the Use of Words in Publicity About Communism', 1948, Box: Anti-Communist propaganda, wartime/1947–50, Labour Party International Department, National Museum of Labour History.

13.7 **The military press for action, 1948**

The transformation of the defensive-offensive strategy into a complex programme of propaganda, economic warfare and liberation, most conspicuously in Albania, enjoyed a number of instigators. The propaganda element owed its origins to officials such as Ivone Kirkpatrick, Christopher Warner and others in the Foreign Office. In contrast, the paramilitary element owed more to a simultaneous disquiet on the part of elements in the military that the British prosecution of the Cold War lacked teeth. Montgomery's diary for 1948 reveals this and the tension between the military and the diplomats. By 1949, a number of figures at the Imperial Defence College

had developed this theme as an explicit critique of Ernest
Bevin and his well-known reservations in this area.

In August 1948 the C.O.S [Chiefs of Staff] instructed the Secretary to
ask the Minister of Defence to approach the Foreign Secretary for a
forecast of Russian moves ... It was thought that this appreciation
might prove the first step in setting up a proper 'cold war' organisation ...

Before the [Foreign Office] paper was taken by the C.O.S., the Directors of Intelligence of the three Services set about it in no uncertain
way. Their paper reviewed Communist policy, emphasised that the
key-stone of this policy was the inevitability of a struggle in order to
establish Communism throughout the earth, and summed up the
Communist policy by saying that the only method of preventing the
Russian threat is by utterly defeating Russian directed Communism.

The paper went on to say that for the first time in our history a
totalitarian organisation of states is attempting to impose its will
upon us by undiplomatic means other than armed conflict – conven-
iently described as 'cold war'. We couldn't win the 'cold war' unless
we carried our offensive inside Russia and the satellite states. In fact
what was required was a world-wide offensive by every available
agency. To date we had failed to unify our forces to oppose the Soviet
'cold war' aggression. One sentence of this paper was particularly
apt, and was as follows: -

'At present we are in danger of losing the 'cold war'. We have *not*
integrated with our Allies, we have *not* selected our strategic aim, we
have *not* got a high-level integrated plan, we have *not* allocated our
world resources, and we have *not* designated our 'cold war' forces.

The paper concluded that an organisation was required capable
of:-

(a) Exercising the higher direction of the 'cold war'.

(b) Controlling and co-ordinating all executive action.

and it recommended that a high level official of Ministerial rank and
with an appropriate staff should be appointed ...

At the Staff Conference on 9 September with the Minister of Defence, C.A.S. [Tedder], speaking for the C.O.S., told the Minister
plainly that the present efforts to prevent the spread of Communist
domination were completely inadequate and that the 'cold war' required the employment of all our resources, short of actual shooting,
and a proper organisation to co-ordinate them, but he emphasised

that the control of this organization should not be taken out of the hands of the Foreign Secretary. The Minister of Defence ... again lost his nerve ... he wished to water down the C.O.S. recommendations ... as far as the C.O.S. were concerned the Memorandum which they put up to the Minister should be forwarded in its original state to the Foreign Secretary who should be absolutely clear as to the views of the C.O.S. on this subject ...

On 10 September the Minister of Defence said he had submitted the C.O.S. memorandum to the Foreign Secretary ... He even said that he had pointed out that the C.O.S. would be the last to criticise or embarrass the Foreign Secretary in achieving this objective, and that the C.O.S. memorandum should be regarded in that light ...

Furthermore, at their meeting on 29 June [probably September not June], Sir Ivone Kirkpatrick, as the Foreign Secretary's representative, met the C.O.S. to discuss their memorandum on the 'cold war'. Sir Ivone Kirkpatrick agreed that the time had come to review the machinery, but added that the C.O.S. were incorrect when they said that the only body charged with the task of conducting the 'cold war' was the Information Research Department, which had not responsibility other than propaganda. He explained that the task of planning and co-ordinating all the other measures was the responsibly of the 'Russia Committee', which met once a week, and consisted of the Parliamentary Under Secretary, the Political Under Secretaries and the Chairman of the J.I.C., calling on experts as required.

In the propaganda field it was assisted by the Information Research Department and by the Head of the European Service of the B.B.C.

Sir Ivone admitted, however, that hitherto military factors had not been considered, and that the time was now advantageous to strengthen the Committee by the addition of a representative of the C.O.S.

In reply to further questions, Sir Ivone said that the Russia Committee was, in fact, the Cold War Planning Staff. He emphasised the difficulties in waging the 'cold war' from this side, saying that some of the tactics open to the Russians were not open to ourselves, and also that it was not easy to co-ordinate measures with our Allies. The Foreign Secretary was inclined to the view that covert activities would not pay a dividend.

As a result of the meeting it was agreed that Sir Ivone Kirkpatrick would suggest to the Foreign Secretary that a representative of the

C.O.S. should be attached to the Russia Committee, and that the whole issue of intelligence about Russia should be reviewed with the Chairman of the J.I.C., the J.I.S. and 'C'. Perhaps at this late hour there will be a proper set-up to control and direct this very important aspect of our national defence. It must be hoped that the clock is not on the point of striking.

Diary of the Chief of the Imperial General Staff, Field Marshall Bernard Montgomery, September–October 1948, 'SECTION D – The Cold War', Montgomery Papers, BLM 186/1, Reel 18, Imperial War Museum.

13.8 **IRD in 1949**

In 1949 British officials gave the American Ambassador in London a useful summary description of the nature of the work of IRD in its first year of operation.

Following expansion data re confidential UK anti-Communist program ... obtained May 19 from Ralph Murray and Adam Watson, Foreign Office Information Research Department ...

1. IRD produces two categories material:

Category A is secret and confidential objective studies re Soviet policies and machinations which are designed for high-level consumption by heads of states, cabinet members, et cetera none of this material (e.g. evidence WFTU [World Federation of Trade Unions] Communist connections; evidence re forced labor USSR, et cetera) publishable or quotable for obvious reasons.

Category B is less highly-classified information suitable for dissemination by staff of British missions to suitable contacts (e.g., editors, professors, scientists, labor leaders et cetera) who can use it as factual background material in their general work without attribution. Success category B operations depend on activity [by] British representatives in various countries.

2. IRD has been disseminating category A material to older Commonwealth countries and Brussels treaty powers. Category B materials now being disseminated in most non- [Iron] curtain countries.

3. Murray explained that IRD has been slow starting its program in new Commonwealth countries but that following consultation with CRO [Commonwealth Relations Office] instructions were sent

short time ago to British High Commands [Commissioners] India, Pakistan and Ceylon to approach governments at top level to explain that British Government would supply henceforth confidential category A studies ...

4. Foreign Office and CRO are agreed that dissemination category B material should begin henceforth in India, Pakistan and Ceylon on exactly the same lines as used in non-Commonwealth countries without embarrassing GOI [Government of India] or GOP [Government of Pakistan] by asking their permission.

US Ambassador in London, Douglas, to US Secretary of State, 20 May 1949, No. 1993, Top Secret, Assistant Chief of Staff (G2 Army Intelligence) files, TS Incoming and Outgoing Cables, Box 189, Entry 58, RG 319, USNA.

13.9 **UK–US co-operation and propaganda, 1950**

Between 11 and 13 May 1950, the British Foreign Secretary, Ernest Bevin, met in London with his American and French counterparts, Dean Acheson and Robert Schuman, to discuss the world situation. Detailed issues were delegated to working groups of senior officials. Lengthy bilateral (not trilateral) discussions were held on information policy, an area of rapid expansion for London and Washington. Anglo-American 'working groups', similar to this, were increasingly the way in which joint planning for covert activities was co-ordinated in the 1950s and 1960s. This document makes clear the importance that the British attached to 'black', or unattributable, propaganda by 1950, especially in the Third World. At this time Ralph Murray was head of IRD and not, as this document suggests, in the Information Policy Department.

Present:
Christopher Warner	FO Information Policy Department
Ralph Murray	FO Information Policy Department
P.L. Carter	FO Information Policy Department
Edward Barrett	US Assistant SoS for Public Affairs
W.T. Stone	US Chairman, Interdepartmental Foreign Information Staff
Mallory Browne	Counsellor, US Embassy, London

185

The following topics were discussed at the first meeting: (1) general aims and objectives of U.S. and British information services; (2) information functions of the NAT [North Atlantic Treaty] organisation, and (3) arrangements for closer co-operation between our services in promoting common objectives and combatting Communist propaganda ...

MR. WARNER reviewed British information objectives since the Cabinet directive of 1948 authorizing anti-Communist activities and noted the difference between U.S. and British target area priorities. The Foreign Office gives a higher priority to areas outside the Iron Curtain and concentrates its effort on parts of the free world in danger of Communist penetration. Thus, first priority is given to France, Italy and Germany in Europe, and South East Asia in the Far East. Second priority is given to India, Pakistan and the Middle East. The European satellite states are regarded as more important than the Soviet Union.

MR. WARNER stressed the importance attached by the Foreign Office to the use of local channels for the dissemination of anti-Communist propaganda, rather than flooding the market with publicly identified British propaganda. British experience shows that overt propaganda has very little value in areas like South East Asia or the Middle East, and the danger of over-reaching the saturation point in other areas should not be lost sight of ...

... General Jacob, BBC Director of Overseas Broadcasting, has the full confidence of the Foreign Office and participates in policy conferences as though he were a permanent member of the F.O.

MR. MURRAY described the methods and techniques of anti-Communist propaganda. Basic materials are developed by a central research staff in London [IRD], and processed for specific areas by a group of writers who work through an agency set up outside of the Foreign Office for this purpose. Trade Union organizations and various groups are used to place articles published under the by-line of well known writers; these articles and additional anti-Communist materials are then sent to regional field offices in Singapore and Cairo, or to Information Officers in individual countries for adaption to meet local needs. The materials are never used directly by BIS [British Information Service], but are placed in local journals or made available to local groups. Careful attention is given to the selection of the most effective channels and target groups and themes.

MR. BARRETT expressed our interest in developing similar techniques for effective use of gray propaganda, particularly in South East Asia, and in learning more about the British experience in this field. However, we believe that much could be done to strengthen the effect of our positive propaganda, through the overt media, by using public statements stressing the unity of purpose of the free nations of the world.

III. Arrangements for US–UK Cooperation
It was agreed that close and continuous liaison in both Washington and London will be essential if our present general co-operation in the information field is to be strengthened effectively. MR. WARNER said that the Foreign Office was ready to appoint a qualified Foreign Service officer to the British Embassy in Washington. They have in mind a man like Adam Watson, who would be attached to the Chancery, rather then to Goore-Booth's information staff [Director, BIS in the United States].

MR. BARRETT said that we would welcome such an officer in Washington, and would like to establish a similar officer in London.

Both liaison officers should be in a position to cover all aspects of current information activities, including broadcasting and certain special activities ...

Notes on the First Meeting Between Messrs Christopher Warner and Edward Barrett, at London, Secret, Saturday 20 May 1950, *FRUS*, 1950, Vol. III, *Western Europe*, pp. 1641–4.

13.10 **IRD and the trade unions, 1951**

The Labour Party, moderate trade unionists, Foreign Office departments such as IRD, and MI5 worked together to reduce Communist influence within British trade unions and British national life generally. This is an example of IRD addressing British domestic political and industrial activity, rather than foreign policy, and helps to explain why the work of IRD is still considered a sensitive subject. The papers of IRD are being opened to public inspection when they are close to fifty years old, rather than following the usual thirty-year rule. This document illustrates the close relationship of the prominent trade unionist Victor Feather with IRD. In 1952 Feather was chosen to join a confidential government

enquiry into Overseas Information Services. The real fears of
Communist penetration of trade unions entertained by the
Prime Minister, Clement Attlee, in his last years in office are
also indicated here.

We spoke on the telephone about Victor Feather's note on Communism in the British trade unions, and I return his paper herewith.

It was agreed at our recent meeting that we should look at this note
together with the longer paper prepared by Feather for our I.R.D.
and a short document prepared in that Department recently for inclusion in the new 'Defence Digest', which is being circulated to Ministers and senior civil servants by authority of the Prime Minister ...

Our views briefly on the document returned herewith are that (a) it
does not give the overall picture of Communist strength in some of
our key industries, notably engineering, transport and the docks, and
is in this respect not objective; (b) it needs checking by M.I.5.; and (c)
unless it is specifically sent out as a Victor Feather product the language would need to be overhauled.

It is however a useful first shot, and I would suggest that your
Industrial Relations Department might take it and re-write it into
something more balanced, omitting of course the more personal references and checking for accuracy with M.I.5 at the same time ...

F. C. Mason, Foreign Office, to A. Greenhough, Ministry of Labour and
National Service, 18 October 1951, LAB 13/697, PRO.

14

Special operations against Russia in peace

14.1 Winding down the SOE, 1945

In November 1945 the wartime SOE was already being wound down. Many policy-makers who had been alienated by its wartime activities wished to see it terminated immediately. Attlee had declared bluntly that he had no interest in running a 'British Comintern'. However, others saw the potential long-term value of SOE and its network of contacts. The Chiefs of Staff in particular pressed for its survival on a 'care and maintenance basis'. The Foreign Office agreed only on condition that it was allowed a veto over any operational activities. Although the decision to incorporate the remnants of SOE into SIS was not finalised until early 1946, it was clearly pre-figured here in Austria where the two organisations were now working closely on the ground. This document underlines that the Chiefs of Staff were making early and detailed covert preparations for a possible Soviet invasion of Europe.

1. Tasks of S.O.E. abroad have been agreed as follows:-

(a) to create an organisation capable of quick and effective expansion in time of war. This will necessitate maintenance of adequate clandestine contacts, collection of up-to-date information regarding potential objectives of the special types required for planning S.O.E. operations and preparation of adequate covert communications.

(b) to serve the clandestine operational requirements of His Majesty's Government abroad by giving covert support to British national interests where threatened, but only in cases where the appropriate department of His Majesty's Government or the Chiefs of Staff may think fit, and subject always to the express approval of the Foreign Office.

2. In carrying out these tasks, S.O.E. have been directed to accord priority to those countries which are likely to be overrun in the earliest stages of conflict with Russia, but which are not, at present, under Russian domination ...

Draft telegram for Chiefs of Staff to H.Q. British Troops Austria, COS (45) 671 (0), 22 November 1945, AIR 20/7997, PRO.

14.2 The fusion of SIS and SOE, 1946

At the end of 1945 most SOE activity had been wound down, with only small elements continuing their work in Austria, Germany and the Middle East. Unofficially Mountbatten retained the services of SOE to deal with complex occupational problems in South East Asia. In London the decision was taken to abolish SOE, merging its remnants with SIS to provide a residual special operations capability. This decision reflected not only a presumption that there was no peacetime requirement for SOE activities, but also a dislike of SOE on the part of SIS and the Foreign Office that had grown during the war.

1. FUTURE S.O.E. ACTIVITY
THE COMMITTEE had before them -
(i) a letter from the Foreign Office concerning certain aspects of the future of S.O.E. activity and expressing the view that S.O.E. should not have any active functions anywhere abroad at present except for certain activities in the Middle East ...
MR CACCIA [Chairman of the JIC] said that the origin of the Foreign Office letter lay in the directive on the future of S.O.E. activity date 10th November. That directive gave the Foreign Office the right of veto throughout ... it would be seen that they wished to use that veto rather drastically ...
It was over the recruitment of conscious and unconscious agents that the Foreign Office saw the difficulty. In their view, such recruitment would be politically dangerous. Mr. Caccia quoted as an example his own experience in Greece, and said that somewhat similar considerations apply in almost every other country.
SIR STEWART MENZIES [head of SIS] said that under the terms of his directive, he was required to prepare an S.O. organisation ca-

pable of rapid expansion in an emergency. In view of the strong arguments put forward by the Foreign Office, he had been considering a compromise method of discharging this responsibility. Most of the information required could be obtained through S.I.S. channels and from the Joint Intelligence Bureaux [sic]. There would, however, be a definite need for a qualified staff at home trained in the operational side, for which he would need about 20 officers versed in S.O. methods. Under this scheme no contacts would be made abroad that were contrary to Foreign Office policy. The fact that S.I. officers, versed in S.O. technique, were in foreign countries and employing agents, would considerably reduce the time required to build up a resistance movement if and when required. The officers working on S.O. problems in London would keep alive the experience gained by S.O.E. in this war, and would be available in the event of expansion. This proposal, if acceptable, would involve an extra expenditure of some £40,000 a year.

LORD ALANBROOKE [Chief of the Imperial General Staff] said that there should be no necessity in peacetime for any subversive operations in any part of the world. The experience of the recent war had emphasised the importance of achieving the complete amalgamation of S.I.S. and S.O. This was the main reason for bringing these two activities under one head. The S.O. problems that might arise in the various countries in war-time, should be studied in peace by S.I. methods ...

COS (46) 12th meeting (1) 23 January 1946, AIR 19/816, PRO.

14.3 **SIS and 'Cold War fighting', 1948**

As we have seen in the previous section, by mid-1946 a new British attitude to waging the Cold War was emerging. Pressure for a vigorous Cold War counter-offensive came from the Chiefs of Staff. The military were dismayed by the ambivalence and lack of vision displayed by other bodies, including SIS. This is conveyed in a minute by the senior RAF officer, John Slessor, written in his inimitably outspoken style.

With reference to the letter you showed me from Orme Sargent [Permanent Under-Secretary, Foreign Office] about the Chiefs of Staff

191

'cold war' proposals, I thought it might be of interest to mention that I had a word with 'C' about it at lunch-time. I was somewhat dismayed at what appears to be his conception of the scale of Psychological warfare and S.O.E. operations he might undertake. He said that, of course, everything depended on whether the Government would cough up the money required to enable him to operate effectively – it might be a formidable addition to the Secret Service vote. I immediately had visions of something of the order of at least £10 million a year, which seems to me to be the minimum sort of scale on which our secret operations to win the Cold war should be considered. I was alarmed to find that 'C' was thinking in terms of £½ million, which seemed to me derisorily inadequate. I wonder what the enemy are spending!

Incidentally I don't see why all this sum need necessarily come on the Secret Service vote. A lot of our 'cold' operations could, and it seems to me should, be overt. There will, however, have to a very substantial covert expenditure; but I don't believe Parliament would strain at even £10 million for the Secret Service vote if they were told frankly what it was for.

I thought possibly this might interest you and C.A.S.

Air Chief Marshal Sir John Slessor to Vice Chief of the Air Staff, Air Marshal Sir James Robb, JCS.37, 21 January 1948, Top Secret, AIR 75/116, PRO.

14.4 The Russia Committee and the Soviet orbit, 1948

The Russia Committee had been formed in 1946 to consider centrally the problem posed by the Soviet Union and Communism on a global basis, drawing in individuals from many different geographically based departments. With individuals co-opted from the Chiefs of Staff and the BBC, it became Whitehall's 'cold war planning staff'. By late 1948 it was considering plans for 'winning' the Cold War, set out in a Foreign Office paper by Robin Hankey. Strong pressure for a more forward policy was now coming from the Chiefs of Staff. The majority of the individuals involved in these conversations had extensive experience with both SOE and PWE during the war and this informed the discussion to a considerable degree. Despite some important reservations, the Russia

Committee decided to press ahead and one result was the un-
successful operation mounted from Italy and Malta against
the Communist government of Albania from 1949.

SIR IVONE KIRKPATRICK said that, in the present state of our fi-
nances and in view of public opinion, he thought that it would be best
to start any kind of offensive operations in a small area and suggested
for consideration in this regard Albania. Would it not be possible to
start a civil war behind the Iron Curtain and by careful assistance to
produce a state of affairs in Albania similar to the state of affairs in
Greece? MR JEBB pointed out that United Nations observers would
certainly come to hear of any operations we were undertaking and
would complain to the United Nations with possibly unpleasant consequences. MR. BATEMAN suggested that though Albania was a
very weak point in the Soviet orbit there might be some advantage in
allowing the rift there to widen without our interference especially as
the Russians were in Albania in some force. SIR IVONE
KIRKPATRICK enquired whether it would not be possible to arrange
that the operations should be undertaken by members of resistance in
Albania. We knew that there was opposition to the present regime
and it should be possible to make use of it. MR. ROBERTS pointed
out that it was simple for the Russians to arrange for offensive operations in other countries without formally committing the Soviet Government since they worked through the local Communist parties. We
had no similar instrument and the position of H.M.G was therefore
more difficult. MR. DENING stressed the dangers of becoming involved in political commitments in Albania by using part of the population against the rest. It meant that you became beholden to the
people on whom you depended. This had produced complications in
the last war and might well do again. MR. MAKINS said that in his
opinion the value of underground movements was doubtful. He felt
that, in the last war, if the effort expended on underground operations had been put into straight military operations the results would
have paid us better.

MR. WRIGHT said that any action we undertook must be co-
ordinated with the Americans. THE COMMITTEE agreed ...

LORD TEDDER stressed the importance of setting up a planning
staff to examine the various means available to us. He said that he
was sceptical of the value of SOE unless followed up by military
action. He likened these operations to a barrage laid down before

attack by troops; if it was laid down too far ahead your friends were simply annihilated.

MR. JEBB stressed the importance of having, firstly, a Cabinet decision on the proposal to indulge in anything like SOE operations and, secondly, of setting up the requisite organisation. It was important to decide whether we should undertake activity of this sort; if so, whether the present was the best time to do so. Generally speaking, we ought to clarify our objectives. The Committee discussed these objectives and decided that our aim should certainly be to liberate the countries within the Soviet orbit by any means short of war ...

LORD TEDDER said that he thought we should aim at winning the 'cold war' (by which he meant the overthrow of the Soviet regime) in five years time. MR. ROBERTS said that, in his opinion, if we aimed at unseating the Soviet Government in five years by means other than war, we were undertaking an impossible task. LORD TEDDER suggested that there should, in any case, be a small permanent team which would consider plans which would subsequently be executed by ourselves and the Americans. He agreed that it was important to bring in the Americans at as early a stage as possible. Frankly he thought that unless we reformed our present machinery for conducting the 'cold war', we might lose it, in which case the Services would have to conduct a hot war, which was the last thing they wanted to do ...

Summing up, MR. JEBB suggested that a sub-committee should be set up to examine this question and report back to the Russia Committee. He read out terms of reference for the Sub-Committee with which the Committee agreed (copy attached).

RC (48) 16 (2), Russia Committee minutes, 25 November 1948, N3016/765/38, FO 371/71687, PRO.

14.5 PUSC attempts to retard US covert action, 1952

In late 1951 the Foreign Office's main planning authority, PUSC, carried out a major review of Britain's long-term policy on the Cold War. The final version was not completed until January 1952. This paper was important. A summary of it was used by the Foreign Office to try and blunt Churchill's desire for a summit with Stalin on his return to office in

November 1951. In a slightly different form it constituted one of two key papers taken to Washington by officials for high-level strategy talks in January 1952 (document 14.6). The other paper taken to Washington was a version of the fabled 'Global Strategy Paper'. Although at the outset this paper reviewed liberation in a moderately optimistic tone, it turned to argue decisively against attempts to stir up revolt in the Eastern Bloc. The arguments for and against liberation were set out in Annex B, 'Liberation of the Satellites', which was given a more restricted circulation than the main paper. Having decided against liberation, the paper then turned its attention to how best to restrain the United States.

The Implications of United States Policy

28. The long-term aims of United States policy are not clear. They are already engaged in attempts to weaken the structure of the Soviet empire by various means including broadcasting, refugee organisations working from outside and covert activities and propaganda behind the Iron Curtain; and there are some indications that they rate the possibility of detaching the satellites by subversion and revolt a good deal higher than we do. As their strength grows, they will no doubt be impatient to see what results can be achieved by these means and indeed they may at present be more concerned with means than ends. But it is clear that they are dealing with very delicate questions and the end result of activities of this kind could be very far-reaching. There are very evident risks that subversive activities involving anti-Soviet elements in the satellite countries may at a certain stage get out of control. We might then be faced with a choice between supporting the revolutionary movement by force of arms or abandoning the revolutionaries to their fate – an alternative which would inevitably lead to a strengthening of the Soviet hold over the whole of the Soviet empire and the liquidation of all potential supporters of the West. It is therefore important to ensure that American activities of this kind have taken full account of the risks involved and that they do not press harder on Russian sore spots than their other Atlantic partners would approve. For it is clearly on the European nations rather than on the United States that the first repercussions would fall.

29. It is therefore desirable that the United Kingdom should be in a position to exercise an influence for moderation on this aspect of United States policy. But the United States Government may be reluctant to pay much heed to British criticisms which seem to them to be

only obstructive and negative. They might be more ready to listen if the United Kingdom was able to indicate agreement in principle to study the possibilities of a more forward policy aimed not at fomenting revolt in the satellites but at weakening the whole fabric of the Soviet empire: and was then in a position to put forward suggestions and criticism as a partner from the inside. This course then would clearly involve the United Kingdom in going some way with the Americans towards a more active policy.

PUSC (51) 16 (Final), 'Future Policy Towards Soviet Russia', Secret, 17 January 1952, ZP10/4, FO 371/125002, PRO.

14.6 British policy and American reactions, 1952

The Americans were less than delighted to hear British misgivings about covert activities. On 12 March 1952 the high-level State Department–JCS Co-ordinating Committee met at the Pentagon and considered the 'British paper on covert operations'. They were not entirely taken in by British attempts to present this new line as a mere change of direction. The Chairman of the US JCS, General Omar Bradley, was particularly vociferous. These minutes also bring out the differences between British and American records of such discussions, the former being dry and depersonalised, the latter often being delightfully verbatim, as here.

MR. BOHLEN: I think Mr. Nitze is right. This paper had its start in discussions on covert operations which we held with the British some time ago. The British are quite concerned about political warfare behind the iron curtain. This involves such questions as the use that we should make of Ukrainian nationalists, Russian emigres, etc. The British line has been that they are interested in intelligence gathering, not subversion. From our discussion on these matters it became clear that the difference in U.S. and British views on covert operations stemmed from a somewhat different analysis of the Soviet system ...

GENERAL BRADLEY: What worries me is that this paper has an appeasement ring to it.

MR. NITZE: I think you are right about that.

MR. MATTHEWS: Of course this is not a new position. The British appear to have moved some distance forward from the position they took last December in the discussions we had with the MI-6 people.

ROBERT JOYCE: The kick-off on this paper was that the British and American services began to foul each other up in some of their covert operations. For that reason it became important to review these problems with the British. I went over last December for that purpose. I outlined to the British as best I could the NSC-68 policies and indicated why Bedell Smith [Director of the CIA] desired to beef up his covert operations ... I tried to obtain their approval for our point of view and to obtain their agreement that they would not foul up our operations. I must say that in December I got a very negative reaction. The British were strongly inclined to accept the status quo. I think Mr. Matthews is right and that this paper represents a step forward although of course there is still a long way to go. The pitch is that the U.K. wants a voice in decisions on these matters. They are worried that the Americans will go too far too fast. They repeatedly emphasised that they are only 25 miles away from the Continent and that this is much too close for comfort. They want to influence us a little and perhaps even control us a little. This is the guts of the matter.

Minutes of the JCS–SD Co-ordinating Committee, 12 March 1952, File: JCS-SD Meetings, Box 77, Policy Planning Staff Records, Lot Files 64D 563, RG 59, USNA.

14.7 **The Chiefs of Staff and liberation, 1952**

Although the Foreign Office had turned British official policy decidedly against liberation by 1952, this did not reflect a complete consensus within Whitehall. Field Marshal William Slim, now Chief of the Imperial General Staff, had no qualms about contradicting the main British line when addressing fellow senior British, American and French commanders at SHAPE in August 1952. Slim had accompanied Prime Minister Churchill on his visit to the United States in 1952, the purpose of which was to sell Truman the idea of detente with the Soviets. Accordingly, he was aware how far this speech directly contravened British policy at the highest level.

To end this cold war, we ought to be very much more aggressive. We, the British especially I think, are too much on the defensive. And as our strength grows, so should our aggression in the cold war. We should aim first of all at separating the satellites from Russia. It is not an impossible objective, especially in a country like Czechoslovakia, where the people can still remember freedom. Or in Poland, where they can still remember freedom. In Russia they can't. There is no-one living in Russia who's ever been free. They don't understand it, they don't know what it means. But in those other countries, in the satellites, they still can, in some of them. And the idea of separating a national movement from Russia, as has happened in Yugoslavia, is not all that impossible and we should aim at doing it. And we should not bother too much to start with whether, being separated, they remain Communist or not. Our propaganda should not be so much against Communism in the satellite countries. It should be against Russia, the domination of Russia. It should be nationalist propaganda. And I think we very often miss a lot by that. We forget this separation between Russia and Communism. Get them away from Russia, and then their Communism won't matter. Russia won't go to war for that reason, they don't care much. They'll tell you that half of them are bourgeois deviationists anyway. But if you do something – if you go and put a big American airbase in Finland, for instance – if you do something like that, which touches on the historic and continuing national interests of Russia, the thing that the Czars kept their eye on, then you are taking a risk. And that is why I ask you to consider the difference between Russia and Communism. I'm not asking you to sympathise with Communism, but I'm asking you, merely as a means of combatting both of them, to keep that distinction in mind.

Chief of the Imperial General Staff, Field Marshal William Slim, 'Address to SHAPE Staff', 22 August 1952, Papers of General Matthew Ridgway, SHAPE Correspondence file 1952, Box 24, US Army Military History Institute, Carlisle Barracks, Pennsylvania, USA.

14.8 **From revolution to 'evolution': the Satellites in 1961**

This paper, produced by the Foreign Office Steering Committee in mid-1961, outlined the manner in which the British hoped to encourage gradual and gentle liberation in the Eastern Bloc. It reflected the experience of the crushing of the revolts in East Berlin in 1953 and in Hungary in 1956, both of which confirmed the worst fears of liberation's detractors in the Foreign Office. This 1961 paper caused lengthy disagreement in Whitehall about the extent to which its text needed to be agreed with the Americans before it was presented to NATO partners, pointing to a new climate of Allied relations in the 1960s.

3. The underlying assumptions of the policy recommended in the present paper do not differ significantly from those set out in the earlier one [1959]. The events of [Hungary] 1956, however, have now receded further into the past; Soviet control over the Bloc has been further consolidated and the Communist regimes in the Satellites have become more firmly entrenched. The Satellite peoples have become more acquiescent, their discontent having been appeased to some extent by an improvement in living conditions. At the same time the pattern of Satellite-Soviet relations has been developing towards that of a 'Socialist Commonwealth' in which there is now much more mutual consultation and, perhaps, more scope for the pursuit of national interests by individual Satellites. The main thesis of the present paper is that if there is eventually to be any weakening of the Soviet hold over the Satellites it will come about through evolution rather than revolution and that the West should do more to encourage favourable evolutionary trends, particularly by fostering a spirit of nationalism in the Satellites and laying up to their sense of national identity. This will involve both developing closer relations with the regimes and intensifying our efforts to keep in touch with the populations. The paper argues that there need not be any incompatibility between these two different lines of approach.

4. The paper recommends, in particular, that we should devote more attention to information work and should increase our cultural activities substantially ...

Note by the Steering Committee Secretary, P. S. Ziegler, on S.C. (61) 25, 'United Kingdom Policy towards the Satellites', 27 June 1961, Secret, FO 371/177821, PRO.

15

Special operations against Russia in a future war

15.1 SIS special operations for war in the Middle East, 1948

The small special operations section of SIS was busy in the late 1940s. As we have seen, it was called upon to implement a brief enthusiasm for fighting the Cold War more energetically, most obviously inAlbania. It was also busy carrying out contingency planning for special operations in the context of a 'hot' war, which many believed would begin in the Middle East. In 1947–48 Kim Philby was stationed in Turkey and conducted detailed survey work on the ground in support of these plans.

Object.
8. To consider the scale of M.I.6 effort that can be made available in the event of war breaking out with RUSSIA with little warning before July, 1949. This scale to be considered in 3 phases : -
 D Day to D Day + 3 months
 D + 3 months to D + 6 months
 D + 6 months onwards

Types of activity.
9. Depending on local circumstances, Special Operations may be of ten main types :-
 (a) The supply of information – tactical and strategical, military, political economic and scientific.
 (b) Covert Propaganda (spreading rumours, false information, 'black broadcasts', etc.)
 (c) The organisation of bases, areas and Safe Houses.
 (d) The marking of targets.
 (e) The organisation of escape routes.

200

(f) The infiltration and exfiltration of personnel and stores to and from enemy occupied countries by air and sea.

(g) Industrial and other sabotage, including organising strikes, etc.

(h) The stimulation of indigenous resistance.

(i) Cooperation with S.A.S. and L.R.D.G. [Long Range Desert Group] type units.

(j) 'Coup de main' operations to attack special targets or carry out demolitions.

D Day to D + 3 months

10. At present there is a Foreign Office ban on carrying out any preparatory measures for Special Operations. This is unlikely to be lifted, unless war appears inevitable, for the following reasons:-

(a) It means taking Foreign Governments into our confidence, which may well precipitate alarm and despondency.

(b) With any prolongation of the peace period, there would probably be a leakage of plans.

(c) Special personnel would have to be infiltrated, and if left in countries for a long time would become suspect.

11. In view of the above, the S.O. effort from D to D + 3 months would be strictly limited to the following : -

(a) General.

(i) The collection and distribution of intelligence.

(ii) Broadcast propaganda of all types.

(iii) Very limited assistance in marking of vital targets.

(iv) 'Coup de main' operation, provided these are planned, and the necessary personnel, equipment, etc. is provided before D Day.

(b) PERSIA, IRAQ AND PALESTINE.

These are probably the most difficult countries in the MIDDLE EAST in which we could operate in the early phases of a war with RUSSIA, owing to the unsuitability of the population for this type of work. Success in these countries also largely depends on allied policy before the outbreak of war, and on the degree of organised resistance offered to the Russians. It is possible that some of these countries may be actively hostile to us, in which case Special Operations would not succeed in the early stages of the war.

(c) TURKEY and GREECE.

It should be easier to organise Special Operations in these counties as it is probable that they will be friendly to us. They should have the will to resist, and as they are unlikely to be completely overrun in less than two months, operations can be carried out with collaboration of the Governments and Staffs concerned ...

'Scope of Possible Special Operations in the Event of Hostilities in the Middle East Before July, 1949', Appendix 'H', British War Plan SANDOWN, August 1948, AIR 8/1605, PRO.

15.2 Control of UK–US special operations in war, 1952

As during the Second World War, Britain and the United States had great difficulty in compromising on the issue of control of secret service activities, which they viewed as important instruments of national policy. The British favoured control by the national headquarters of SIS in London, while the Americans preferred to give more authority to the regional military commander. This was not a mere academic question, for General MacArthur had imposed rigid control upon the activities of clandestine agencies as theatre commander during the Korean War. By 1952, the question of how to reconcile this approach with the authority of a regional NATO commander, in whose areas these activities would take place, was a live one. It was not easily resolved. This document also sheds some light on the CIA–SIS agreement, concluded in the late 1940s.

1. In the light of a memorandum by the Deputy U.S. Representative to the Standing Group (S.G.0, North Atlantic Military Committee (NAMC), DUSM-40-52), dated 18 January 1952 (Enclosure to J.C.S. 1735/105), to provide guidance on definitions and control for 'Clandestine Operations' by Supreme Allied Commanders during war ... The Joint Intelligence Committee, the Joint Strategic Plans Committee, and the Central Intelligence Agency have been consulted in the preparation of this report ...

ENCLOSURE 'C'
FACTS BEARING ON THE PROBLEM AND DISCUSSION
1. In a memorandum for the U.S. Military Representative on the S.G. [NATO Standing Group], NAMC, SM-2876-51, dated 28 November 1951 (Enclosure 'A' to J.C.S. 1735/94), the Joint Chiefs of Staff in coordination with the Director of the Central Intelligence Agency

provided guidance on Clandestine Operations within the Northern Atlantic Treaty Organisation (NATO).

2. Agreement with the British and the French Representatives of the S.G. has been obtained on all aspects of the above guidance except with regard to:

a. Wartime Control by Supreme Allied Commanders; and

b. Certain definitions.

3. With regard to control over wartime clandestine operations by Supreme Allied Commanders, NATO, the Deputy U.S. Representative to the S.G., NAMC, in DUSM-40-52 has requested guidance from the Joint Chiefs of Staff on views of the British representatives, who state that such control should be as follows:

'a. In active theaters in wartime Supreme Allied Commanders will exercise general control of clandestine resources operating in direct support of their military operations to the extent necessary to insure coordination.

'b. In order to insure this coordination a Theater Clandestine headquarters will be set up in each Theater the basic composition of which will be drawn from the Clandestine Services which have most to contribute in that Theater as a whole; the clandestine representatives of any other nations involved being called for consultation when their particular interests are concerned.

'c. The Theater Clandestine headquarters will be in charge of an officer drawn from one of the Clandestine Services forming the basic composition of the headquarters. This officer will advise the Supreme Allied Commander on all clandestine matters affecting the Theater, but other basic members of the Clandestine Headquarters will have the right of direct approach to the Supreme Commander if they consider that their interests are being jeopardised.'

4. Subparagraph 3 a above is the verbatim guidance that the Joint Chiefs of Staff previously furnished the S.G. in SM-2876-51 (subparagraph 3 f) except that the British have used the word 'general' instead of 'operational' in the phrase, 'will exercise general control of clandestine resources, ...' neither word should be used because the degree of control is specified by the phrase, 'operating in direct support of their military operations to the extent necessary to ensure coordination.'

5. Subparagraphs 3 b and c above concern the wartime mechanisms to implement 3 a above and were not treated in the guidance furnished to the S.G. in SM-2876-51.

6. It should be noted that the British views in 3 b and c above stem from a fundamental difference in national policy as compared with the United States on the wartime organization and control of clandestine operations in active theaters of war. U.S. policy (NSC 10/2 and NSCID No. 5) directs that the conduct of such operations will be commanded by the American theater commander in active theaters of war where American forces are engaged. Also the Central Intelligence Agency points out that, pursuant to NSCID No. 5, the conduct of U.S. espionage and counterespionage cannot be subject to the approval of an international group. British policy directs that such wartime operations will be under the operational control of British military commanders with the command and over-riding authority retained by the British clandestine authorities at the national level.

7. Although British and U.S. policies on the wartime organization for clandestine operations at the NATIONAL levels are divergent, there is general agreement on the degree of control that will be exercised by a Supreme Allied Commander (NATO) as an INTERNATIONAL commander. The meaning of the word 'control' is interpreted to be that control exercised over clandestine resources operating in direct support of military operations and only to the extent necessary to insure coordination. This interpretation is in consonance with paragraph 3 a above, with the previous guidance furnished the S.G. by the Joint Chiefs of Staff in SM-2876-51 (subparagraph 3 f), and is consistent with the policy provisions of the CIA–SS [CIA–SIS] agreement.

8. The organization to discharge the responsibilities of the Supreme Allied Commander (NATO) will differ in each instance as a result of differing requirements. Further, it should be a cardinal principle that organisation of his headquarters is his responsibility subject to the approval of the S.G. on matters of policy.

9. Supreme Headquarters Allied Powers Europe (SHAPE) is formulating a structure for such matters, the final position on which is not yet formed.

10. In adhering to the view in paragraph 3, above, the British cite an agreement between their Clandestine Services and the Central Intelligence Agency. This agreement recognized that certain considerations must be taken into account at the international level on clandestine operations as differentiated from military operations by regular forces. These considerations are:

a. Resistance movements invariably provide frequent and complex political problems, often of a sporadic and unforeseen nature, which can be solved only between governments, or in the theater, by political advisers to the theater commander. Allied officers experienced in the politics of the country concerned will also be required to deal with appropriate representatives of that country. Even executive officers in the field should be well versed in the local politics. Theater commanders and their staffs are unlikely to wish to be involved in such questions, at any rate until their political implications have been fully accepted by the Allied political authorities.

b. Logistics alone make it necessary at times to carry out special operations (U.S. Covert Operations) from within a theater into a country outside the military theater boundaries. Such operations may in fact be of little or no concern to the theater from which they are sustained.

c. Though this applies, at times, to any special operations (U.S. Covert Operations), it is of particular importance in the waging of political and psychological warfare. The clandestine side of these types of operations will often require handling on a much broader basis than a theater one.

In the light of the above it is apparent that requirement will exist for continual coordination of clandestine operations as between supreme Allied commanders and national clandestine agencies.

11. In the light of the facts: the SACEUR [Supreme Allied Commander Europe] is studying the wartime organisation required to discharge his responsibilities in this field; that there is U.S.–U.K. agreement on degree of control to be exercised by supreme Allied commanders over such operations during war; that a requirement will exist for wartime coordination of clandestine operations as between SACEUR and the national clandestine agencies; and that a European Clandestine Committee has been established to advise SACEUR on problems in this field; it is advisable to:

a. Concur in that part of the British views which relates to the amount of control that Supreme Allied Commanders will exercise over such operations.

b. Non-concur with the British views which predetermine the organization to discharge responsibilities of Supreme Allied Commanders.

c. Recognize that the organization to discharge responsibilities of Supreme Allied Commanders will differ in each instance and that these commanders are most capable of determining their organizational requirements.

d. Recognise that policy approval of these organizations is necessary due to the extreme sensitivity of operations in this field.

12. The S.G. proposes to define 'Clandestine Operations' as those operations which are normally under national governmental control in peacetime and requests guidance thereon.

13. In paragraph 6 of SM-2876-51, the U.S. Representative to the S.G. was informed that definitions in this field were under consideration by the Joint Chiefs of Staff and would be forwarded as soon as possible.

14. The term, Clandestine Operations, as used by the S.G., embraces BOTH 'Unconventional Warfare,' which includes Covert Operations as an integral part thereof, and 'Espionage and Counterespionage.'

15. In light of the decision by the Joint Chiefs of Staff on J.C.S. 1969/15, it is now possible to forward definitions for Unconventional Warfare.

16. The U.S. conducts espionage and counterespionage on an organized basis outside the U.S. However, SHAPE recognized that such operations as may be conducted by the U.S. in NATO countries should remain outside his purview due to the extreme sensitivity of such operations. SHAPE limited his responsibilities for such operations to those that are conducted in enemy countries. It follows that Supreme Allied Commanders should concern themselves, infosar as this field is concerned, only with espionage and counter-espionage conducted against enemy countries. The Central Intelligence Agency recommended that the phrase, 'in enemy countries' be changed to read 'against enemy countries.'

JCS 1735/132, Report by the Joint Subsidiary Plans Division to the Joint Chiefs of Staff on Clandestine Operations, 24 June 1952, Top Secret – Limited Distribution, RG 218, USNA.

16

Special operations in the Third World

16.1 Operation BOOT: Iran, 1953

In 1951 Iran's President Mussadiq nationalised the Anglo-Iranian Oil Company, in which Britain had a 50 per cent share-holding. Subsequently, diplomatic relations between Britain and Iran were ruptured and overt military intervention was briefly considered. SIS developed plans for Mussadiq's overthrow and replacement by the exiled Shah. Robert Zaehner, Britain's longest-serving covert specialist in Iran (an ex-PWE officer), was pessimistic about the possibility of overthrowing Mussadiq. Officials in the Foreign Office and State Department were also unenthusiastic. However, in 1953 'Monty' Woodhouse, an SIS officer responsible for special operations, was able to secure CIA support and the newly installed President Eisenhower was well-disposed towards the CIA and special operations in general. Thereafter, although the plan was designed by the British, the operation was largely implemented by the United States, which still had a functioning embassy in Teheran. The final stages of the coup were dramatic, ending in a tank battle at Mussadiq's headquarters.

When I saw Eden in the Foreign Office, Zaehner was also present at my request. He had left Iran some weeks before me, and I had not realised how disillusioned he was with the plans which he had helped to launch. To my dismay, he gave Eden an extremely defeatist account of the capabilities of the Brothers [a pro-Western faction in Iran].As I had asked for him to be present as the leading authority on Iran, I was quite unable to counter his gloomy advice.

That seemed likely to terminate the whole project. The officials present were visibly relieved, but Eden left one loop-hole open. He

207

remarked that an operation such as we contemplated would have no chance of success without American support. This had always been my view. I took his words as tantamount to permission to pursue the idea further with the Americans ...

Not wishing to be accused of trying to use the Americans to pull British chestnuts out of the fire, I decided to emphasize the Communist threat to Iran rather than the need to recover control of the oil industry. I argued that even if a settlement of the oil dispute could be negotiated with Mussadiq, which was doubtful, he was still incapable of resisting a *coup* by the Tudah Party, if it were backed by Soviet support. Therefore he must be removed ... The plan which came with me to Washington was called, rather too obviously, Operation Boot ...

It was presupposed that the *coup*, once it succeeded, would be immediately welcomed by the western powers and followed by a vigorous programme of reforms. It would be costly: perhaps half a million pounds would be needed, in addition to the £10,000 a month which we were currently supplying to the Brothers. For all these reasons American support would be indispensable.

C. M. Woodhouse, *Something Ventured* (London: Granada, 1982), pp. 117–18.

16.2 **Eden, Suez and Nasser, 1956**

There is little evidence that SIS had much enthusiasm for assassination, in contrast to the secret services of countries such as France and Israel. However, in 1956 the Prime Minister, Anthony Eden, whose judgement was undoubtedly affected by serious ill-health, ordered plans to assassinate the President of Egypt, Gamal Abdel Nasser, who had nationalised the Suez Canal. Peter Wright's *Spycatcher* memoirs offer the fullest account of these deliberations and a rare glimpse into the surreal world of technical support. Peter Wright's memoirs are wrong on many issues, not least his obsession with the supposed treachery of the MI5 Director, Roger Hollis, and must be approached with caution. Nevertheless they are probably reliable here, since Eden's ardent desire to 'get Nasser down' is confirmed by a multitude of sources.

At the beginning of the Suez Crisis, MI6 developed a plan, through the London Station, to assassinate Nasser using nerve gas. Eden initially gave his approval to the operation, but later rescinded it when he got agreement from the French and Israelis to engage in joint military action. When this course failed, and he was forced to withdraw, Eden reactivated the assassination option a second time.

... I was consulted about the plan by John Henry and Peter Dixon, the two MI6 Technical Services officers from the London Station responsible for drawing it up. Dixon, Henry and I all attended joint MI5/MI6 meetings to discuss technical research for intelligence services at Porton Down, the government's Chemical and Biological Weapons Research Establishment.

... Their plan was to place canisters of nerve gas inside the ventilation system, but I pointed out that this would require large quantities of gas and would result in massive loss of life amongst Nasser's staff. It was the usual MI6 operation – hopelessly unrealistic – and it did not remotely surprise me when Henry told me later that Eden had backed away from the operation.

... after the gas canisters plan fell through, MI6 looked at some new weapons. On one occasion I went down to Porton to see a demonstration of a cigarette packet which had been modified by the Explosives Research and Development Establishment to fire a dart tipped with poison.

P. Wright, *Spycatcher: The Candid Autobiography of a Senior Intelligence Officer* (New York: Viking, 1987), pp. 160–2

16.3 **Indonesia 1958: prime ministerial authorisation**

The British and Australians agreed to co-operate with an American plan, approved by Eisenhower in late 1957, to put pressure upon the Indonesian Premier, Sukarno, whom they perceived as neutralist and toying with Communism. This was to be implemented by supporting rebel groups. The short minute by Harold Macmillan below is revealing on the matter of authorisation. It shows that such matters received attention at the highest level, albeit they were dealt with more informally, in contrast to the more elaborate National Security Council structure evolved by the Americans for planning and approving special operations. During the 1950s, both British and American premiers took a detailed interest in such special operations.

2. There is a proposal by the Americans which we have agreed to offer disavowable help. It involves the use of the Singapore air base and the RAF. We have agreed in principle if Sir Robert Scott and the Governor of Singapore agree. Keep an eye on this.

Prime Minister, Harold Macmillan, minute to Mr Bishop, 'Points discussed with Foreign Secretary last night', 4 March 1958, PREM 11/2320, PRO.

16.4 Indonesia 1958: UK–US–Australian co-operation

Britain had been sceptical of the idea of special operations against Sukarno in 1957, partly because of instability in Singapore, but had warmed to it in 1958. The scheme required the use of facilities in Australia, Singapore and the Philippines. By 1958, with the exception of the Governor of Singapore, British officials and ministers were sympathetic and had believed that a veil of plausible deniability could be maintained. The views of the British Commissioner General for South East Asia, Sir Robert Scott, who favoured the operation, carried weight in London and Washington.

In private conversation with me evening May 6, Lloyd [the British Foreign Secretary] said he thought most recent news from Indonesia encouraging and we should not rpt not give up hope of keeping on the pressure through the rebellious forces now rpt now principally in the Celebes. He expressed the view that it not rpt not impossible that activity in Sumatra might revive if there were success in the Celebes. He said his Ambassador Djakarta strongly favored trying for a political solution and abandoning any assistance to the rebels, but that Rob Scott, whose judgement Lloyd valued more highly, did not rpt not share this view.

Copenhagen to Washington (signed Dulles), Dulte 15, 7 May 1959, 756D.00/5-758, USNA. Quoted in A. R. and G. McT. Kahin, *Subversion as Foreign Policy: The Secret Eisenhower and Dulles Debacle in Indonesia* (London: IB Tauris, 1965), p. 175.

16.5 Indonesia, June 1958: reactions to defeat

Some of the assistance to the rebels in Indonesia came in the form of black-painted American B-28 bombers with no insignia, which were flown by CIA pilots. One of these was captured in May 1958 and this effectively marked the end of the operation. By June 1958 the British were disenchanted with the US-inspired covert operation to support rebels in Indonesia against Sukarno. They hoped to encourage the Americans in their efforts to draw Sukarno away from Communism by more overt political means. There was some concern in London that the United States would not persevere with this for long before resorting to covert measures once again.

Present Situation:-
1. The rebellion against the central Government has failed militarily, but guerilla activities continue in Sumatra and in the Celebes, the Central Government has yet to launch a major attack against the dissidents.
   2. The Americans have stopped helping the dissidents and are working through the Army and political channels to reverse the trend of the central Government towards Communism. This will take time, if it works at all. There is little confidence in Washington that it will. The U.S. and we are keeping our clandestine planning and assets in being.

Prospects.
3. The Americans should be encouraged to give their new policy of using political means to improve the situation fair trial. It cannot transform the scene but it may improve matters appreciably. If this policy looks like failing, the Americans may want to change back to more active measures, before all their dissident assets are lost. This will not be easy and might have serious consequences. We need to keep in very close touch with the Americans as both we and the Commonwealth are directly concerned. The Working Group is very useful in this, and the Americans are also much impressed with Sir R. Scott's judgment.

The Dutch

It is important to keep the Dutch informed about any aid given to Indonesia, in pursuance of the new policy, and to remember their extreme sensitivity (which the Americans are very apt to ignore). [Sentence deleted and retained under Section 3(4).]

Briefing Note for the Prime Minister's Washington Visit, 'Indonesia', 8 June 1958, PREM 11/2324, PRO.

16.6 US–UK co-operation on counter-subversion, 1958

The failure of the British and Americans to co-ordinate their covert efforts properly during the Lebanon crisis, and the failure of covert action in Indonesia, prompted British officials to reflect on the alliance mechanisms in this area. Macmillan was advised to raise this during his visit to Washington in June 1958 and his brief is reproduced below.

It would be better to take these as two subjects and if possible to take counter-subversion first as it is wider.

Counter-subversion

It is easiest to think of this in terms of concrete examples, e.g. Indonesia, the Lebanon, the Yemen.

On the British side there is a fairly expert staff covering the Foreign Office, M.I.6, the Information Research Department, and to an increasing degree the Ministry of Defence (and Service Departments), the Colonial Office, and the Commonwealth Relations Office. The basic principle is the direct responsibility of the Minister concerned and the planning is best carried out at the working level, general and specific political or financial approval being given as required.

On the American side the organisation is not so tight and the co-ordination between the State Department and the C.I.A. is not complete. Neither side trusts the other.

There is a need on both sides for better forecasting of possible trouble spots, quicker provision of the type of intelligence required to launch counter-subversive operations, and above all quicker financial and logistical provision of military and other supplies for all these operations. This can best be done on a national basis.

212

As between the American and ourselves the best way to proceed is to develop the Working Group principle in Washington and [Passage deleted and retained under Section 3(4)] in the field. If the Working Group system is to work properly the Working Groups must be attended by suitably high-level people who can speak authoritatively on policy and operational matters and they must meet at frequent intervals. In the case of the Lebanon the Working Group met but State Department representation was inadequate.

In the case of Indonesia the preliminary intelligence was not very much good and the logistic support was in general inadequate and too late.

If an operation is to be mounted in the Lebanon we shall need much more intelligence and more careful planning.

To sum up, no new machinery is required but a development and strengthening of the existing procedure particularly at the Working Group level.

Briefing Note for the Prime Minister's Washington Visit, 'Propaganda/Counter-Subversion', 8 June 1958, PREM 11/2324, PRO.

PART VII

LIAISON AND DECEPTION

Liaison and deception, although rather different activities, are complementary partners for the final section of this volume and share some characteristics. They are both activities that involve all the other main functional areas of secret service. Liaison is the technical term for the 'diplomacy' of intelligence, or the management of relations between one's own intelligence services and those of other countries. It is complex because there are usually a multitude of links between the intelligence specialists of co-operating countries, working in fields as diverse as economic intelligence or underwater sound monitoring. A neglected aspect of liaison is co-operation between domestic security services against internal enemies. It is from co-operation against individual 'agitators' at the start of the twentieth century, rather than co-operation against enemy states in wartime, that the modern Western intelligence alliance of European, Commonwealth and American agencies probably originates.

Liaison is an ambiguous subject. Co-operation can be very close, as between the partners in the UKUSA signals intelligence alliance, which extends to jointly operated stations in which national boundaries begin to dissolve. Alternatively it might be more qualified, as with liaison with European states which were considered insecure, or with the services of Third World states which received intelligence support and training from Britain. The difficulties of maintaining simultaneous co-operation with American and Commonwealth services were notorious.

Deception, like liaison, also involved the deployment of many different types of intelligence organisation, but in a much more co-ordinated manner. This form of activity, which had been developed to a high level of sophistication during wartime, was placed on a care and maintenance basis in 1945. But in 1950 British deception skills were dusted off and redeployed in a Cold War context. Almost all these post-war deception operations remain classified and unknown to us.

Deception and liaison are also linked by the theme of immense sensitivity. Governments have gone to great lengths to protect secrets in these areas. In the early 1990s, the Directors of the CIA repeatedly promised that its files on Operation BOOT/AJAX, the UK–US operation that restored the Shah of Iran to the throne in 1953 (document 16.1), would be declassified. But in the mid-1990s, when officials finally turned their hand to the declassification process, they discovered that these files had been destroyed at an earlier point. It is likely that they were destroyed in the 1970s, to prevent the exposure of British SIS activities in the course of the major congressional investigations into the CIA that were active at that time.

17

Co-operation with foreign services

17.1 British JIC papers supplied to Washington

Britain deluged the Washington bureaucracy with multiple
copies of its JIC papers. This was part of a deliberate policy of
encouraging liaison. These documents were sometimes copies
of proper London-produced JIC papers, but more often they
were subtle variants, produced specifically for American consumption by Britain's JIC Washington, part of the British
Joint Staff Mission. A proportion of these papers dealt with
subjects on which London wished to influence opinion in
Washington, such as Palestine.

1. On 25 February 1948 five copies, 77–80 and 80A inclusive, of a
[UK JIC Washington] paper entitled 'Short Term Intentions of the
Soviet Union in Palestine' dated 13 February 1948 were handed to
the Secretary, U.S. Joint Intelligence Committee by the Secretary JIC,
British Joint Services Mission, with the following written request:
'The British Chiefs of Staff have requested that this paper be shown to
the U.S. Chiefs of Staff.'
2. Copy number 77 is accordingly transmitted herewith.
3. Remaining copies with copies of this memorandum are being
distributed as follows:

	Copy No.
Lieut. General S.J. Chamberlin, USA	78
Major General G.G. McDonald, USAF	79
Rear Admiral T.B. Inglis, USN	80
*JIC File	80A

*For circulation to Major General W.E. Todd, USAF and JIG
Copies to:
JIG Members
Intelligence Section, JIG

E. W. Rawlins, Commander, US Navy, Secretary US JIC, to Secretary, US JCS, 26 February 1948, Top Secret, Memo: 'Short Term Intentions of the Soviet Union in Palestine', Director of Intelligence USAF HQ files, File 2-1000/2-1099, Box 40, RG 341, USNA.

17.2 The British JIC and American views of the Soviet Union, 1948

Britain and the United States worked hard to achieve some commonality of view in their estimates of the Soviet Union in the late 1940s, even seeking to produce documents called 'ABAIs' or 'Agreed British-American Intelligence'. A major sticking point was the likelihood of war before 1956, which the British were not prepared for, and therefore were most unwilling to contemplate.

1. In arriving at an appreciation of the situation which would face a conference of British and American intelligence Staffs, a review of available British staff papers has been accomplished. The two British papers which were forwarded by the JSM as a possible basis for a combined estimate of the situation were studied and found to be inadequate for the purpose. These [UK] papers are J.I.C. (48) 26 (0), 'Strategic Intentions of the Soviet Union,' and J.I.C. (47) 42 (0), 'Forecast of the World Situation in 1957.' In addition to these, a study was made of J.I.C. (47) 46 (00, 'Possibility of War before the End of 1956,' J.I.C. (48) 11 (0), 'Increase in the Likelihood of a Major War After the End of 1956,' and J.I.C. (48) 39 (0), 'Basic Assumptions for Planning.'

2. It is apparent from an analysis of the foregoing papers and a comparison with the latest approved American estimate, J.I.C. 380/3, that there exists a fundamental difference in concept. This springs largely from the fact that the British accept and use as hypotheses some basic factors which American Intelligence considers as problems to be studied and solved. One of these in particular will require detailed analysis. This factor is in relation to the possibility of war prior to the period 1956 – 1957.

3. From a standpoint of Air Intelligence there are few differences in estimates of Soviet capabilities that could not be resolved after Combined consideration ... Basically the British tend to believe that American Intelligence over-rates Soviet capabilities in a number of

respects. These differences, however, should be readily amenable to solution in a conference. The greater difficulty may be expected to arise from differences in basic concept and estimates of Soviet intentions ...

Colonel USAF, Chief Air Intelligence Division, DFI/USAF – ONI, J. F. Olive, Jr., to Director of Intelligence USAF, 19 July 1948, Top Secret, Memo: 'Proposed Intelligence Conference', Director of Intelligence USAF HQ files, File 2-2200/2-2299, Box 42, RG 341, USNA.

17.3 **The wartime legacy of camaraderie, 1951–52**

The importance of wartime associations in facilitating US-UK intelligence relations is hard to assess. They were probably most important during the early 1950s when Walter Bedell Smith was head of the CIA and Eisenhower was Chief of Staff, then President, while many former British senior figures who had worked with them, including Ismay, Macmillan, Portal, Sinclair, Strong and Tedder, rose to top positions in Whitehall and Westminster. A key factor for Eisenhower was his good experience with staff at the Supreme Headquarters Allied Expeditionary Force, including his intelligence chief, the British General Kenneth Strong. An important common denominator amongst this 'in' group was fly-fishing.

My dear Kenneth,

I have just returned from a brief fishing trip – which was most successful – to find your package containing a wealth of fly-tying materials. You certainly did not buy all this for five dollars – did you? Please let me know what they really cost, as I will want you to act as my purchasing agent again.

It was good, as always, to see you, and I hope to visit you later in the year. All my best.

Faithfully,
Bedell.

General Walter Bedell Smith, Director CIA, to Major General K. W. D. Strong, 16 April 1952, File 1952 Personal Correspondence 'S', Box 20, Walter Bedell Smith Papers, Dwight Eisenhower Library, Abilene, Kansas.

17.4 **Third parties, 1952**

The numbers of alliance partners collected by Britain and the United States increased steadily in the 1950s and 1960s. The inclusion of third or fourth parties often rendered Anglo-American intelligence co-operation hugely complicated. By the 1960s many smaller states, such as Greece, had well-developed secret services of their own.

Special Handling Required, Not Releasable to Foreign Nationals ...
A. Various Greek Gen[eral] Staff Off[icers], upon query, agree talks taking place and exchange Bulg OB [order of battle intelligence] under discussion. Brigadier Nikodopoulos of [Greek] Central Information and Control Branch of National Defence General Staff (comparable to CIA) expresses personal opinion exchange must begin slowly in order to insure quid pro quo. No further details aval.
B. Procedure of G2 [US Army Intelligence] Bulg OB summary to go to Greek Gen Staff desirable: believe UK now doing this; however exchange Bulg OB with Yugs [Yugoslavs] without UK knowledge might jeopardise the excellent US and UK joint intell collections effort in Greece at SIC. SIC opn plus agreement with NDGS received jointly all Greek agency intell reports on satellites true examples this co-ordination ...

US Military Attaché, Athens, to G-2, Army Intelligence Washington DC, Top Secret, 24 June 1952, Assistant Chief of Staff (G2 Army Intelligence) files, TS Incoming and Outgoing Cables, Box 189, Entry 58, RG 319, USNA.

17.5 **Restrictions upon liaison**

British and American intelligence in Hong Kong was important and offered a major window upon events in Communist China. Yet liaison was problematical. Britain was at pains to avoid provoking Communist China and insisted that all liaison business be conducted in Singapore, the home of Britain's JIC Far East and its regional political authorities. However, the British military in Hong Kong, who wanted direct contact with the Americans and more active operations, chaffed under these restrictions.

Special Handling Required, Not Releasable to Foreign Nationals.

Gen Airey informed me this date he has formally recommended to FARELF Singapore early establishment of 'Anglo American Intel Committee' in Hong Kong to specialize in Commie Chi mil intell. French will not rpt not be informed existence this group. He believes he has way paved with GOC FARELF and with General Shortt [Director of Military Intelligence] in London to approve this favourite project of his. He has recommended that Hong Kong USAIRLO, ASTALUSNA and USARMLO [American service liaison officers] be officially invited thru Washington to participate as full members of the committee. Informed him your recent decision provide weekly summary of Watch Committee Intel, Commie order of battle changes, etc, and he was tremendously pleased, saying this more than he expected even from my participation in Intell Committee if approved. Believe Gen Airy's formal recommendation is based entirely on his personal desire to 'get out from under the academic and unreasonable restrictions imposed by Singapore mil and civil auth on exchange of Far East infor anywhere except Singapore' and to have official auth to overrule the Hong Kong Civil govt, if necessary, when they object to the release of sensitive, though vital information to US. From American viewpoint consider establishment such committee will have little or no effect either way. Gen Airey is now giving US all info he has though it currently not much. Based on various comments of past, believe Gen Airey and General Shortt also considering plan to greatly increase Brit covert agent orgn on mainland China though this my present conjecture only. Will keep you informed any further info to this end.

US Army Liaison Officer, Hong Kong, to G-2, Army Intelligence Washington, 6 June 1952, Top Secret, Assistant Chief of Staff (G2 Army Intelligence) files, TS Incoming and Outgoing Cables, Box 189, Entry 58, RG 319, USNA.

17.6 British intelligence and NATO partners, 1953

The relatively large number of NATO partners rendered the British and the Americans reluctant to disclose sensitive intelligence information in a NATO context. Accordingly, intelligence circulated in NATO tended to be in the form of assessments and could be rather bland.

Intelligence

1. You are now authorised to pass UK intelligence information collated or obtained locally up to TOP SECRET to NATO officers integrated in HQ, Northern Army Group, or to any foreign or international echelon thereon, and to such NATO formations as may, in the future, be placed under your command.

2. The principle of the 'need-to-know' will be most strictly applied individually in the case of all recipients.

3. Sources will be protected and their identity will not be disclosed other than to UK Eyes.

4. No intelligence will be passed which can be identified by a third party as the property of another country, or as being the combined property of the UK and any other country. This proviso applies equally to intelligence of US or UK/US origin and to that of any other origin.

5. No intelligence on individual NATO countries will be passed.

6. Classified Intelligence should normally be passed to higher, lower, or flank formations through COSMIC channels ...

Co-ordination Branch STIB to Director Security Analysis, STIB, 10 March 1953, Secret – UK Eyes Only, 10 March 1953, DEFE 41/70, PRO.

17.7 **CIA views of liaison with the British, 1954**

CIA views of British intelligence are interesting because many traced the antecedents of the CIA to British inspiration in the early years of the Second World War. The memoirs of the CIA covert action specialist J. B. Smith are particularly noteworthy because they were one of the few memoirs published without being submitted for sanitisation by the CIA, which is cautious on the subject of liaison. The memoir is also widely regarded as accurate. This section recounts his thoughts on being posted to Singapore, the British intelligence centre in Asia, in 1954.

There were two views of liaison with the British. One was that it was a rare and beautiful thing to be nurtured with every care, because the British were the most sagacious spies in the business, with a long and remarkable tradition of success. The other was that it was a waste of time, the British officers were a bunch of supercilious snobs toward whom we should show an equivalent disdain. In time, the unmasking of Kim Philby, impeccable MI-6er and the most useful agent the Soviets ran during the cold war, may have brought the weight of the argument down on the second side, but in 1954 the first side had the upper hand. Allen Dulles enjoyed mulling over the exploits of Sir Francis Walsingham, the spymaster of Elizabeth I, whose hand, Dulles liked to point out, lay behind most of the major undertakings of Elizabeth's reign, such as manipulating the plotters around Mary Queen of Scots to the point where Elizabeth finally had the pretext to execute her cousin. Frank Wisner enjoyed the opportunity of going over operational details with such an astute intelligence officer as Kim Philby.

As a result of being briefed by representatives of both schools of thought, however, I arrived at my post with a formula for guiding my conduct that went something like this: our liaison with the British is one of our greatest assets; don't tell the bastards anything important. I would learn how things really worked from Bob Jantzen, the chief of station, Singapore, who belonged to a school all his own. Perhaps he could fashion his way through the maze because he had not been successfully indoctrinated into an Eastern prep school, as had many of the pro-British school, nor by poor Irish nuns at a parochial school, who hated even English muffins, as I suspected was the case with many of the anti-British school. In any case he made British liaison work for the CIA and for the good of his own career with impressive results.

J. B. Smith, *Portrait of a Cold Warrior: Second Thoughts of a Top CIA Agent* (New York: Putnam, 1976), pp. 148–9.

17.8 **MI5 liaison and the Baghdad Pact, 1956**

The various regional alliances concluded by Britain, the United States and their allies often provided a framework for enhanced co-ordination between secret services, as well as overt military services. In 1956 it was the UK that drafted the agreement governing the Liaison Committee which was concerned with counter-Communism and dealt with relations between the security services of each country. This document also underlines the importance of prior relationships with Commonwealth secret services in steering wider international groupings.

The Liaison Committee held five meetings under Iranian Chairmanship with Pakistani rapporteur. To begin with the Iranian and Turkish delegates were utterly confused as to the purpose and scope of the Liaison Committee and the first two meetings were largely wasted, but with effective assistance from the Pakistani delegate succeeded by end of second meeting in explaining, and persuading them to abide by, terms of reference of the Liaison Committee as originally laid down in Baghdad in December 1955. The following day was devoted by each delegation to composing individual draft proposals and at a third meeting the paper submitted by the United Kingdom delegate was immediately adopted as a basis for a working agreement between the security authorities of the member countries.

2. This United Kingdom paper subsequently amplified and amended and entitled a 'Memorandum for Guidance of the Liaison Committee' forms the substance of the final report to which it is appended and is in effect a permanent agenda for the future work of the Liaison Committee and recommends the strengthening of the security forces of the member countries through mutual cooperation and the exchange of information on:

(a) methods and techniques of Communist bloc espionage and sabotage and means of countering them and successes obtained;

(b) Communist subversion in the member countries and a wide range of subjects dealing with the strength and activities of National Communist Parties.

3. An amendment included in this paper proposed that before all future meetings of the committee the security authorities of each member country shall draw up an assessment of the threat of Communist subversion both internal and external to the respective member country, to enable the committee to provide an appreciation for the Council of the immediate objectives of Communist subversive activities, methods by which the Communists are seeking to subvert the member countries, social groups which are the prime targets of Communist subversion and the factors which have helped in those successes. These assessments are to be circulated one month before all future meetings of the Liaison Committee by each security service to all the others direct and not through the Secretariat and will form

the basic agenda for the following meeting of the Liaison Committee. These assessments will be collated by the full committee and will form periodic progress reports for the Council.

4. I am satisfied that the paper is perfectly satisfactory from the United Kingdom point of view ...

Head of SIME to Foreign Office, No. 271, Top Secret, 7 April 1956, V10710/G, FO 371/121283, PRO.

17.9 **Attempts to disguise UK–US co-operation, 1957**

Britain and the United States were agreed on the importance of maintaining a veil of secrecy over intelligence co-operation. One of the most persistent irritants in the Anglo-American intelligence relationship was periodic leaks on this subject. This irritation was particularly acute when it resulted in high-level public embarrassment, as in 1957 when there were press leaks about the Anglo-American-Canadian summit at Bermuda. References to discussions on intelligence and 'planning' (often a euphemism for covert action and psychological warfare) were omitted from the final communique, but were then revealed in the British and American press. Eisenhower felt that the UK delegation was responsible and, as a result of the leak, he might appear to have been disingenuous with Congress. Macmillan's reply was courteous, but he did not accept responsibility for the leak.

Dear Harold,

I enclose herewith a copy of the article to which I referred today in my cable, sent to you at Bermuda. I likewise send a copy of that cable.

The part of the article that disturbs me so deeply appears in the first two columns. Here is practically a verbatim account of the detailed incidents and events surrounding the elimination of the words 'intelligence and planning' from the draft communique. The writer, of course, did not know the background that led to the original suggestion, that is, your thought that Canada, yourselves and ourselves should co-ordinate our efforts to detect any hostile move on the part of the Russians in periods of tension.

Of course the writer himself proves that he did not have the good of either your country or ours in mind in writing the article because he gives the logical reason for its elimination in the two sentences 'The announcement was eliminated from the final draft of the document by Secretary of State Dulles. It is understood that Mr Dulles felt that this evidence of a more intimate British-United States Relationship would offend other allies of the United States, notably France.' In other words, he cared nothing for the soundness of national reasons, only for the story.

This article came out this morning, after Foster [Dulles] and I had held a meeting with Congressional leaders last evening in which we outlined the general character of our talks, carefully avoiding however, operational or planning details which could, if publicised, cause embarrassment to either or both of us. Nevertheless we made the truthful assertion that no 'secret agreements' were arrived at. This morning some of them may be wondering!

I am sure, of course, that you share my disappointment at such an occurrence, with its implications that even the members of such friendly governments as yours and ours cannot talk frankly and freely with one another without the danger of serious leaks to the public press. I earnestly hope that both of us may be successful in preventing things like this in the future so that there may be no interruption of the close communion and coordination that we consider so important to our future security and welfare.

With warm personal regard,
Yours ever DE

The Right Honorable Harold Macmillan, M.P.
The Prime Minister,
London

Eisenhower to Macmillan, 26 March 1957, Eyes Only, DDRS 1997/518.

Dear Mr President,

I have seen Middleton's article in the New York Times of March 26. I deplore particularly the reference to the drafting of the communique. You will remember that we were as anxious as you were that nothing should be said publicly to suggest that special bi-lateral machinery was being set up for intelligence and planning.

I have made very full enquiries about this. I find that although Middleton's article is dated March 25 (Monday), mention of secret agreements and joint planning machinery was current among press correspondents in Bermuda on the previous Saturday evening and Sunday ... Much of course of the article could be based on intelligent guess-work ... I can find nothing to suggest that this was the fault of any member of the United Kingdom Delegation ...

I dislike publicity as much as you do. I hate newspapers and am very bad at handling them, and I remember you saying that you never read them. This modern technique of doing everything in public makes life almost intolerable. For my part, I would certainly be relieved if our meetings in future could be on a quite different basis – that they should be more personal, with a very limited number of advisers, and with no publicity at all. But I do hope that the embarrassment of this article will not make us lose faith in the need for us to talk frankly and with confidence in each other.

Since Dean [British JIC Chairman] is already in Washington, I hope that his programme can go ahead as planned.

Yours ever,

Harold.

P.S. Anyway, if we write to each other, nobody need read our letters.

Harold Macmillan to Eisenhower, 29 March 1957, DDRS 1997/745.

17.10 **Denis Healey, DIS and Israel, 1965**

This document relates to Denis Healey's tenure as Minister of Defence. It reveals the way in which intelligence could form part of the wider fabric of diplomatic relations and was often seen as a key constituent of close relationship with Britain by other countries. Britain enjoyed a close intelligence relationship with many Gulf Arab countries at this time.

When Mrs. Meir, the Israel Foreign Minister, met Mr. Healey, she expressed disappointment at the lack of response to repeated Israeli invitations to the Director of Sales and to the Director General of Intelligence to visit Israel. Mr Healey asked what lies behind Foreign Office objections to the acceptance of such invitations. Following a telephone conversation, Mr. Thomas of the DIS called on me on 29 September to discuss the question.

2. I told Mr. Thomas that we were opposed to any action which could contribute to the build-up of a 'special relationship' between Israel and Britain, particularly in the military field on the grounds that it was in Israel's interests to achieve identification of Britain with the Israel cause in Arab eyes, whereas our interests lay in maintaining our public position of impartiality. Particular invitations might in themselves seem insignificant but the cumulative effect was damaging. I also gave Mr. Thomas an account of the past difficulties with the Israelis over the formalization of intelligence exchanges ...

Minute by C. McLean of conversation with Thomas of the DIS, Secret, 29 September 1965, ER 1691/5, FO 371/180917, PRO.

18
Deception

18.1 The Directorate of Forward Plans, 1950

The highly successful centre for wartime deception against the Axis, the London Controlling Section, was not closed down at the end of the war. Until 1950 it was preserved with the main objective of maintaining a reservoir of the specialist skills and knowledge learned during the war. In 1950 it was revived on an operational basis, renamed the Directorate of Forward Plans (DFP) and deployed in a Cold War context.

MINISTER OF DEFENCE

Your Ministry includes, I understand, a Directorate concerned with the techniques which we evolved during the war for misleading the enemy about our future plans and intentions.

... How large an organisation is maintained for this purpose? What is its cost? What is the scope of its present activities? ...

W.S.C

PRIME MINSTER

With reference to your Minute No. M.457/52 of 26th of August the facts are as follows.

2. The deception organisation (cover name 'Directorate of Forward Plans') derives from the wartime 'London Controlling Section' which operated first under the late Colonel Oliver Stanley and subsequently under Colonel Bevan. Between the end of the war and the middle of 1950, it existed on a care and maintenance basis. Then, after a review by the Chiefs of Staff, it was decided that the technique of deception, suitably modified to present conditions, could play a useful part in our defence preparations and the present organisation was set up.

229

3. There are, in all, 8 officers in the organisation, 5 in London, 1 in the Middle East, and 2 in Singapore ...

4. I think that, provided the organisation sticks, as it does, to military matters, its existence is well justified. We are under continuous and vigorous attack by a hostile Intelligence Organisation, and it is most important to confuse and mislead that organisation and to put ourselves in a position to continue to do this if war comes ... We have good reason to believe the Russians are attempting the same kind of activity.

Churchill to Minister of Defence, M457/52, 26 August 1952, and reply 2 September 1952, PREM 11/257, PRO.

18.2 **The Joint Concealment Centre, 1951**

In 1949 a centre for the study of operational deception techniques was set up called the Visual Inter-Service Training and Research Establishment (VISTRE), which worked under the overall direction of the DFP. By 1951 it had changed its name to the Joint Concealment Centre and its remit included the study of physical deception, radio deception and the enemy intelligence system for deception purposes.

Mr Drew [of the Directorate of Forward Plans] explained that it had long been realised by the Chiefs of Staff that there was a need for an organisation at the higher level to control deception. Such an organisation [DFP] was in existence on a world-wide basis. Its responsibilities were primarily strategic. Since it was impossible to draw a clear cut line between strategic and tactical deception, it was inevitable that the co-ordinating agency should in addition be vested with general policy direction of tactical deception organisations of the three Services. In the same way at the lower level, it was vital to have a central agency where the principles and techniques of physical deception could be jointly studied by all three Services. Every Service had an interest, to varying degrees, in all methods of deception. Typical examples of such methods were the radar camouflage of equipment and decoy lighting sets. It was only in the implementation on operations of individual techniques, jointly studied and perfected at VISTRE, that separate forces, such as the Army's R Force, were needed.

Deception

Minutes of 'Inter-Service Meeting on the Future of VISTRE', 79/Mob/
9914 (SWVI), 24 August 1951, AIR 20/11420, PRO.

Appendix of key personnel

(This is a list of key figures in the British overseas policy process, many were not engaged on duties related to secret service activities.)

1. Cabinet committees

Cabinet Office Co-ordinator on Intelligence and Security
Sir Dick Goldsmith White, 1969–72

Counter-Subversion Committee, Chairman
John Nicholls, 1963–

Joint Intelligence Committee (JIC), London, Chairman
(a Cabinet committee from 1957)
Victor Cavendish-Bentinck, 1939–45
Sir Harold Caccia, 1946–47
Sir William Hayter, 1947–49
Sir Patrick Reilly, 1949–53
Sir Patrick Dean, 1953–60
Sir Hugh Stephenson, 1960–63
Sir Bernard Burrows, 1963–66
Sir Denis Greenhill, 1966–68
Sir Edward Peck, 1968–70

Official Committee on Communications Electronics, Chairman
Captain Michael Hodges, 1963–68

Permanent Secretary's Committee on Intelligence and Security
Sir Burke Trend, 1960s

Appendix of key personnel

2. Foreign Office

Head of the Cultural Relations Department
William Montagu-Pollock, 1945–49
John Finch, 1949–52
Anthony Haigh, 1952–62
Robert Cecil, 1962–67
C. C. B. Stewart, 1967–72

Head of the Economic Intelligence Department
Edward Radice, 1946–49
Paul Falla, 1949–52

Head of the Information Policy Department (IPD)
Alan Dudley, 1948–49
Richard Speaight, 1948–50
Angus Malcolm, 1950–53
R. H. K. Marret, 1954–55
C. C. B. Stewart, 1955–58
Paul Wright, 1958–60
Reginald Burrows, 1960–61
Antony Moore, 1962–64
Francis Brooks Richard, 1964–65
George Littlejohn Crook, 1965–69
Bernard Curson, 1969–70

Head of the Information Research Department (IRD)
Ralph Murray, 1948–51
John Peck, 1951–53
John Rennie, 1954–58
Donald Hopson, 1958–62
Christopher Barclay, 1962–66
Nigel Clive, 1966–69
Kenneth Crook, 1969–71

Head of Permanent Under Secretary's Department (PUSD)
Norman Brain, 1949–50
Archibald Ross, 1950–52
Cecil King, 1952–53
Geoffrey McDermott, 1953–56

Robin Hooper, 1956–60
Peter Wilkinson, 1960–63
Geoffrey Arthur, 1963–67
Christopher Ewart-Biggs, 1967–69

Head of the Security Department
George Carey-Foster, 1947–53
Arthur de la Mare, 1953–56
Adrian Samuel, 1956–59
Philip Adams, 1959–63
John Street, 1963–66
S. J. L. Olver, 1966
Derick Ashe, 1966–69

3. The secret services

MI5 / Security Service Director-General
Sir David Petrie, 1940–46
Sir Percy Sillitoe, 1946–53
Sir Dick Goldsmith White, 1953–56
Sir Roger Henry Hollis, 1956–65
Sir Martin Furnival Jones, 1965–72

Chief ('C') of the Secret Intelligence Service / MI6
Major General Sir Stewart Menzies, 1939–53
Major General John Sinclair, 1953–56
Sir Dick Goldsmith White, 1956–69
Sir John Rennie, 1969–73

Director of Government Communications Headquarters (GCHQ)
Sir Edward Travis, 1944–52
Sir Eric Jones, 1952–60
Sir Clive Loehnis, 1960–64
Sir Leonard Hooper, 1965–73

London Communications-Electronic Security Agency (LCESA)
Captain R. F. T. Stannard, 1959–69

Appendix of key personnel

4. Ministry of Defence

Director of Joint Intelligence Bureau (JIB)
Major General Sir Kenneth Strong, 1946–64

Director-General, Defence Intelligence Staff (DIS)
Major General Sir Kenneth Strong, 1964–66
Air Chief Marshal Alfred Earle, 1966–68
Air Marshal Sir Harold Maguire, 1969–

Department of Atomic Energy Intelligence Unit
(transferred to JIB in the mid-1950s, see below)
Commander Eric Welsh, 1945–54

Deputy Director of JIB for Atomic Energy Intelligence
Archie Potts, 1957–64

Head of Intelligence Division, Germany
Major General John Lethbridge, 1945–47
Major General Charles Haydon, 1948–50
Major General John Kirkman, 1950–54

Director of Forward Plans / Planning
John A. Drew, 1950s

5. Scientific intelligence

*Chairman of the Joint Scientific / Technical Intelligence Committee
(JS/TIC)*
Sir David Brunt, 1948–49
Colonel John Neville, 1949–50

Director of Scientific Intelligence
Dr Bertie Blount, 1950–52
Professor R. V. Jones, 1952–54

Scientific Adviser, Intelligence, Ministry of Defence
Eric Williams, 1955–60

Appendix of key personnel

Director of Scientific and Technical Intelligence
Archie Potts, 1964–74

6. Service intelligence

Director of Military Intelligence, –1965
Major General Francis Davidson, 1940–43
Major General John Sinclair, 1944–45
Major General Gerald Templer, 1946–48
Major General Arthur Shortt, 1949–53
Major General Valentine Boucher, 1953–56
Major General Cedric Price, 1956–59
Major General Richard Lloyd, 1959–62
Major General Marshall St J. Oswald, 1962–65

Deputy Director DIS (Army), 1965–
Brigadier R. C. Lempiere, 1966–67
Brigadier R. E. Coaker, 1967–68
Brigadier D. J. Wilson, 1968–70

Director of Naval Intelligence, –1965
Admiral Sir John Godfrey, 1939–42
Rear Admiral Edmund Rushbrooke, 1942–46
Rear Admiral W. E. Perry, 1946–48
Vice Admiral Eric Longley-Cook, 1948–51
Rear Admiral Anthony Buzzard, 1951–54
Rear Admiral John Inglis, 1954–60
Rear Admiral Norman Denning, 1960–64
Rear Admiral, P. W. W. Graham, 1965

Deputy Director DIS (Navy), 1965–
Captain M. D. Kyrle Pope, 1966–67
Commodore E. M. B. Hoare, 1968–69
Commodore C. R. Sims, 1970–

Assistant Chief of Air Staff (Intelligence), –1965
Air Vice Marshal Sir Thomas Elmhirst, 1945–47
Air Vice Marshal Lawrence Pendred, 1947–49
Air Vice Marshal Sir Hugh Constantine, 1950–51

Guide to further reading

The development of espionage, security and intelligence in Britain should be considered in a broad historical context. The best account of the genesis of the British intelligence community, and required reading for those who wish to understand this field, is C. M. Andrew, *Secret Service: The Making of the British Intelligence Community* (London: Heinemann, 1985). Two outstanding studies of British intelligence in the Second World War, which add new research and synthesise a mountain of recent scholarship, are R. Bennett, *Behind the Battle: Intelligence in the War with Germany, 1939–45* (London: Sinclair Stevenson, 1995), and D. Stafford, *Churchill and Secret Service* (London: John Murray, 1997). Amongst the more important official histories are the landmark study of SOE, M. R. D. Foot, *SOE in France, 1940–1944* (London: HMSO, 1966) and the magisterial multi-volume series, F. H. Hinsley *et al.*, *British Intelligence in the Second World War*, Vols I–IV (London: HMSO, 1979–90). The latter is now rendered more accessible to the general reader in a useful abridged single volume. Short contextual assessments are available in recent general studies of the Second World War, one conventional in tone offered by G. L. Weinberg, *A World at Arms: A Global History of World War II* (Cambridge: Cambridge University Press, 1994), pp. 544–58, and one enjoyably iconoclastic by J. Keegan, *The Second World War* (London: Hutchinson, 1989), pp. 483–502. British intelligence during the Far Eastern War as yet remains without substantial analysis, official or unofficial.

There is as yet no well-documented account of British secret service during any decade of the Cold War, although substantial archival materials have been available since the mid-1980s. A detailed and somewhat controversial account, based on interviews and press material, is J. Bloch and P. Fitzgerald, *British Intelligence and Covert*

Action (Dingle, Ireland: Brandon, 1983). A valuable debate on the role and place of intelligence in the history of the Cold War is available in J. L. Gaddis, 'Intelligence, Espionage and Cold War Origins', *Diplomatic History*, 13, 2 (1989) 191–213, together with the subsequent response, D. C. Watt, 'Intelligence and the Historian',*Diplomatic History*, 14, 2 (1990) 199–205.

The history of SIS is dominated by an obsession with the figure of Kim Philby. But the best literature on this subject is now sophisticated, see in particular P. Knightley, *The Master Spy: The Story of Kim Philby* (London:Andre Deutch, 1988). Kim Philby's own memoirs are still essential reading, but need to be accompanied by the critical commentary in E. D. R. Harrisons's, 'More Thoughts on Kim Philby's *My Silent War*', *Intelligence and National Security*, 10, 3 (1995) 514–26. Newly opened archives are beginning to shed light on specific aspects of SIS, for example J. L. Schecter and P. S. Deriabin, *The Spy Who Saved the World: How a Soviet Colonel Changed the Course of the Cold War* (New York: Scribner, 1992). GCHQ in the post-war period remains, appropriately perhaps, a cipher, but the story of Britain and the emerging post-war English-speaking signals intelligence alliance is given in B. F. Smith, *The Ultra-Magic Deals and the Most Secret Special Relationship, 1940–1946* (Shrewsbury: Airlife Publishing, 1993).

Scientific intelligence is discussed in a combative manner in R. V. Jones, *Reflections on Intelligence* (London: William Heinemann, 1989), and the related issue of defectors to the West is illuminated in a valuable way by an essay on the motivation of defecting Soviet soldiers, W. K. Wark, 'Coming in from the Cold: British Propaganda and the RedArmy Defectors', *International History Review*, 9, 1 (1987) 48–73.

Outstanding studies of aerial reconnaissance are available in P. Lashmar, *Spy-Flights of the Cold War* (London:Alan Sutton, 1996) and R. C. Nesbit, *Eyes of the RAF: A History of Photo Reconnaissance* (London: Alan Sutton, 1996). Army intelligence is surveyed by A. Clayton,*Forearmed: A History of the Intelligence Corps* (London: Brasseys, 1993) and T. Geraghty, *BRIXMIS* (London: Hodder and Stoughton, 1997). British naval intelligence remains almost completely unknown.

The outstanding commentary upon the general management of intelligence and security within Whitehall remains P. Hennessey, *Whitehall* (NewYork: The Free Press, 1989). Valuable historical insights, mixed with contemporary discussion and prescription, are to be found in M. Herman, *Intelligence Power in Peace and War* (Cambridge: Cambridge University Press, 1996). The general survey literature on British overseas policy produced by historians and especially by international relations specialists is remarkably devoid of discussions on this subject (or indeed British secret service generally), partly reflecting an inexplicable neglect of the core-executive machinery as a whole. Exceptions to the rule include J. W. Young, *Britain and the World in the Twentieth Century* (London: Arnold, 1997).

Two substantial accounts of internal security in modern Britain contain chapters on post-war developments: B. Porter, *Plots and Paranoia: A History of Political Espionage in Britain, 1790–1988* (London: Routledge, 1989) and R. Thurlow, *The Secret State: British Internal Security in the Twentieth Century* (London: Blackwell, 1994). Positive vetting is discussed in P. Hennessey, and G. Brownfield, 'Britain's Cold War Security Purge: The Origins of Positive Vetting', *Historical Journal*, 25, 4 (1982) 965–75, and also in M. Hollingsworth and R. Norton-Taylor, *Blacklist* (London: Heritage, 1988).

A vast miasma of literature confronts those wishing to consider the complex issues of moles and mole-hunters. The classic account, which revealed the identity of Anthony Blunt and provoked a surge of public interest, is A. Boyle, *The Climate of Treason: Five Who Spied For Russia* (London: Hutchinson, 1979). A study which continued Boyle's programme of research is T. Bower, *The Perfect English Spy* [biography of Sir Dick White] (London: Heinemann, 1995). C. M. Andrew and O. Gordievsky, *KGB: The Inside Story* (London: Hodder and Stoughton, 1990) is also essential reading in this area. Much scholarly endeavour has focused upon the activities of Donald Maclean and carefully considered assessments are available in R. Cecil, *A Divided Life: A Biography of Donald Maclean* (London: The Bodley Head, 1988) and also in S. Kerr, 'The Secret Hotline to Moscow: Donald Maclean and the Berlin Crisis of 1948', in A. Deighton (ed.), *Britain and the First Cold War* (London: Macmillan, 1990), pp. 71–87, and 'NATO's First Spies: The Case of the Disappearing Diplomats – Guy Burgess and Donald Maclean', in B. Heuser and R. O'Neill (eds), *Securing the Peace in Europe, 1945–62* (London: Macmillan, 1991), pp. 293–312. An overview of intelligence, security and the end of empire is offered by K. Jeffery, 'Intelligence and Counter-Insurgency Operations: Some Reflections on the British Experience', *Intelligence and National Security*, 2, 1 (1987) 118–50.

IRD and the associated fields of cultural and political warfare generated enormous scholarly interest in the mid-1990s, with the release of some early IRD papers and revelations about clandestine contacts with figures such as George Orwell. The two pathbreaking essays remain R. Fletcher, 'British Propaganda Since World War II –A Case Study', *Media, Culture and Society*, 4, 9 (1982) 96–109, and L. Smith, 'Covert British Propaganda: The Information Research Department, 1944–1977', *Millenium*, 9, 1 (1980) 676–83. British post-war special operations have not been subject to sustained analysis and this field remains dominated by memoir literature on specific episodes, such as C. M. Woodhouse, *Something Ventured* (London: Granada, 1982).

Relations with allies are, by their nature, a fragmentary subject. They are discussed substantially in many accounts of foreign services: C. M. Andrew, *For the President's Eyes Only: Secret Intelligence and the American Presidency from Washington to Bush* (London: Harper Collins, 1995); T. Mangold, *Cold Warrior: James Jesus Angleton, the CIA's Master Spy Hunter* (London: Simon and Schuster, 1991); D. McKnight, *Australia's Spies and their Secrets* (London: University College London Press, 1994); F. Cain, *The Australian Security and Intelligence Organization: An Unofficial History* (London: Frank Cass, 1994); B. Toohey and B. Pinwill, *Oyster: The Story of the Australian Intelligence Service* (Sydney: Heinemann, 1989). An account of allied relations, replete with technical detail and mostly focused on the period after 1970s, is available in J. T. Richelson and D. Ball, *The Ties that Bind* (London: Allen and Unwin, 1985). Nothing has been written on post-war deception.

An invaluable aid to further study is an extended and annotated guide to the literature, P. Davies, *British Intelligence: A Bibliography* (Oxford: ABC Clio, 1996). Much of the literature is concentrated in the dominant academic journal in this field, *Intelligence and National Security*, published by Frank Cass, London, since 1986.

Index